BEHAVIORAL
MANAGEMENT GUIDE

BEHAVIORAL MANAGEMENT GUIDE

Essential Treatment Strategies
for Adult Psychotherapy

Muriel Prince Warren, DSW, ACSW

JASON ARONSON INC.
Northvale, New Jersey
London

This book was set in 11 pt. Goudy by Alabama Book Composition of Deatsville, AL, and printed and bound by Book-mart Press, Inc. of North Bergen, NJ.

Library of Congress Cataloging-in-Publication Data

Warren, Muriel.
      Behavioral management guide : essential treatment strategies for adult psychotherapy / Muriel Prince Warren.
          p.   cm.
      Includes index.
      ISBN 0-7657-0300-9
      1. Mental illness — Treatment — Planning — Handbooks, manuals, etc.   2. Psychiatric records — Handbooks, manuals, etc.   3. Managed mental health care — Handbooks, manuals, etc.   I. title.

RC480.5 .W277   2000
616.89'1 — dc21   00-061059

Printed in the United States of America on acid-free paper. For information and catalog write to Jason Aronson Inc., 230 Livingston Street, Northvale, NJ 07647-1726, or visit our website: www.aronson.com

In memory of my father, Sidney Prince,
whose treatment plan went awry.

Contents

PART III
TREATMENT AIDS

PART IV
APPENDIX

Acknowledgments

I wish to give thanks to some wonderful people who made this book possible. First I thank Jason Aronson, publisher extraordinaire, whose enthusiasm and wise counsel propelled me into writing this book. Next, Norma Pomerantz who helped initiate the birth of the book and gave support along the way.

A special thanks goes to my husband and consultant Howard Matus, whose editorial acumen and research capability made the book possible. I want him to know that I appreciate his perseverance, encouragement, and forbearance.

I am grateful to my two research assistants, Caitlin Burck and my granddaughter Ashleigh Siriotis, who spent hours helping to select the books included in the Bibliotherapy.

I also would like to thank Elaine Lindenblatt, Anne Marie Dooley, and David Kaplan for their help in organizing the manuscript.

PART I

INTRODUCTION

1

The Changing Face of Psychotherapy

CONFRONTING MANAGED CARE

The language of psychotherapy changed when therapists contracted with insurance companies and became "service providers."

The treatment process was once regarded as the "talking cure" in which the patient engaged in a frank and open dialogue with a therapist who intervened with interpretations and clarifying questions. In this process most patients gained a greater understanding of themselves and insights into problems and their causes. They felt better, and often the problem that brought them into therapy was dissipated or reduced to tolerable levels. Although the process worked over time, it was perceived by managed care as too lengthy and too expensive. Managed care found it more expeditious to cover measurable, short-term behavioral change rather than long-term structural change in the patient's psyche.

Managed care's overnight rise to dominance brought with it more than just behavioral management. A fundamental concern with cost-effectiveness led logically to the basic business techniques of project management: establishing long-term goals, choosing short-term tasks or objectives to get there, and tracking the progress from start to finish. Suddenly these issues were incorporated into the mental health lexicon, and psychoanalysis was considered archaic. Gone were the concepts of working through the resistance, repetition compulsion, maintaining a holding environment, and exploring the underlying transference. Even establishing a therapeutic alliance was considered suspect. Free association, a standard treatment mode since the early days of Freud, was replaced by a more focused interaction that could be charted step by step along a predetermined path to the final achievement of its treatment goal.

Psychotherapists, who spent years studying the giants of psychiatry and mastering the proven techniques of listening and intervening, suddenly discovered they could not talk to managed care case managers in terms they understood. The language of psychotherapy had changed as the concept of mental disorders gave way to behavioral impairment. Patients became "clients," and psychotherapists became "service providers."

Managed care is concerned with Axis I impairments. If you have a client with an Axis II personality disorder, it becomes a red flag warning of potential long-term treatment for which managed care is not prepared to pay. However, if you have a client with a severe borderline personality disorder, the diagnosis can be coded on Axis II, and the behavioral symptoms treated as Axis I impairments. Most, if not all, personality disorders also have Axis I impairments. Managed care does not want to pay for treatment of irresolvable diagnoses, and Axis II diagnoses are usually considered irresolvable by insurance companies.

Managed care is also concerned with therapists treating a client for one long-term disorder and transforming him/her over time into a dependent personality disorder. So, if managed care case managers spot a provider with a cluster of long-term clients, they are more apt to refer future clients to other providers who provide short-term treatment.

Managed care is interested in quick, cost-effective change using modalities that are consistent with the client's needs. Acceptable treatment modalities include cognitive, behavioral, interpersonal, brief dynamic, supportive, group, psychopharmacology, psychological testing, biofeedback, and, depending on the insurance company, hypnosis, sometimes referred to as relaxation technique. Check with each company, since some will accept biofeedback or hypnosis; others will only accept relaxation techniques. However, it is mostly a matter of semantics, and as a provider you need to be sensitive to the particular buzz words of individual companies.

Treatment frequency is usually crisis-driven. Once a week is standard, and may temporarily be increased to twice a week. Some companies also may reduce sessions to every other week or once a month as a prelude to termination. Prior approvals are normally required for evaluation of medication by a psychiatrist or for psychological testing.

In today's managed care environment, the players may change without notice to subscribers or providers. One insurance company may gobble up another or assign a subcontractor to handle utilization review and payment or other services. Health Care Financing Administration (HCFA) forms and treatment reports now must be sent to a new company at a new address. Patients and therapists will find out about the changes eventually, but until they do there is a great deal of confusion. There are no ground rules to cover prior notification.

For example, Aetna was managed by Merit Behavioral Health, which merged with Magellan, and Magellan has now contracted with a capitation company to manage treatment for many of their subscribers, or "covered lives," in New Jersey and Pennsylvania. Although you may be certified by Aetna, Merit, and Magellan, you would not get paid unless you were now a provider for the new capitation company. Capitation companies are paid a set annual fee to handle treatment for an assigned population. The fewer services they provide, the more money the capitation company makes.

In another case, one client was notified that her insurance company was bought out by another and her provider was not in the new network. She was given ninety days to find a new network provider. Upon further investigation, it was learned that the notification was a mistake. A number of letters were mistakenly sent by the insurance company to subscribers. Can you imagine the impact of such an error on the basic trust between client and therapist? At this point, there is no penalty for the insurance companies when they make mistakes. In contrast, when providers miss the deadline for an outpatient treatment report, they are not paid.

MEDICAL NECESSITY

Medical necessity is the criterion used by managed care companies to authorize sessions.

There are various definitions of medical necessity in use today. The term and its meaning are usually published in the insurance companies' provider manuals. Value Options, another of the nation's larger behavioral management organizations, defines medical necessity treatment as "that which is intended to prevent, diagnose, correct, cure, alleviate or preclude deterioration of a diagnosable condition (ICD-9 or *DSM-IV*) that threatens life, causes pain or suffering, or results in illness or infirmity" (Value Options 1999, p. B-2). Medical necessity is usually limited to resolvable issues. The term *resolvable* is vague and subject to definition by the insurance company's case manager.

There are other qualifications. The treatment must also be:

1. expected to improve the client's condition or level of functioning;
2. consistent with the symptoms, diagnosis, and nationally accepted standards of care;
3. representative of a safe level of service where no effective, less expensive treatment is available;
4. not intended for the convenience of client or provider;
5. no more restrictive than necessary to balance safety, effectiveness, and efficiency.

Medical necessity is open to interpretation by a case manager who determines just what is appropriate and what is not. In my private practice, I have been authorized to provide thirty sessions for one patient and ten for another with the identical diagnosis, both from the same insurance company.

If you feel the authorization decision has been made unfairly, you can usually appeal. Most insurance companies provide for at least two levels of appeal. However, the process is different for each company and is outlined in the provider handbooks or is available from the company's provider service center.

WHEN THE APPEAL PROCESS FAILS

It may seem as if the insurance companies have the last word, but that is not always true. The National Association of Insurance Commissioners (NAIC) is an organization of insurance regulators from each of the fifty states, the four U.S. territories, and the District of Columbia. NAIC helps state regulators protect the interests of insurance consumers.

National Association of Insurance Commissioners
2301 McGee (Suite 800)
Kansas City, MO 64108-2604
(816) 842-3600

If you are an insurance subscriber or a provider who feels he/she has been treated unfairly or has an insurance problem that defies resolution, NAIC is a good place to start. They are also available on-line at www.naic.org. They may refer your problem to a funded consumer representative in your area or to your state insurance department. A list of State Insurance Departments is contained in Chapter 28.

DEVELOPING A COMPREHENSIVE
TREATMENT PLAN

This book is a guide for the development of a comprehensive treatment plan for adult patients based on a diagnosis and presenting problem. It includes essential instructions for tracking patient sessions and alerting you that outpatient treatment reports (OTRs) are due. It also provides tips on preparing the required treatment progress notes and discharge summary.

The major diagnostic categories listed in the *Diagnostic and Statistical Manual of Mental Disorders*, fourth edition (*DSM-IV*), published by the American Psychiatric Association, are discussed. Mental disorders are presented as behavioral problems, which are more readily understood and accepted by managed-care case managers. A comprehensive outline of broad, long-term treatment objectives, measurable, sort-term behavioral goals to be achieved, and possible interventions is provided. This book will take you step by step through the authorization process, show you how to monitor payments and authorization dates, and guide you through the required reports and progress notes.

2

The Paper Trail

In this electronic age, paper is still king. Under state law, the entire treatment process must be documented from the first phone call to the final discharge summary. If it is not documented, it never happened.

In addition to the Outpatient Treatment Reports, discussed below, the forms that you may need include:

- Medical Management-Psychiatrist's Report
- The Psychosocial Intake Report
- Payment and Session Monitor
- Progress Notes
- Billing: Form HCFA-1500
- Discharge Summary

Chapter 27 contains a sample form for each of the above, and guidelines for its use. If you are a provider and have contracted with any of the managed care companies, be aware that they have a right to request any of these documents.

Many companies follow the guidelines prepared by the National Committee for Quality Assurance or the Institute for Healthcare Quality, organizations that have researched, developed, and written position papers on each diagnosis. The papers include a description, approved treatment—usually psychotherapy and pharmacology—with a strong emphasis on the cognitive behavioral, interpersonal, and brief dynamic treatment modalities.

The Institute for Healthcare Quality, a subsidiary of Health Risk Management, develops and maintains evidence-based guidelines for clinical decisions by managed care organizations. The guidelines are available in published reports and can be accessed on-line by computer. The institute's QualityFIRST Behavioral Health Guideline package covers 90 percent of cases encountered in typical behavioral practices, including psychiatric and substance abuse. The guidelines, based on research findings and clinical evidence, cover over thirty-five behavioral health guidelines and 285 treatments. The institute maintains a staff of board-certified medical experts and allied professionals, representing sixty-three subspecialties, who review guideline decision logic in accordance with standards developed by the Agency for Health Care Policy and Research (AHCPR) and the Institute of Medicine (IOM).

These groups advise insurance companies on the number of treatment sessions that should be authorized, under normal circumstances, for the more prevalent diagnoses. These guidelines, now integrated into the curriculum at more than a dozen medical schools in the United States, are changing the way psychotherapy is taught.

Some managed care companies have developed their own detailed formulas as the basis for authorizing sessions. Others say they use "medical necessity" (discussed in Chapter 1) as the criterion.

THE OUTPATIENT TREATMENT REPORT

The purpose of this book is to guide you in writing an effective outpatient treatment report. The first step is to make a multiaxial assessment. Based upon this assessment, you will establish both broad, long-term objectives and measurable, behavioral short-term goals that can be met within a specific time frame. You must be able to estimate when you will reach a short-term behavioral goal and how far you are from achieving that goal at any given time. There is usually more than one short-term behavioral goal for each diagnosis. The goals must be concrete events. Vague goals are unacceptable.

Part II of this book includes a list of suggested objectives, behavioral goals, and therapist's interventions for each diagnosis. You will choose those you consider appropriate for your client; additionally, you will develop and include some of your own goals and interventions. Be sure that they have been translated into behavioral terms and are measurable (see Chapter 22). Managed care companies expect treatment plans to include homework assignments and referrals to self-help groups. See Chapter 23 for suggested homework assignments and Chapter 25 for a listing of telephone numbers for major self-help groups.

Following these guidelines, you will develop a viable behavioral treatment plan for every client, a smoother relationship with behavioral case managers, and outpatient treatment reports that assure optimum treatment certification for your clients. In actual practice, treatment may be considerably more complicated than the plans outlined in this book.

To begin, you must develop a multiaxial assessment.

MULTIAXIAL ASSESSMENT

DSM-IV uses a multiaxial system for the comprehensive clinical evaluation of a client which focuses on mental disorders, general medical conditions, psychosocial and environmental problems, and a general level of functioning. As mentioned in Chapter 1, managed care will pay only for diagnoses that are resolvable. Therefore, the behavioral symptoms of Axis II diagnoses should be coded as Axis I impairments. The *DSM-IV* system includes five different axes of information designed to aid the clinician in planning treatment:

Axis I: Clinical Disorders and Other Conditions that May Be the Focus of Clinical Attention

Axis I is designed for reporting the various clinical disorders or conditions listed in *DSM-IV* with the exception of personality disorders and mental retardation, which are reported on Axis II. Also reported on Axis I are other conditions that may be the focus of clinical attention. If a client has two or more mental disorders, they should be reported on Axis I, with the principal diagnosis listed first. If the client has both an Axis I and an Axis II disorder, it is assumed that the Axis I disorder is the principal reason for the office visit unless otherwise noted. If no Axis II disorder is present, it is coded as V71.09. If the diagnosis is deferred pending the collection of additional information, it is coded as 799.9.

Axis I clinical disorders include:

- Disorders usually first diagnosed in infancy, childhood, or adolescence (excludes mental retardation, which is diagnosed on Axis II)
- Delerium, dementia, amnesia, and other cognitive disorders
- Mental disorders due to a general medical condition
- Substance-related disorders
- Mood disorders
- Anxiety disorders
- Somatoform disorders
- Factitious disorders
- Dissociative disorders
- Sexual and gender identity disorders
- Eating disorders
- Sleep disorders
- Impulse-control disorders not otherwise classified
- Adjustment disorders
- Other conditions that may be a focus of clinical attention

Axis II: Personality Disorders and Mental Retardation

Axis II is for reporting personality disorders and mental retardation. It may also be used for recording maladaptive personality features and defense mechanisms that do not meet the threshold for a personality disorder. Axis II disorders include:

- Paranoid personality disorder
- Schizoid personality disorder
- Schizotypal personality disorder
- Antisocial personality disorder
- Borderline personality disorder
- Histrionic personality disorder
- Narcissistic personality disorder
- Avoidant personality disorder
- Dependent personality disorder
- Obsessive-compulsive personality disorder
- Personality disorder not otherwise specified (NOS)
- Mental retardation

Axis III: General Medical Conditions

Axis III is for current general medical conditions that are relevant to the understanding and management of the individual's mental disorder. When a mental disorder is considered to be the direct result of a general medical condition, it should be diagnosed on Axis I. The general medical condition should be coded on Axis III in the following manner: 316 (indicating a psychological factor) affecting ICD-9-CM (indicating the general medical condition) (see Appendices F and G of *DSM-IV* [American Psychiatric Association 1994]).

When the relationship between the general medical condition and the mental symptoms is unclear or insufficient to warrant an Axis I diagnosis of mental disorder due to a general medical condition, the mental disorder should be coded on Axis I and the general medical condition coded on Axis III. If no disorder is coded on this axis, the word "none" is acceptable. Axis III general medical conditions include:

- Infectious and parasitic diseases
- Neoplasms
- Endocrine, nutritional, and metabolic diseases and immunity disorders
- Diseases of the blood and blood-forming organs
- Diseases of the nervous system and sense organs
- Diseases of the circulatory system
- Diseases of the respiratory system
- Diseases of the digestive system
- Diseases of the genitourinary system
- Complications of pregnancy, childbirth, and the puerperium
- Diseases of the skin and subcutaneous tissue
- Diseases of the musculoskeletal system and connective tissue
- Certain conditions originating in the perinatal period
- Symptoms, signs, and ill-defined conditions
- Injury and poisoning

Axis IV: Psychosocial and Environmental Problems

Psychosocial and environmental problems that may affect the diagnosis, treatment, and prognosis of Axis I and Axis II mental disorders are reported on Axis IV. If more than one psychosocial or environmental problem exists, all that are considered relevant should be listed. Psychosocial and environmental problems include:

- Problems with primary support group
- Problems related to the social environment
- Educational problems
- Occupational problems
- Housing problems
- Economic problems
- Problems with access to health care services
- Problems related to interaction with the legal system or the criminal justice system
- Other psychosocial and environmental problems

Axis V: Global Assessment of Functioning (GAF)

Axis V requires that you score the client on a special Global Assessment of Functioning (GAF) scale. This information is helpful in planning treatment, measuring impact, and predicting outcome. The GAF scale relates only to psychological, social, and occupational functioning, and does not include impairment in functioning due to physical or environmental limitations. The GAF rating (1 to 100) is usually followed by the time period (e.g., current or past). Normally, insurance companies consider scores lower than 50 as irresolvable and therefore not covered. Scores of 70 or more are regarded as too high functioning to require treatment.

THE GLOBAL ASSESSMENT OF FUNCTIONING (GAF) SCALE

Consider psychological, social, and occupational functioning on a hypothetical continuum of mental health–illness. Do not include impairment in functioning due to physical (or environmental) limitations.

Code (**Note:** Use intermediate codes when appropriate, e.g., 45, 68, 72.)

100 **Superior functioning in a wide range of activities, life's problems never seem to get out of hand, is sought out by others because of his or her many positive qualities. No**
91 **symptoms.**

90 **Absent or minimal symptoms** (e.g., mild anxiety before an exam), **good functioning in all areas interested and involved in a wide range of activities, socially effective, generally satisfied with life, no more than everyday problems or concerns** (e.g., an occasional argument with
81 family members).

80 **If symptoms are present, they are transient and expectable reactions to psychosocial stressors** (e.g., difficulty concentrating after family argument); **no more than slight impairment in social, occupational, or school functioning** (e.g.,
71 temporarily falling behind in schoolwork).

70 **Some mild symptoms** (e.g., depressed mood and mild insomnia) **OR some difficulty in social, occupational, or school functioning** (e.g., occasional truancy, or theft within the household), **but generally functioning pretty well, has**
61 **some meaningful interpersonal relationships.**

60 **Moderate symptoms** (e.g., flat affect and circumstantial speech, occasional panic attacks) **OR moderate difficulty in social, occupational, or school functioning** (e.g., few
51 friends, conflicts with peers or co-workers).

50 **Serious symptoms** (e.g., suicidal ideation, severe obsessional rituals, frequent shoplifting) **OR any serious impairment in social, occupational, or school functioning** (e.g.,
41 no friends, unable to keep a job).

40 **Some impairment in reality testing or communication** (e.g., speech is at times illogical, obscure, or irrelevant) **OR major impairment in several areas, such as work or school, family relations, judgment, thinking, or mood** (e.g., depressed man avoids friends, neglects family, and is unable to work; child frequently beats up younger children, is defiant
31 at home, and is failing in school).

30 **Behavior is considerably influenced by delusions or hallucinations OR serious impairment in communication or judgment** (e.g., sometimes incoherent, acts grossly inappropriately, suicidal preoccupation) **OR inability to function in almost all areas** (e.g., stays in bed all day; no job, home,
21 or friends).

20 **Some danger of hurting self or others** (e.g., suicide attempts without clear expectation of death; frequently violent; manic excitement) **OR occasionally fails to maintain
minimal personal hygiene** (e.g., smears feces) **OR gross
impairment in communication** (e.g., largely incoherent or
11 mute).

10 **Persistent danger of severely hurting self or others** (e.g.,
recurrent violence) **OR persistent inability to maintain
minimal personal hygiene OR serious suicidal act with
1 clear expectation of death.**

0 Inadequate information.

From *Diagnostic and Statistical Manual of Mental Disorders, 4th Ed. (DSM-IV)*,
copyright © 1994 American Psychiatric Association, and reprinted by permission.

EXAMPLES OF MULTIAXIAL EVALUATION

Example 1:

Axis I	296.23	Major Depressive Disorder, Single Episode, Severe Without Psychotic Features
	305.00	Alcohol Abuse
Axis II	301.6	Dependent Personality Disorder
		Frequent use of denial
Axis III		None
Axis IV		Threat of job loss
Axis V	GAF = 35 (current)	

Example 2:

Axis I	300.4	Dysthymic Disorder
	315.00	Reading Disorder
Axis II	V71.09	No diagnosis
Axis III	382.9	Otitis media, recurrent
		Victim of child neglect
Axis V	GAF = 53 (current)	

Example 3:

Axis I	293.83	Mood Disorder Due to Hypothyroidism, with Depressive Features
Axis II	V71.09	No diagnosis, histrionic personality features
Axis III	244.9	Hypothyroidism
	365.23	Chronic angle-closure glaucoma
Axis IV		None
Axis V	GAF = 45	(on admission)
	GAF = 65	(at discharge)

Example 4:

Axis I	V61.1	Partner Relational Problem
Axis II	V71.09	No diagnosis
Axis IV		Unemployment
Axis V	GAF = 83	(highest level past year)

From *Diagnostic and Statistical Manual of Mental Disorders*, 4th Ed. (*DSM-IV*), copyright © 1994 American Psychiatric Association, and reprinted by permission.

PART II

THE TREATMENT PLANS

3

Abuse- and Neglect-Related Problems

Abuser (in which case, a V code applies):

Physical abuse of child (V61.21)
Sexual abuse of child (V61.21)
Neglect of child (V61.21)
Physical abuse of adult (V61.21)
Sexual abuse of adult (V61.21)

NOTE: *Solitary V-codes are not reimbursed by insurance companies and should be used on Axis IV to qualify as Axis I diagnosis.*

(See Chapter 19 for behavioral symptoms and treatment plan for physical and sexual abuse—treatment of abuser.)

Victim (code on Axis I):

Physical abuse of child (995.54)
Sexual abuse of child (995.53)

Neglect of child (995.52)
Physical abuse of adult (995.81)
Sexual abuse of adult (995.83)

Behavioral Symptoms—Victim
(severity index: 1, mild; 2, moderate; 3, intense)

Severity

1. Persistent reexperience of the abuse as a recollection or dream _____
2. Flashbacks or feelings of reliving the abuse _____
3. Intense distress at cues that are reminiscent of the abuse _____
4. Avoidance of thoughts, feelings, activities, people, or places associated with the abuse _____
5. Inability to remember an important aspect of the event _____
6. Reduced interest in significant activities _____
7. Feeling of detachment from others _____
8. Restricted range of feelings _____
9. Heightened sense of limited future _____
10. Sleep problems _____
11. Irritability or angry outbursts _____
12. Inability to concentrate _____
13. Increased vigilance/easily startled _____
14. Symptoms cause serious impairment to activities of daily living (ADLs) _____

Other Diagnostic Considerations

Posttraumatic stress disorder (309.81)
Hypoactive sexual desire disorder (302.71)
Sexual aversion disorder (302.79)
Female orgasmic disorder (302.72)
Male erectile disorder (302.72)

Premature ejaculation (302.72)
Dyspareunia—not due to a general medical condition (302.76)
Vaginismus—not due to a general medical condition (306.51)
Major depressive disorder (296.xx)
Dysthymia (300.4)
Generalized anxiety disorder (300.02)
Substance dependence (303.90)
Dissociative disorders (300.14)
Personality disorders (301.xx)

TREATMENT PLAN
PHYSICAL/SEXUAL ABUSE—VICTIM

Client: _____ Date: _____

I. OBJECTIVES OF TREATMENT
   (*select one or more*)

   1. Eliminate stressors associated with the abuse.
   2. Relieve distress associated with the abuse.
   3. Return client to premorbid level of functioning.
   4. Prevent recurrence of symptoms.

II. SHORT-TERM BEHAVIORAL GOALS AND
   INTERVENTIONS
   (*select goals and interventions appropriate for your client*)

CLIENT'S SHORT-TERM BEHAVIORAL GOALS	THERAPIST'S INTERVENTIONS
Confirm diagnosis.	Confirm diagnosis.
Agree with therapist on target problem.	Develop treatment plan. Agree with client on target problem.
Feel less alienated and more hopeful that problems can be resolved.	Establish therapeutic or collaborative alliance with client.
Be aware of requirements for therapist to report certain incidents.	Discuss therapist's obligation to report deviant behavior if and when mandated by law.
Continue under revised treatment plan.	Investigate for sadomasochism in partners. If positive, see appropriate treatment plan.
Report continuing abuse if client is in danger.	If client is partnered, determine whether or not abuse continues.
Learn nature of reactions to abuse.	Teach client features of reactions to abuse.

Verbalize feelings toward the abuse.	Encourage client to verbalize his/her feelings about the abuse.
Relate in detail the trigger event and your reactive feelings.	Investigate with client the traumatic event and his/her feelings and reactions.
Maintain daily log of your feelings and the triggers that touch off physical and emotional reactions.	Instruct client to maintain daily log of persons, places, activities, and things related to the traumatic event that trigger fear or anxiety.
Irrational beliefs and myths toward abuse are reframed with evidence-based reality.	Explore issues of self-blame or irrational beliefs about the abuse.
Work on issues related to the abuse that impinge on normal sexual activity.	Investigate interpersonal issues that impinge on sexual activity due to the abuse.
Overcome sexual inhibitions.	If abuse causes sexual inhibitions in victim, assign pleasuring and sensate focus exercises.
Improve sexual response.	Explore ways to increase feelings of security and improve sexual arousal and satisfaction.
Record flashbacks and dreams of the event.	Explore flashbacks and analyze dreams to reduce their impact on the client.
Follow-up with referral for medical evaluation and maintain regular medication schedule.	Refer client for medical evaluation and possible medication. Instruct client on medication regimen.
Provide feedback on reactions to meds and lapses in planned medication schedule.	Instruct client on importance of feedback and need to report reactions to the meds.

Read recommended self-help books.	Assign client to read self-help book (see Chapter 24).
Examine distortions in reaction to the event stressors.	Discuss reactions to identify exaggerated and distorted reactions.
Replace exaggerated reactions with positive reactions, using evidence-based reality.	Reframe negative reactions with positive reality-based cognitions.
Check urge to blame victim for the abuse.	Investigate issue of blaming the victim.
In relaxation technique or hypnosis, revisit traumatic event replacing stress reactions with positive cognition.	Using relaxation technique or hypnosis, attempt to desensitize client. Reexperience the traumatic event replacing negative reactions with new cognitions.
Practice coping skills in real-life situations. Report reactions and self-reward successes.	Instruct client to challenge persons, places, activities, and things related to the event and record reactions. Reinforce successes.
Repeat real-life challenge to gradually diminish and eliminate anxiety reactions.	Urge client to repeat real-life challenge strategy to ameliorate fear and stress reactions.
Investigate and resolve termination issues with therapist—separation anxiety, dependence.	Explore with client issues of separation and dependence.
Attend self-help group meetings to reinforce coping skills.	Refer client to self-help group or group therapy for abuse victims.

4

Attention Deficit and Disruptive Behavior Disorder

ATTENTION-DEFICIT/HYPERACTIVITY DISORDER (AD/HD) (314.xx)

Combined type (.01)
Predominantly inattentive type (.00)
Predominantly hyperactive-impulsive type (.01)

Attention-deficit/hyperactivity disorder (AD/HD) is character-ized by a persistent pattern of inattention and/or hyperactivity-impulsivity. Symptoms, displayed singly or in combination, usually appear before age 7, but may not be diagnosed until later in life. Recently, there has been a surge in the number of adults diagnosed with AD/HD that was apparently undetected in childhood. Symptoms must be present in at least two settings (home, work, school, or social settings). The disorder is associated with significant academic and occupational underachievement as well as higher than average divorce and substance abuse rates. Psychostimulants are the single most effective intervention in the treatment of AD/HD. Antidepressants are also used. Nonpharmacologic interventions are critical for the treatment of low self-esteem and subsequent psychosocial problems associated with the disorder.

Behavioral Symptoms
(severity index: 1, mild; 2, moderate; 3, severe)

<u>Severity</u>

Attention:

1. Fails to pay close attention to details at work or in social situations _____
2. Does not seem to listen when spoken to directly _____
3. Does not follow through on instructions _____
4. Fails to finish tasks _____
5. Has difficulty organizing tasks and activities _____
6. Avoids or dislikes tasks that require sustained mental effort _____
7. Loses things that are necessary for tasks and activities _____
8. Is easily distracted by extraneous stimuli _____
9. Is forgetful in daily activities _____

Hyperactivity-Impulsivity:

1. Fidgets or squirms in seat _____
2. Cannot remain in seat when expected to _____
3. Inappropriately overactive _____
4. Has subjective feelings of restlessness _____
5. Has difficulty engaging appropriately in leisure activities _____
6. Feels or acts "driven by a motor" _____
7. Talks excessively _____
8. Blurts out answers before questions are completed _____
9. Has difficulty awaiting turn _____

10. Interrupts or intrudes on conversations or
    activities of others   _____

Other Diagnostic Considerations

AD/HD NOS (314.9)
Conduct disorder NOS (312.8)
Oppositional defiant disorder (313.8)
Disruptive behavior disorder NOS (312.9)
Obsessive-compulsive disorder (300.3)
Generalized anxiety disorder (300.02)
Major depressive disorder (296.xx)
Substance abuse (see Chapter 20)

TREATMENT PLAN
AD/HD

Client: _____ Date: _____

I. OBJECTIVES OF TREATMENT
   (*select one or more*)

   1. Increase frustration tolerance.
   2. Reduce aggression and anxiety.
   3. Improve self-esteem.
   4. Assure compliance with medical regimen.
   5. Focus concentration for increased time span.
   6. Develop a balanced life plan.

II. SHORT-TERM BEHAVIORAL GOALS AND
    INTERVENTIONS
    (*select goals and interventions appropriate for your client*)

CLIENT'S SHORT-TERM BEHAVIORAL GOALS	THERAPIST'S INTERVENTIONS
Understand nature of AD/HD. Discuss treatment plan with therapist and agree on target problem.	Instruct client on nature of AH/DH, and develop a treatment plan. Determine target problem.
Cooperate with therapist in confirmation of AD/HD diagnosis.	Rule out differential diagnoses: depression, anxiety, obsessive-compulsive disorder (OCD), or substance abuse.
Client feels that change is possible, becomes more hopeful as prognosis improves.	Develop a therapeutic or collaborative alliance to enhance outcome of treatment.

Follow through with psychiatric and medical referrals.	Refer client for psychiatric and medical evaluation and follow-up to confirm client has kept appointments.
Start medication log. Maintain regular meds schedule. Report reactions and urges to ignore or discontinue meds.	Instruct client on importance of medication and use of meds log. Review log with client for possible medication adjustment and lapses in motivation.
Become more focused and think before acting impulsively.	Explain self-talk to encourage client to focus on tasks at hand.
Maintain a thought and behavior log. Review periodically with therapist to improve ability to focus.	Assign client to keep a thought and behavior log (see homework assignments) to improve ability to focus. Review periodically with client.
Learn how to improve control over unfocused behavior.	Practice focused behavior in school or work role playing with client.
Apply new learned techniques in the real world.	Urge client to externalize the learned control in the actual school or work environment.
Significantly improve behavior.	Build client's confidence to level where he understands he can control his unfocused behavior.
Develop and use an organizational system to address tasks at hand.	Help client develop and implement an organizational system to help complete tasks.
Learn how to prioritize tasks to assure completion of project.	Teach client how to prioritize tasks.
Maintain a daily log to track progress in handling work and school tasks. Confidence builds.	Assign client to maintain a daily log to record progress in handling work and school tasks.

Identify and understand issues that disrupt optimal functioning.	Investigate issues of depression or anxiety that impede client from becoming task-oriented. See treatment plans for anxiety and depression (Chapters 5 and 7) as applicable.
Learn new techniques for control of impulsive behavior. Practice techniques at home.	Introduce client to relaxation or hypnosis techniques to improve skills in dealing with impulsive behavior. Provide audiotape for home use.
Use new techniques in real-life school and work situations.	Guide client in use of new skills in external world.
Learn to use diaphragmatic breathing to calm self in critical situations.	Introduce client to diaphragmatic breathing as a technique for self-calming (see behavioral techniques, Chapter 22).
Recognize triggers for impulsive behavior and thinks before taking action.	Urge client to confront and challenge triggers for impulsive behavior.
Further improve behavior with understanding of AD/HD dynamics.	Further clarify the underlying dynamics of AD/HD to reinforce behavioral gains.
Participate in self-help group increases client's understanding and control, provides feedback from peers.	Refer client to self-help group.
Feel supported and less alienated.	Educate family about AD/HD to promote acceptance of client.
Relationship with family becomes less stressful and communication is improved.	Conduct family therapy session to improve communications and reduce anger toward client.

Address and resolve issues of dependency and separation anxiety.	Discuss termination plan and resolve termination issues with client.

5

Anxiety Disorders

ACUTE STRESS DISORDER (308.3)

Acute stress disorder typically occurs within one month after a traumatic event and is marked by dissociation and other symptoms common to posttraumatic stress disorder. Symptoms occur within one month after a traumatic event, last for at least two days, and cause significant impairment or distress in the client's activities of daily living (ADLs). In contrast, posttraumatic stress disorder requires a history of more than one month of symptoms. If the acute stress symptoms persist for more than one month, a revised diagnosis of posttraumatic stress disorder should be considered.

Behavioral Symptoms
(severity index: 1, mild; 2, moderate; 3, intense)

Client witnessed or experienced an actual or threatened event that placed him/her or another person in danger of death or serious injury and reacted with feelings of intense fear, horror, or helplessness.

Severity

1. Numbing, or lack of emotion _____
2. Feeling of being disconnected or dazed _____
3. Derealization or depersonalization _____
4. Inability to recall an important part of the event _____
5. Traumatic event is reexperienced as recurring images, thoughts, dreams, flashbacks, or distress at reminders of the event _____
6. Avoidance of places, people, activities, or things associated with the event _____
7. Anxiety, sleep difficulties, irritability, difficulty concentrating, exaggerated vigilance, restlessness _____
8. Restlessness, or extreme startle response _____
9. Major impairment in activities of daily living (ADLs) _____

Other Diagnostic Considerations

Posttraumatic stress disorder (309.81)
Adjustment disorders:
   with depressed mood (309.0)
   with anxiety (309.224)
   with mixed anxiety and depressed mood (309.28)
   with disturbance of conduct (309.3)
   with mixed disturbance of emotions and conduct (309.4)
   unspecified (309.9)
Major depressive episode (296.2)
Brief psychotic disorder (298.8)

Malingering should be ruled out.

TREATMENT PLAN
ACUTE STRESS DISORDER

Client: _____   Date: _____

I. OBJECTIVES OF TREATMENT
(select one or more)

1. Reduce client's anxiety symptoms: sleep disturbance, irritability, concentration, vigilance, restlessness.
2. Restore realization and personalization.
3. Eliminate need for avoidance of people, places, things, or activities.
4. Restore client to optimal level of functioning.

II. SHORT-TERM BEHAVIORAL GOALS AND INTERVENTIONS
(select goals and interventions appropriate for your client)

CLIENT'S SHORT-TERM BEHAVIORAL GOALS	THERAPIST'S INTERVENTIONS
Confirm diagnosis of acute stress disorder.	Rule out malingering and confirm diagnosis.
Join in collaborative treatment.	Establish a collaborative or therapeutic alliance to build trust and enhance outcome of treatment.
Determine level of anxiety.	Refer for or administer the Beck Anxiety Inventory (BAI) to determine existence and level of anxiety.
Learn nature of acute stress disorder.	Teach client features and causes of acute stress disorder.

Relate in detail the trigger event and your reactive feelings.	Investigate with client the traumatic event and his/her feelings and reactions.
Openly share feelings about the traumatic event.	Encourage client to share feelings about the traumatic event.
Maintain daily log of your feelings and the triggers that touch off physical and emotional reactions.	Instruct client to maintain daily log of persons, places, activities, and things related to the traumatic event that trigger fear or anxiety.
Record flashbacks and dreams of the event.	Explore flashbacks and analyze dreams to reduce their impact on the client.
Undergo evaluation for sleep disorder.	Evaluate client for sleep disorder and if positive, see appropriate treatment plan.
Undergo evaluation for other associated disorders.	Evaluate for other possible disorders associated with acute stress disorder, such as depression and dissociation. See appropriate treatment plans.
Learn laws of anxiety: not dangerous, not permanent, reduced by confrontation.	Teach client laws of anxiety.
Follow-up with referral for medical evaluation and maintain regular medication schedule.	Refer client for medical evaluation and possible medication. Instruct client on medication regimen.
Provide feedback on reactions to meds and lapses in planned medication schedule.	Instruct client on importance of feedback and need to report reactions to the meds.

Relive the traumatic event using relaxation technique or hypnosis.	Using relaxation technique or hypnosis, guide client in reliving the traumatic event.
In relaxation technique or hypnosis, replace stress reactions with positive cognition.	Using relaxation technique or hypnosis in the office, guide client to replace negative reactions with new cognitions. Provide tape for home use to reduce stress.
Examine distortions in reaction to the event stressors.	Discuss reactions to identify exaggerated and distorted reactions.
Replace exaggerated reactions with positive reactions, using evidence-based reality.	Reframe negative reactions with positive reality-based cognitions.
Learn to use diaphragmatic breathing to calm self.	Teach client diaphragmatic breathing for self-calming (see behavioral techniques, Chapter 22).
Practice coping skills in real-life situations. Report reactions and self-reward successes.	Instruct client to challenge persons, places, activities, and things related to the event and record reactions. Reinforce successes.
Repeat real-life challenge to gradually diminish and eliminate anxiety reactions.	Urge client to repeat real-life challenge strategy to ameliorate fear and stress reactions.
Explore with therapist the issues of separation and dependency; review termination plan.	Prepare termination plan. Investigate with client issues of separation and dependency.
Attend self-help group meetings to reinforce coping skills.	Refer client to self-help group or group therapy dealing with acute stress disorder.

BODY DYSMORPHIC DISORDER (300.7)

Body dysmorphic disorder is characterized by preoccupation with an imagined or slight flaw in appearance that causes impairment in the individual's ADLs. Any body part may be involved including hair, face, genitals, breasts, or buttocks. Excessive checking and grooming may be involved. Individuals may frequently ask friends and relatives for reassurance. In severe cases, they may confine themselves to their homes. The disorder usually starts in adolescence, and may be gradual or sudden. Koro, a cultural disorder common to Southeast Asia, may be related to body dysmorphic disorder. It is marked by a preoccupation with the idea that the penis is shrinking into the abdomen and that the condition will be fatal.

Behavioral Symptoms
(severity index: 1, mild; 2, moderate; 3, intense)

	Severity
1. Preoccupation with an imagined defect or slight flaw in appearance	_____
2. Ritualized checking and grooming	_____
3. Social withdrawal	_____
4. Obsessive-compulsive behavior	_____
5. Somatization	_____
6. Delusions	_____
7. Low self-esteem	_____
8. Depression	_____
9. Significant impairment in ADLs	_____

Other Diagnostic Considerations

Anorexia nervosa (307.1)
Gender identity disorder (302.9)
Major depressive disorder (296.xx)

Avoidant personality disorder (301.82)
Social phobia (300.23)
Obsessive-compulsive disorder (301.4)
Delusional disorder—somatic type (297.1)

TREATMENT PLAN
BODY DYSMORPHIC DISORDER

Client: _____ Date: _____

I. OBJECTIVES OF TREATMENT
    (*select one or more*)

     1. Eliminate preoccupation with real or imagined flaw.
     2. Eliminate time spent worrying about the defect.
     3. Resolve conflicts that trigger or exacerbate obsession with the defect.
     4. Reduce need for perfection and accept body as it is.
     5. Eliminate excessive checking and grooming.
     6. Develop improved social skills.
     7. Control delusions.
     8. Reduce and eliminate depression.
     9. Restore optimum level of functioning.

II. SHORT-TERM BEHAVIORAL GOALS AND INTERVENTIONS
     (*select the goals and interventions appropriate for your client*)

CLIENT'S SHORT-TERM BEHAVIORAL GOALS	THERAPIST'S INTERVENTIONS
Review treatment plan with therapist and agree on target problem.	Review treatment plan with client and agree on target problem.
Cooperate with therapist in collaborative effort.	Develop a collaborative or therapeutic alliance to build trust and enhance treatment outcome.
Comply with medical and psychiatric recommendations. Take meds if required.	Refer client for medical and psychiatric evaluation.

Help build genogram to understand family history associated with the disorder.	Create genogram and identify family characteristics that are relevant to the problem (see Behavioral Techniques, Chapter 22).
Maintain daily log of thoughts and actions.	Assign client to keep a daily journal of thoughts and actions recording ritualized behavior.
Evaluate and restructure need for ritualized behavior.	Evaluate preoccupation with imagined defect, time spent, and checking/grooming rituals involved.
Examine the imagined or exaggerated flaw and irrational negative reaction to it.	Explore irrational beliefs about defect with client.
Help investigate underlying disorders. Undergo treatment as required.	Evaluate for underlying disorders and treat as required. See appropriate treatment plan.
Replace irrational beliefs about the defect with realistic view.	Confront and reframe irrational beliefs with evidence-based rational reaction to the so-called defect.
Review discharge plan with therapist. Understand that recovery is not only possible, but expected.	Address the discharge plan, showing client that recovery is expected.
Recognize depression or anxiety that may trigger or exacerbate feelings about the so-called defect.	Explore possible mood disorders that may contribute to imagined or exaggerated defect.

In hypnosis or relaxation technique, reduce automatic reactions toward the flaw and use audiotape at home to reinforce new feelings.	Using hypnosis or relaxation technique, desensitize client reaction to the flaw and resulting rituals. Instruct client on home use of the audiotape.
Use expanded social interactions to practice reframed view of the so-called defect. Self-reward success.	Encourage client to expand social interactions or refer to self-help group.
Read and understand book on obsessive-compulsive disorders and discuss with therapist.	Assign client to read recommended self-help book on obsessive-compulsive disorders and discuss (see Chapter 24).
Replace negative self-talk with positive view of self.	Change pattern of negative self-talk with positive view of self.
Family interaction improves. Client feels less alienated.	If appropriate, involve client's family in treatment. Help them understand and deal with client.
Realize impact of family on negative self-esteem and develop new skills to deal with it.	Clarify family dynamics that contribute to the body dysmorphic disorder and teach new interpersonal skills to deal with the situation.
Expand use of new coping skills to other life situations.	Instruct client to practice and perfect new skills in other life interactions outside the family.
Recognize secondary gains and discards negative behavior as a way of getting attention.	Investigate secondary gains related to retaining negative behavior and the imagined defect.
Self-esteem improves as anger recedes.	Assign client to use home audiotape to reduce anger and improve self-esteem.

Discuss and resolve termination issues with therapist.	Explore termination issues, separation anxiety, and dependence with client and resolve.
Regularly attend self-help group sessions to reinforce new self-outlook.	Refer client to self-help group.

GENERALIZED ANXIETY DISORDER (300.02)

The lifetime prevalence for generalized anxiety disorder is 5 percent with a one-year prevalence rate of 3 percent. The disorder appears more frequently (60 percent) in women than in men. Typically, onset occurs after age 20, although many people report feeling nervous or anxious for most of their lives. Individuals with generalized anxiety disorder frequently also suffer from major depression or other types of anxiety disorders. Medical conditions also can mimic generalized anxiety disorder, making differential diagnosis difficult. These clients often have excessive worries regarding illness.

Behavioral Symptoms
(severity index: 1, mild; 2, moderate; 3, intense)

	Severity
1. Difficult to control anxiety or worry more days than not for six months or more	_____
2. Three of the following:	_____
a. Feeling on edge or restless	_____
b. Fatigues easily	_____
c. Difficulty concentrating	_____
d. Irritability	_____
e. Muscular reactions	_____
f. Sleep problems	_____
3. Multiple physical complaints	_____
4. Clinical impairment of client's ADLs	_____

Other Diagnostic Considerations

Anxiety disorder due to a general medical condition (293.84)
Substance-induced anxiety disorder (substance-specific)
Panic disorder (not codable)
Social disorder (300.23)
Obsessive-compulsive disorder (300.3)

Anorexia nervosa (307.1)
Hypochondriasis (300.7)
Somatization disorder (300.81)
Separation anxiety (309.21)
Posttraumatic stress disorder (309.81)
Adjustment disorder (see subtypes)
Mood disorders (see subtypes)
Psychotic disorders (see subtypes)

TREATMENT PLAN
GENERALIZED ANXIETY DISORDER

Client: _____ Date: _____

I. OBJECTIVES OF TREATMENT
    (*select one or more*)

1. Reduce pervasive worry.
2. Diminish and eliminate symptoms of anxiety: restlessness, fatigue, lack of concentration, irritability, somatization, and sleep disturbance.
3. Restore client to optimum level of functioning.

II. SHORT-TERM BEHAVIORAL GOALS AND INTERVENTIONS
    (select goals and interventions appropriate for your client)

CLIENT'S SHORT-TERM BEHAVIORAL GOALS	THERAPIST'S INTERVENTIONS
Confirm diagnosis of generalized anxiety disorder.	Rule out malingering and confirm diagnosis.
Enter into collaborative relationship.	Establish a therapeutic or collaborative alliance to build trust and enhance the outcome of treatment.
Client's level of anxiety is determined.	Refer client for or administer the Beck Anxiety Inventory (BAI) to determine the level of anxiety.
Review treatment plan and discharge plan with therapist.	Discuss treatment plan and discharge plan with client.
Agree on target problems.	Agree on target problems to be worked on.

Explore underlying issues with therapist.	Explore for underlying disorders that contribute to generalized anxiety. See appropriate treatment plan.
Maintain daily log of anxiety reactions to persons, places, things, and activities.	Instruct client in importance of maintaining an accurate daily log of anxiety reactions.
Determine probable origins of the anxiety.	Investigate origins of client's anxiety.
Assist in preparation of genogram to understand the use of anxiety in the family.	Construct genogram to understand family history and define how family deals with anxiety (see Chapter 22).
Conscientiously complete homework assignments.	Assign appropriate homework (see Chapter 23).
Learn laws of anxiety: not permanent, not dangerous, reduced by confrontation.	Teach client the laws of anxiety and the opportunities it provides for growth.
Confront thoughts of exaggerated and unrealistic consequences—"What if?"	Guide client in confronting distorted reactions to trigger situations.
Identify cognitive distortions.	Weigh the reactions against evidence-based reality.
Restructure distortions with evidence-based consequences.	With client, reframe distortions with reality-based reactions to stressors.
Learn diaphragmatic breathing as relaxation technique.	Teach client diaphragmatic breathing to assist relaxation (see Chapter 22).
Learn new relaxation skills to cope with anxiety. Use audiotape at home.	Using relaxation technique or hypnosis, instruct client on new skills to better handle the anxiety.

Follow-up on referral for medical evaluation and possible medication.	Refer client for medical evaluation and possible medication.
Read self-help book to increase coping skills.	Assign client to appropriate self-help book to expand coping skills (see Chapter 24).
Maintain regular medication schedule and report reactions or failure to take meds.	Instruct client on need for a regular medication schedule and feedback that may indicate the need for revised dosage.
Record in daily log significant changes in anxiety reaction to triggers. Self-reward successes.	Review with client all changes in anxiety reactions. Advise client on self-rewards.
Practice new skills in real-life challenge of persons, places, things, and activities that were anxiety-producing. Self-reward successes.	Urge client to face real-life anxiety-producing situations and record reactions.
Family interactions improve. Anger is diminished, communications skills improved.	Conduct family sessions if appropriate, to reduce anger and improve communications.
Family learns about the disorder. Learns new coping techniques.	Educate family about the disorder and teach new coping techniques.
Family demonstrates alliances, triangles, and emotional currents.	Explore family boundaries through family sculpturing (see Chapter 22).
Continue challenge strategy and use of home tape to gradually diminish and eliminate anxiety in real-life situations.	Reinforce need and encourage client to continue real-life confrontation to reduce anxiety reactions.

Investigate termination issues with therapist—separation anxiety, dependence.	Explore possible feelings of separation anxiety or dependence.
Attend self-help group focused on anxiety.	Refer client to self-help group.

OBSESSIVE-COMPULSIVE DISORDER (300.3)

Obsessive-compulsive disorder has a lifetime prevalence of 2.5 percent and a one-year rate of between 1.5 and 2.1 percent. Although it may begin in childhood, the onset of the disorder is more common in adolescence and early adulthood, appearing earlier in males than in females.

Behavioral Symptoms
(severity rating: 1, mild; 2, moderate; 3, intense)

<u>Severity</u>

Obsessions:
1. Intrusive, inappropriate thoughts, impulses, or images that cause anxiety or distress _____
2. The thoughts, impulses, or images are not just excessive worries about real-life problems _____
3. Tries to ward off or suppress these stimuli by ritualized thought or action _____
4. Recognizes the stimuli as the products of his/her own mind. _____

Compulsions:

1. Driven to perform repetitive physical or mental behaviors according to rigid rules to reduce or eliminate distress or prevent a dreaded event _____
2. The behaviors are not connected in a realistic way with the event _____
3. Recognizes that the obsessions or compulsions are excessive or unrealistic _____
4. The obsessions and compulsions are time-consuming, cause distress, and interfere with client's ADLs. _____

Other Diagnostic Considerations

Body dysmorphic disorder (300.7)
Specific or social phobia (300.29/300.23)
Major depressive episode (296.2)
Generalized anxiety disorder (300.02)
Delusional disorder (297.1)
Psychotic disorder NOS
Schizophrenia (295.xx)

TREATMENT PLAN
OBSESSIVE-COMPULSIVE DISORDER

Client: _____ Date: _____

I. OBJECTIVES OF TREATMENT
   (select one or more)

   1. Ameliorate obsessional thoughts, impulses, and images that cause anxiety or distress.
   2. Eliminate the excessive and unrealistic compulsions that interfere with the client's ADLs.
   3. Restore client to optimal level of functioning.

II. SHORT-TERM BEHAVIORAL GOALS AND INTERVENTIONS
   (*select goals and interventions appropriate for your client*)

CLIENT'S SHORT-TERM BEHAVIORAL GOALS	THERAPIST'S INTERVENTIONS
Discuss treatment plan with therapist and agree on target problems.	Develop treatment plan with client and agree on target problems.
Feelings of hopelessness and isolation are diminished.	Cultivate therapeutic alliance or collaborative relationship with client.
Client's level of anxiety is determined.	Refer client for or administer the Beck Anxiety Inventory (BAI) to determine the level of anxiety.
Comply with psychiatric evaluation.	Refer client for psychiatric evaluation and possible medication.
Follow medication regimen if prescribed.	Instruct client on importance of regular medication schedule.

Learn the nature of obsessive-compulsive disorder.	Instruct client on the nature of obsessive-compulsive disorder.
Complete homework assignments.	Assign homework to monitor automatic thinking and rituals in the face of anxiety.
Identify and monitor automatic thinking.	List client's automatic thoughts and ritualized actions.
Evaluate automatic thoughts for cognitive distortions.	Analyze automatic thoughts and point out cognitive distortions.
Replace distorted thinking with evidence-based reality.	Test distortions and reframe them based on available evidence.
Identify ritualized actions to ward off anxiety.	List and monitor client's ritualized actions.
Use relaxation audiotape to act out ritual in imagined situation and gradually reduce frequency and repetition of ritual.	Use relaxation technique or hypnosis to gradually reduce frequency and repetition of ritualized actions. Provide practice tape for client's home use.
Understand laws of anxiety.	Teach client the laws of anxiety (not dangerous, not permanent, avoidance increases anxiety).
Learn diaphragmatic breathing for relaxation.	Teach client diaphragmatic breathing for relaxation (see Behavioral Techniques, Chapter 22).
Read assigned books and learn new ways to deal with OCD.	Assign self-help books on OCD (see Chapter 24).
Client's family support system is strengthened.	Involve client's family in treatment. Act as family consultant to help them understand the nature of OCD.

Family understanding and interaction with client improves.	Lessen family anxiety and teach new skills for interaction with client.
Challenge anxiety triggers in real-life situations.	Instruct client to face and challenge real-life situations and record outcomes. Suggest self-rewards to reinforce success.
Gradually reduce and eliminate need for ritual in real-life situations.	Reinforce successes and continue to challenge reality, reducing the need for ritualized actions.
Understand nature of symptom recurrence and cope successfully with setbacks as they occur.	Teach client that recurrence of symptoms is a normal reaction and will dissipate with experience.
Investigate with therapist and resolve termination issues of separation and anxiety.	Explore and resolve separation and dependency issues. Develop termination plan.
Regularly attend support group meetings.	Refer client to support group or group therapy dealing with OCD.

PANIC DISORDER WITHOUT AGORAPHOBIA (300.01)

The lifetime prevalence of panic disorder, with or without agoraphobia, is between 1.5 and 3.5 percent worldwide. The one-year prevalence is between 1 and 2 percent. The onset of panic disorder typically occurs between late adolescence and the mid-30s. Some people may have episodes of the disorder with years of remission in between, while others may have continuous severe symptoms. Clients with parents who suffered from panic disorder are more likely to develop the disorder as well.

Behavioral Symptoms
(severity index: 1, mild; 2, moderate; 3, intense)

Severity

1. Recurrent unexpected panic attacks (see below) _____
2. Persistent concern about future attacks _____
3. Worry about the consequences of the attacks _____
4. Significant change in behavior related to the attacks _____

Panic Attack Criteria
(not *DSM-IV* codable)

Intense fear or discomfort in which at least four of the following develop quickly and reach a peak intensity within ten minutes:

1. Palpitations, pounding heart, increased pulse rate
2. Perspiration
3. Trembling or shaking
4. Shortness of breath
5. Sensation of smothering or choking
6. Chest pain or discomfort
7. Nausea or abdominal distress
8. Dizziness or light-headedness

9. Derealization or depersonalization
10. Fear of losing control, going crazy, or dying
11. Numbness or tingling
12. Chills or hot flashes

Other Diagnostic Considerations

Panic disorder with agoraphobia (300.21)
Agoraphobia without history of panic disorder (300.22)
Specific phobia (300.29)

Panic disorder and agoraphobia occur with several other disorders, but are not codable disorders in themselves. Behavioral definitions for both these conditions are included below.

TREATMENT PLAN
PANIC DISORDER WITHOUT AGORAPHOBIA

Client: _____ Date: _____

I.   OBJECTIVES OF TREATMENT
     (*select one or more*)

     1. Reduce frequency of panic attacks.
     2. Restore client to optimum level of functioning.
     3. Prevent recurrence of panic attacks.

II. SHORT-TERM BEHAVIORAL GOALS AND
     INTERVENTIONS
     (*select goals and interventions that are appropriate for your client*)

CLIENT'S SHORT-TERM TREATMENT GOALS	THERAPIST'S INTERVENTIONS
Join in collaborative treatment effort.	Develop a collaborative or therapeutic alliance to build trust and enhance outcome of treatment.
Discuss treatment plan and agree on target problems.	Develop treatment plan, discuss with client, select target problems.
Determine level of anxiety.	Refer client for or administer the Beck Anxiety Inventory (BAI) to determine the level of anxiety.
Explore underlying problems with therapist.	Explore for underlying problems and treat. See appropriate treatment plan.
Cooperate with therapist in building genogram to better understand family history that may impact on the disorder.	Construct genogram (see Chapter 22).

Review panic disorder history in family of origin and explore how your parents dealt with the attacks.	Investigate with client the history of panic disorder in his family of origin to determine the source of the disorder.
Help explore past and present conflicts that are related to panic attacks.	Explore past and present conflicts that exacerbate panic attacks.
Learn that anxiety is temporary and not dangerous.	Instruct client on the dynamics of anxiety.
Family interaction is improved.	Refer for or conduct family therapy to reduce anger and improve communications.
Complete homework assignments on time.	Assign homework to reduce client reaction to situational triggers.
Maintain a daily journal to help track reaction to panic trigger and record effect of medication. Use record to discuss with therapist.	Urge client to maintain a daily log to monitor his reactions and effectiveness of treatment.
Recognize the situational trigger for unexpected panic attacks.	Identity the situational triggers for unexpected panic attacks.
Learn new behavior pattern to deal with the trigger in the future.	Teach client a better way to react to the trigger.
Learn relaxation techniques to reduce the impact of future attacks.	Use relaxation techniques to help client stay calm in critical situations associated with the attacks.
Recognize irrational beliefs associated with the panic attacks.	Identify irrational beliefs associated with the attacks.

Reframe irrational beliefs with reality.	Guide client in reframing irrational beliefs with evidence-based reality.
Follow through with referral for psychiatric evaluation and the need for medication.	Refer client for psychiatric evaluation and possible medication.
Learn to take medication regularly or at first sign of distress.	Confirm client uses meds on a regular schedule and/or at first signs of distress.
Report failure to take medication and efficacy of medication when taken.	Monitor efficacy of medication for possible dosage adjustment.
Learn diaphragmatic breathing for relaxation.	Teach client diaphragmatic breathing to enhance relaxation (see Behavioral Techniques, Chapter 22).
Read self-help book to expand coping skills.	Assign client to read a self-help book to increase coping skills (see Chapter 24).
Discuss with therapist issues of termination, including separation anxiety and dependence. Agree with termination plan.	Investigate with client issues of separation anxiety and dependence. Agree on termination plan.
Regularly attend self-help group or group therapy sessions.	Refer client to self-help group or group therapy focused on panic and/or related disorders.

PANIC DISORDER WITH AGORAPHOBIA (300.21)

The lifetime incidence of panic disorder with or without agoraphobia is between 1.5 and 3.5 percent worldwide. The one-year prevalence is between 1 and 2 percent. Studies indicate that one-third to one-half of individuals diagnosed with panic disorder also have agoraphobia. In some samples, the percentages were even higher.

Agoraphobia and panic attack occur with several other disorders, but are not codable disorders in themselves. Behavioral symptoms for this condition are included below.

Panic attacks as a reaction to a substance or medication, or a general medical condition, should be ruled out.

Behavioral Symptoms
(severity index: 1, mild; 2, moderate; 3, intense)

	Severity
1. Recurrent unexpected panic attacks	_____
2. Persistent concern about future attacks	_____
3. Worry about consequences of the attacks	_____
4. Agoraphobia	_____

Panic Attack Symptoms
(not *DSM-IV* codable)

Intense fear or discomfort in which at least four of the following develop quickly and reach a peak intensity within ten minutes:

1. Palpitations, pounding heart, increased pulse rate
2. Perspiration
3. Trembling or shaking
4. Shortness of breath
5. Feeling of smothering or choking
6. Chest pain
7. Nausea

8. Dizziness
9. Derealization or depersonalization
10. Fear of losing control, going crazy, or dying
11. Numbness or tingling
12. Chills
13. Hot flashes

Agoraphobia Symptoms
(not *DSM-IV* codable)

1. Anxiety over being in a situation or place where escape might be impossible or difficult
2. Anxiety over being in a place where a panic attack would be embarrassing
3. Anxiety over being in situation or place where help may not be available in case of panic attack
4. The situation or place is avoided or endured with distress
5. The situation or place is endured with support of a companion

Other Diagnostic Considerations

Panic disorder without agoraphobia (300.01)
Agoraphobia without history of panic disorder (300.22)
Specific phobia (300.29)
Social phobia (300.23)
Separation anxiety disorder (309.21)

TREATMENT PLAN
PANIC DISORDER WITH AGORAPHOBIA

Client: _____ Date: _____

I. OBJECTIVES OF TREATMENT
   (*select one or more*)

    1. Diminish fear of being trapped in a place or situation.
    2. Diminish fear of embarrassment over panic attack.
    3. Diminish fear that help may not be available in certain places or situations.
    4. Eliminate avoidance of fearful places.
    5. Eliminate need for companion in confronting certain places or situations.
    6. Restore client to optimum level of functioning.
    7. Prevent relapse.

II. SHORT-TERM BEHAVIORAL GOALS AND INTERVENTIONS
   (*select goals and interventions appropriate for your client*)

CLIENT'S SHORT-TERM BEHAVIORAL GOALS	THERAPIST'S INTERVENTIONS
Discuss treatment plan with therapist and agree on target problems to be addressed.	Develop a treatment plan, discuss with client, agree on target problems.
Cooperate with therapist in collaborative treatment.	Cultivate a therapeutic or collaborative alliance to build trust and enhance outcome of treatment.
Determine level of anxiety.	Refer client for or administer the Beck Anxiety Inventory to determine the level of anxiety.

Discuss underlying problems that contribute to your panic attacks.	Explore underlying problems that contribute to panic attacks. See appropriate treatment plan.
Assist in creating genogram and explaining family interactional patterns.	Construct genogram (see Chapter 22).
Recognize and understand the symptoms and nature of panic disorder.	Explain to client the nature of panic disorder and its symptoms, and laws of anxiety: not dangerous, not permanent, avoidance increases it.
Client practices diaphragmatic breathing for relaxation.	Coach client in diaphragmatic breathing to increase relaxation and reduce panic (see Behavioral Techniques, Chapter 22).
Responsibly complete homework assignments.	Provide homework assignments for client to help identify activating events, irrational beliefs, and consequences.
Investigate and determine the origins of panic attack and fear of places or situations.	Track with client the consequences and how they were derived. Identify musts.
Examine and identify the evidence.	Assist client in weighing irrational beliefs against reality.
Develop a rational response to the panic and fears.	With client replace irrational beliefs with rational beliefs and new consequences.
Maintain a daily journal to monitor feelings and reactions to places and situations.	Assign client to keep daily log of his feelings and reactions to activating events.
Build assertiveness skills.	Explain principles of assertiveness—equal respect, you and other, etc.

Learn and practice relaxation techniques or hypnosis.	Use relaxation technique to help client cope with anxiety and panic. Provide audiotape.
Learn and practice concept that anxiety diminishes when confronted and increases when avoided.	Instruct client to confront the first signs of anxiety rather than to flee or give in.
Confront fears with the help of a responsible and trusted friend or relative.	Identify "safe" person who will help client confront fears.
Read assigned self-help book to increase understanding and help overcome anxiety.	Assign client to read self-help book (see Chapter 24).
Reduce and discontinue reliance on companion for support.	Urge client to practice new skills and go it alone.
Participate in family sessions.	Conduct or refer to family therapy to reduce anger. Educate family to develop strategies for coping with agoraphobic client.
Take medications as prescribed and report all side effects.	Refer client to physician medical and psychiatric evaluation.
Overcome fear of specific places and situations. Recognize that avoidance increases anxiety.	Confront and challenge fear of certain places and situations.
Review termination plan. Investigate with therapist issues of separation and dependency.	Prepare termination plan. Discuss with client issues of separation anxiety and dependency.
Regularly attend self-help groups or group therapy dealing with anxiety, panic attacks, and/or agoraphobia.	Refer client to self-help or therapy group dealing with anxiety, panic, and agoraphobia.

POSTTRAUMATIC STRESS DISORDER (309.81)
(Specify: Acute—Duration <3 Months; Chronic—Duration > 5 Months, or Late Onset—After 6 Months)

Studies indicate a lifetime prevalence rate of 1 to 14 percent with substantially higher rates for people in risk situations (military combat, disaster victims, or victims of criminal actions). The disorder can occur at any age, including childhood.

Behavioral Symptoms
(severity index: 1, mild; 2, moderate; 3, intense)

Client witnessed or experienced an actual or threatened event that placed him/her or another person in danger of death or serious injury and reacted with feelings of intense fear, horror, or helplessness.

	Severity
1. Persistent reexperience of the traumatic event as a recollection or dream	_____
2. Flashbacks or feelings of reliving the event	_____
3. Intense distress at cues that are reminiscent of the event or some aspect of the event	_____
4. Avoidance of thoughts, feelings, activities, people, or places associated with the event	_____
5. Inability to remember an important aspect of the event	_____
6. Reduced interest in significant activities	_____
7. Feeling of detachment from others	_____
8. Restricted range of feelings	_____
9. Heightened sense of limited future	_____
10. Sleep problems	_____
11. Irritability or angry outbursts	_____
12. Inability to concentrate	_____
13. Increased vigilance/easily startled	_____
14. The symptoms cause serious impairment to ADLs	_____

Other Diagnostic Considerations

Adjustment disorders:
  with depressed mood (309.0)
  with anxiety (309.224)
  with mixed anxiety and depressed mood (309.28)
  with disturbance of conduct (309.3)
  with mixed disturbance of emotions and conduct (309.4)
  Unspecified (309.9)
Acute stress disorder (308.3)
Obsessive-compulsive disorder (300.3)

Malingering should be ruled out.

TREATMENT PLAN
POSTTRAUMATIC STRESS DISORDER (309.81)

Client: _____ Date: _____

I. OBJECTIVES OF TREATMENT
   (*select one or more*)

   1. Eliminate stressors associated with the traumatic event.
   2. Relieve distress associated with the event.
   3. Return client to premorbid level of functioning.
   4. Prevent recurrence of symptoms.

II. SHORT-TERM BEHAVIORAL GOALS AND
   INTERVENTIONS
   (*select goals and interventions appropriate for your client*)

CLIENT'S SHORT-TERM BEHAVIORAL GOALS	THERAPIST'S INTERVENTIONS
Confirm diagnosis of posttraumatic stress disorder.	Confirm diagnosis. Rule out malingering.
Join in treatment as a collaborative effort.	Develop collaborative or therapeutic alliance to build trust and enhance treatment outcome.
Determine level of anxiety.	Refer client or administer the Beck Anxiety Inventory (BAI) to determine the level of anxiety.
Review treatment plan and agree with therapist on target problems.	Create treatment plan, discuss with client, and agree on target problems to be addressed.
Receive clinical data regarding the effects of trauma.	Refer for or administer the Trauma Symptom Inventory (TSI) to evaluate acute and chronic event-related stress.

Learn nature of posttraumatic stress disorder.	Teach client features and causes of the disorder.
Relate in detail the trigger event and your reactive feelings.	Investigate with client the traumatic event and his/her feelings and reactions.
Maintain daily log of your feelings and the triggers that touch off physical and emotional reactions.	Instruct client to maintain daily log of persons, places, activities, and things related to the traumatic event that trigger fear or anxiety.
Record flashbacks and dreams of the event.	Explore flashbacks and analyze dreams to reduce their impact on the client.
Follow-up with referral for medical evaluation and maintain regular medication schedule.	Refer client for medical evaluation and possible medication. Instruct client on medication regimen.
Provide feedback on reactions to meds and lapses in planned medication schedule.	Instruct client on importance of feedback and need to report reactions to the meds.
Examine distortions in reaction to the event stressors.	Discuss reactions to identify exaggerated and distorted reactions.
Replace exaggerated reactions with positive reactions, using evidence-based reality.	Reframe negative reactions with positive reality-based cognitions.
Learn new coping techniques.	Coach client in developing new strategies to cope.
Learn new breathing technique for relaxation.	Teach client diaphragmatic breathing to increase relaxation (see Behavioral Techniques, Chapter 22).

Using relaxation technique or hypnosis, revisit traumatic event replacing stress reactions with positive cognition.	Use relaxation technique or hypnosis in the office to desensitize client. Reexperience the traumatic event, replacing negative reactions with new cognitions. Provide tape for home use.
Read self-help book to expand understanding of the disorder.	Assign client to read self-help book (see Chapter 24).
Practice coping skills in real-life situations. Report reactions and self-reward successes.	Instruct client to challenge persons, places, activities, and things related to the event, and record reactions. Reinforce successes.
Repeat real-life challenge to gradually diminish and eliminate anxiety reactions.	Urge client to repeat real-life challenge strategy to ameliorate fear and stress reactions.
Review termination plan. Investigate and resolve termination issues with therapist—separation anxiety, dependence.	Build termination plan. Explore with client issues of separation and dependence.
Attend self-help group meetings to reinforce coping skills.	Refer client to self-help group or group therapy dealing with posttraumatic stress disorder.

SOCIAL PHOBIA (300.23)

Studies indicate a lifetime prevalence of social phobia of about 13 percent. Average age at presentation is 30 years. However, the onset of social phobia is typically in the midteens after a childhood marked by shyness.

Behavioral Symptoms
(severity index: 1, mild; 2, moderate; 3, intense)

<u>Severity</u>

1. Persistent fear of social interactions where evaluation by others is possible   _____
2. Fear of acting in social situations in an embarrassing or humiliating way   _____
3. Exposure to social situations leads to panic attack   _____
4. Client recognizes fear as excessive and unreasonable   _____
5. Feared social situations are avoided or endured under duress   _____
6. The fear and distress interfere with the client's ADLs   _____
7. The fear or avoidance is not the result of drugs, medication, or general medical condition   _____

Other Diagnostic Considerations

Panic disorder with agoraphobia (300.21)
Agoraphobia without history of panic disorder (300.22)
Separation anxiety disorder (309.21)
Specific phobia (00.29)
Avoidant personality disorder (301.82)
Schizoid personality disorder (301.20)

If the fears of social phobia include most social situations, consider the added diagnosis of avoidant personality disorder.

TREATMENT PLAN
SOCIAL PHOBIA

Client: _____   Date: _____

I. OBJECTIVES OF TREATMENT
    (*select one or more*)

    1. Diminish and eliminate fear of embarrassment or humiliation in social interactions.
    2. Control and eliminate panic attacks.
    3. Eliminate need for avoidance of social interactions.
    4. Restore client to optimum level of functioning to prevent relapse.

II. SHORT-TERM BEHAVIORAL GOALS AND
    INTERVENTIONS
    (*select goals and interventions appropriate for your client*)

CLIENT'S SHORT-TERM BEHAVIORAL GOALS	THERAPIST'S INTERVENTIONS
Feel more hopeful that phobia can be treated and resolved.	Establish a therapeutic alliance or collaborative working relationship.
Agree on treatment plan and problems to be addressed.	Develop a treatment plan and select target problems to work on.
Help determine the level of his/her anxiety.	Refer client for or administer the Beck Anxiety Inventory (BAI) to determine the level of anxiety.
Learn the symptoms and nature of social phobia.	Instruct client as the nature of social phobia.
Cooperate in building genogram and identify patterns of interaction.	Construct genogram (see Chapter 22).

Recognize social phobia history and how family has dealt with social anxieties.	Investigate history of social phobia with client and in family of origin.
Recognize situational triggers and avoidance behavior.	Identify situational triggers for phobia and avoidance behaviors.
Follow through on referral and maintain a medication regimen if prescribed.	Refer client for psychiatric evaluation and possible medication for anxiety. Rule out drug abuse.
Understand nature of anxiety.	Explain nature of anxiety—not dangerous, not permanent, increased by avoidance.
Learn new breathing technique to help control anxiety.	Teach client diaphragmatic breathing to help in relaxation (see Behavioral Techniques, Chapter 22).
Learn that anxieties are diminished by confrontation and increase when avoided.	Instruct client to confront first signs of anxiety rather than run from it.
Keep a daily journal to record feelings and reactions in different social situations.	Urge client to start and maintain a daily journal to record feelings and reactions in social situations.
Complete homework as assigned.	Assign homework in which client can identify irrational beliefs and negative consequences.
Identify irrational or exaggerated beliefs.	Discuss homework with client.
Evaluate beliefs for negative consequences and reframe them.	Help client examine and reframe irrational and exaggerated beliefs for positive consequences.

Read recommended self-help book to learn more about his/her disorder and how to deal with it.	Suggest that client read self-help book (see Chapter 24).
Adjust performance requirements from "perfect" to "good enough."	Help client to lower his self-expectations.
Learn to focus on task, not audience.	Instruct client to ignore the audience in social interactions, but concentrate on the task at hand.
Explore issues of shame, rejection, and abandonment as they may impact phobia.	Investigate history of shame, rejection, or abandonment that foster phobias.
Recognize the destructive nature of negative self-talk and replace with positive affirmations.	Instruct client to recognize negative self-talk and replace it with positive messages.
Build and practice assertiveness skills.	Explain principles of assertiveness—equal respect for self and others.
Use hypnosis to confront phobias. Avoidance behaviors are eliminated.	Teach client self-hypnosis to help cope with phobias. Provide audiotape for home use.
Visualize being able to overcome phobia in hypnosis.	Use hypnosis to gradually desensitize phobia.
Challenge real social interactions that were formerly troublesome and provide feedback.	Have client increase exposure gradually to real social situations and record/review feelings and reactions.
Participate in self-help group and develops new skills in interacting with others.	Refer to self-help group and urge active participation.
Practice control of anxieties psychodramatically.	Conduct role-playing exercises that address phobias.

Overcome fear of certain places and situations. Gains confidence.	Encourage client to externalize his role-playing skills and challenge fears of certain places and situations.
Develop termination plan.	Develop termination plan.
Discuss with therapist termination issues of separation and dependence.	Investigate and resolve issues of separation anxiety and dependence.

SPECIFIC PHOBIA (300.29)

Studies indicate the one-year prevalence of specific phobia is 9 percent of the population with a lifetime rate of 10 to 11 percent. There are several types of specific phobia that should be specified with the diagnosis, including animal, natural environment, blood-injection, injury, situational, and other.

Agoraphobia and panic attack occur with several other disorders, but are not codable disorders in themselves. Behavioral symptoms for both of these conditions are included below.

Panic attack as a reaction to a substance or medication, or a general medical condition, should be ruled out.

Behavioral Symptoms
(severity index: 1, mild; 2, moderate; 3, intense)

	Severity
1. Excessive and unreasonable fear of an object or situation	_____
2. Immediate anxiety upon exposure to object or situation	_____
3. Client recognizes unreasonable nature of fear	_____
4. The object or situational trigger is avoided or endured	_____
5. The avoidance or distress significantly interferes with the client's daily life.	_____

Other Diagnostic Considerations

Panic disorder with agoraphobia (300.21)
Agoraphobia without history of panic disorder (300.22)
Social phobia (300.23)
Separation anxiety disorder (309.21)
Obsessive-compulsive disorder (300.3)
Posttraumatic stress disorder (309.81)
Avoidant personality disorder (301.82)

TREATMENT PLAN
SPECIFIC PHOBIA

Client: _____ Date: _____

I. OBJECTIVES OF TREATMENT
   (*select one or more*)

   1. Diminish excessive fear of object or situation.
   2. Decrease anxiety when exposed to object or situation.
   3. Eliminate need to avoid or endure object or situation.
   4. Eliminate interference with ADLs.
   5. Restore client to optimum level of functioning.

II. SHORT-TERM BEHAVIORAL GOALS AND
    INTERVENTIONS
    (*select goals and interventions appropriate for your client*)

CLIENT'S SHORT-TERM BEHAVIORAL GOALS	THERAPIST'S INTERVENTIONS
Discuss treatment plan and agree on target problems to be addressed.	Develop treatment plan and agree with client on target problems to be addressed.
Collaborate with therapist in treatment; feels less alienated, more hopeful.	Develop therapeutic or collaborative alliance to encourage trust and enhance treatment outcome.
Reduce severity of fears.	Examine the client's fear and help to look at reality issues related to fears.
Assist therapist in creating genogram in order to better understand family of origin.	Construct genogram (see Chapter 22).
Explore and understand origins of specific fear.	Explore with the client the original source of his/her fear.

Responsibly complete homework assignments.	Assign homework to underline client's irrational belief.
Maintain a daily journal to monitor the trigger that induces fear and his subsequent feelings and reactions.	Instruct client to maintain a notebook to record thoughts, feelings, and reactions to object or situation that triggers fear.
Recognize the irrational belief that ends in fear.	Using homework, identify the irrational belief that leads to the fear.
Investigate rational beliefs to replace the irrational reaction to the trigger.	Collect evidence and replace the irrational belief with a rational belief system.
Learn diaphragmatic breathing.	Instruct client in diaphragmatic breathing to help in relaxation.
Build assertiveness skills.	Teach client principles of assertiveness—equal respect for self and other.
Learn and practice relaxation techniques.	Introduce client to relaxation techniques or hypnosis and provide audiotape for home use.
Recognize that avoidance increases anxiety.	Instruct client in the laws of anxiety: avoidance increases anxiety, confrontation lessens it. Panic is not dangerous, never permanent, exposure decreases anxiety.
Diminish and eliminate need for avoidance.	Gradually build client's confidence to a level where avoidance is no longer a rational response.

Confront and challenge trigger for phobia.	Urge client to confront and challenge the object or situation that once triggered a fear reaction. Reward and repeat success.
Read self-help book; realize other people have similar problems.	Assign client to read self-help book to increase understanding and reinforce new skills (see Chapter 24).
Discuss with therapist issues of termination: separation anxiety and dependence.	Investigate with client termination issues of separation anxiety and dependence.
Regularly attend self-help support groups or group therapy dealing with phobias.	Refer client to self-help group if needed to further integrate the gains and prevent relapse.

6

Bipolar Disorders

Bipolar disorders include recurrent mood disorders in which episodes of mania occur with or without major depression. Included in this category are bipolar I disorder, bipolar II disorder, cyclothymia, and bipolar disorder NOS.

BIPOLAR I DISORDER (296.xx)

Most recent episode:

Single manic episode (296.0x)
Hypomanic (296.40)
Mixed (296.4X)
Depressed (296.5X)
Unspecified (296.7)

Bipolar I disorder is characterized by one or more manic episodes, or mixed episodes. Often clients have had one or more major depressive episodes as well. There are six subsets of bipolar I disorder depending on whether the individual is experiencing a first episode characterized as a single manic episode, or a recurrence. Recurrence may be marked by a shift in polarity (major depressive episode to a manic or mixed episode, or a manic episode into a depressive or mixed episode). However, a hypomanic episode that evolves into a manic or mixed episode, or vice versa, is considered a single episode. Recurrent bipolar I disorders are specified by the current or most recent episode as follows:

Single manic episode characterized by manic symptoms for one week or requiring hospitalization, with no past depressive episodes. Marked impairment in functioning.

Most recent episode: hypomanic characterized by manic symptoms for at least four days without significant impairment in social or occupational functioning. At least one previous manic or hypomanic episode.

Most recent episode: manic characterized by manic symptoms for one week or requiring hospitalization. At least one previous manic, major depressive, or mixed episode. Marked impairment in functioning.

Most recent episode: mixed characterized by both manic and depressive symptoms nearly every day for one week. With significant impairment in functioning or requiring hospitalization.

Most recent episode: depressed characterized by depressive symptoms for a two-week period with at least one previous manic or mixed episode. Impairment is clinically significant.

Most recent episode: unspecified characterized by manic, hypomanic, mixed, or depressive symptoms but not meeting the duration criteria listed above. At least one previous manic or mixed episode. Impairment is clinically significant.

Genetics and gender contribute to the incidence and severity of bipolar symptoms. The incidence of bipolar I disorder or major depressive disorder among first-degree biological relatives of individuals with bipolar I disorder may be as high as 24 percent. More than 90 percent of individuals who have experienced a single manic episode will go on to have future episodes. More than 60 percent of manic episodes occur immediately before or after a major depressive episode.

Completed suicides occur in 10 to 15 percent of individuals with bipolar I disorder.

Although most individuals with bipolar I disorder return to a functional level, some 20 to 30 percent continue to exhibit interpersonal and occupational difficulties.

While medication is the primary treatment modality for bipolar disorders, the therapeutic alliance among the patient, family, and clinician is important in managing the disorder. Mood swings may alter a patient's willingness to comply with a treatment plan (including medication). An assessment of the patients' risk to themselves or others must determine the appropriate level of care. Patients experiencing a severe manic episode are often hospitalized. After hospitalization, regular outpatient sessions may be necessary to fine-tune medication.

Behavioral Symptoms—Manic Episode
(severity index: 1, mild; 2, moderate; 3, intense)

Abnormal, persistent elevated, expansive, or irritable mood lasting for one week, including three of the following, and causing significant impairment in social or occupational functioning or the need for hospitalization. There are psychotic features.

<u>Severity</u>

1. Abnormally talkative, pressured speech   _____
2. Flight of ideas or racing thoughts   _____
3. Marked increase in goal-directed activity   _____
4. Psychomotor agitation   _____
5. Easily distracted by external stimuli   _____
6. Excessive involvement in pleasurable activities with a high potential for negative consequence   _____
7. Decreased need for sleep   _____
8. Inflated self-esteem or grandiosity   _____

Behavioral Symptoms—Depressive Episode
(severity index: 1, mild; 2, moderate; 3, intense)

Depressed mood or loss of pleasure or interest and three or more of the following for a two-week period:

	Severity
1. Depressed mood most of the day	_____
2. Decreased pleasure or interest in activities	_____
3. Significant weight change (± 5 percent) in past 30 days	_____
4. Insomnia or hypersomnia	_____
5. Retardation or psychomotor agitation	_____
6. Fatigue or loss of energy	_____
7. Feelings of worthlessness or excessive guilt	_____
8. Diminished ability to think or concentrate	_____
9. Recurrent thoughts of death	_____
10. Recurrent suicidal ideations with or without a specific plan	_____
11. Suicide attempt	_____

Behavioral Symptoms—Mixed Episode
(severity index: 1, mild; 2, moderate; 3, intense)

Symptoms for both manic and depressive episodes (listed above) persisting almost every day for one week. See Objectives of Treatment for both manic and depressive episodes.

Behavioral Symptoms—Hypomanic Episode
(severity index: 1, mild; 2, moderate; 3, intense)

An elevated, expansive, or irritable mood persisting for at least four days and including three of the following, four with only irritable mood. The episode is not acute enough to cause major impairment in occupational or social functioning or to require hospitalization. There are no psychotic features.

	Severity
1. Abnormally talkative, pressured speech	_____
2. Flight of ideas or racing thoughts	_____
3. Marked increase in goal-directed activity	_____
4. Psychomotor agitation	_____
5. Easily distracted by external stimuli	_____
6. Excessive involvement in pleasurable activities with a high potential for negative consequence	_____
7. Decreased need for sleep	_____
8. Inflated self-esteem or grandiosity	_____

See Objectives of Treatment for manic episodes.

Other Diagnostic Considerations

Bipolar II Disorder (286.89)
    Specify current or most recent episode: hypomanic or
        depressed
Cyclothymic disorder (301.13)
Bipolar disorder NOS (296.80)
Mood disorder due to a general medical condition (293.83)
Substance-induced mood disorder (293.83)
Mood disorder NOS (296.90)

TREATMENT PLAN
BIPOLAR DISORDER I

Client: _____ Date: _____

I.   OBJECTIVES OF TREATMENT—Manic Episode
     (*select one or more*)

     1. Control pressurized speech.
     2. Reduce psychomotor agitation.
     3. Increase ability to maintain concentration.
     4. Curtail potentially destructive activities.
     5. Restore normal sleep pattern.
     6. Reduce grandiosity.
     7. Increase ability to focus on a single thought or task.

I.   OBJECTIVES OF TREATMENT—Depressive Episode
     (*select one or more*)

     1. Reduce persistent depression.
     2. Restore interest in former pleasurable activities.
     3. Restore normal eating pattern.
     4. Restore normal sleep pattern.
     5. Eliminate feelings of worthlessness, guilt.
     6. Improve energy level.
     7. Eliminate or control suicidal ideations.

II. SHORT-TERM BEHAVIORAL GOALS AND
     INTERVENTIONS
     (*select goals and interventions appropriate for your client*)

CLIENT'S SHORT-TERM BEHAVIORAL GOALS	THERAPIST'S INTERVENTIONS
Understand nature of bipolar I disorder.	Review nature of disorder with client.

Review treatment plan and agree on target problems for treatment.	Formulate treatment plan and review with client. Agree on target problems for treatment.
Join in collaborative effort.	Cultivate a therapeutic alliance or collaborative relationship to build trust and enhance treatment outcome.
Confirm and define depression.	Refer for or administer the Beck Depression Inventory–II (BDI-II) to confirm existence of the disorder and level of intensity of the depression.
Clinically assess intent.	Refer for or administer the Beck Scale for Suicidal Ideation (BSS) to help evaluate intent.
Be hospitalized or enter into a "suicide pact" with the therapist to report all suicidal ideations and active plans.	If client is actively suicidal, hospitalize immediately. Call 911 or ambulance. Do not leave client unattended. If client is not active but has suicidal ideations, suggest and implement a "suicide pact" in which the client agrees to inform you of active plans, and promises to inform you before taking action.
Undergo medical evaluation.	Refer client for medical evaluation.
Be treated for physical problems.	Confirm or revise diagnosis. Rule out disorder due to a general medical condition.
Undergo substance abuse evaluation, and if positive attend twelve-step program.	Investigate and rule out substance abuse. Revise diagnosis and treat if necessary. See appropriate treatment plan.

Follow through with referral for psychiatric evaluation to assess need for medication and possible antisuicide measures.	Refer client for psychiatric evaluation and follow-up to confirm he/she kept appointment.
Maintain regular medication schedule and report urges to ignore or discontinue meds.	If medication is prescribed, confirm that prescription is filled and meds are taken on schedule.
Provide prompt feedback on the effectiveness of the medication and possible side effects.	Refer client to psychiatrist for possible dosage adjustment and feedback on side effects.
Confirm or rule out sexual abuse.	Evaluate for and rule out sexual abuse. Treat if necessary. See appropriate treatment plan.
Understand possible need for hospitalization.	Explain to client possible need for hospitalization and resolve any anxiety.
Accept hospitalization as necessary to protect self or others.	Hospitalize client when advisable to prevent suicide or harm to others.
Report to therapist all destructive self-talk and thoughts of harm to self or others.	Explain self-talk to client; closely monitor destructive thoughts and urges.
Replace destructive self-talk with positive affirmations of self-worth and the ability to cope successfully with ADLs.	Replace destructive thoughts and urges with positive affirmations drawing on past successes with ADLs.
Reduce alienation from family.	Conduct or refer for family counseling to improve family dynamics.
Family better understands how to deal with client and the disorder.	Educate family about the disorder.

Understand feelings that result in acting out and learn to think before acting.	Explore and clarify underlying feelings that lead to pathological behavior.
Accept that he/she has a chronic disorder.	Educate client about chronicity of disorder to reduce anger and denial.
Learn technique to help slow down when manic.	Teach client diaphragmatic breathing to slow down pressurized speech or flight of ideas (see Behavioral Techniques, Chapter 22).
Build new assertiveness skills.	Teach client principles of assertiveness—equal respect for self and others.
Responsibly complete homework assignments designed to affirm self-worth.	Discuss with client positive premorbid experiences with ADLs and feelings of self-worth. Provide trigger to reframe negative thoughts and feelings.
Diminish need to "hide out" because of guilt or anger over having this disorder.	Gradually build client's confidence to a level where avoidance behavior is no longer a rational response.
Realize that he/she is more than the disorder and use unique skills to deal with problems.	Empower client by further reinforcing strengths and new skills.
Recognize grandiosity and reframe thinking and behavior.	Investigate client's grandiose thinking and behavior.
Become more aware of behavioral triggers and how to control actions.	Discuss psychomotor agitation and its triggers.
Gradually become aware of the negative consequences of acting out.	Explore excessive involvement in pleasurable activities that have negative consequences.

Participate in recreational activities with others.	Review with client past interests in recreational activities (sports, exercise, chess, cards, etc.) and urge client to join external exercise or recreational group to renew pattern of contact and communication with others.
Maintain a daily journal to record continuing depressive feelings and situations that trigger them. Record success in overcoming these feelings. Discuss with therapist.	Assign client to keep a daily journal to record feelings of depression and successes in overcoming those feelings.
Begin to listen to others and reduce pressurized speech.	Teach client active listening skills.
Improve sleep pattern. Symptoms of sleep deprivation are diminished.	Investigate sleep disorder and see that client gets appropriate treatment if required.
Identify triggers for dreams or nightmares that disturb sleep.	Explore dreams or nightmares that may interfere with sleep.
Renew personal contact with relatives, friends, and neighbors.	Urge client to reach out and renew contacts with relatives and former friends and neighbors.
Review termination plan. Investigate issues of termination, including separation anxiety and dependency.	Review termination plan. Discuss with client issues of termination, specifically separation anxiety and dependency.
Regularly attend and actively participate in recommended self-help groups or group therapy sessions.	Recommend to client active participation in an appropriate self-help group or group therapy focused on depression.

BIPOLAR II DISORDER (296.89)
(Specify if Hypomanic or Depressed)

Bipolar II disorder is characterized by one or more major depressive episodes in conjunction with at least one hypomanic episode. The most recent episode should be specified as hypomanic or depressed. The existence of a manic or mixed episode would preclude the diagnosis of bipolar II disorder. The symptoms must cause significant distress or impairment in social, occupational, or other areas of functioning. Completed suicide occurs in 10 to 15 percent of cases of bipolar II disorder.

Behavioral Symptoms—Depressive Episode
(severity index: 1, mild; 2, moderate; 3, intense)

Depressed mood or loss of pleasure or interest and three or more of the following for a two-week period:

	Severity
1. Depressed mood most of the day	_____
2. Decreased pleasure or interest in activities	_____
3. Significant weight change (± 5 percent) in past 30 days	_____
4. Insomnia or hypersomnia	_____
5. Retardation or psychomotor agitation	_____
6. Fatigue or loss of energy	_____
7. Feelings of worthlessness or excessive guilt	_____
8. Diminished ability to think or concentrate	_____
9. Recurrent thoughts of death	_____
10. Recurrent suicidal ideations with or without a specific plan	_____
11. Suicide attempt	_____

Behavioral Symptoms—Hypomanic Episode
(severity index: 1, mild; 2, moderate; 3, intense)

An elevated, expansive, or irritable mood persisting for at least four days and including three of the following, four with only irritable mood. The episode is not acute enough to cause major impairment in occupational or social functioning or to require hospitalization. There are no psychotic features.

	Severity
1. Abnormally talkative, pressured speech	_____
2. Flight of ideas or racing thoughts	_____
3. Marked increase in goal-directed activity	_____
4. Psychomotor agitation	_____
5. Easily distracted by external stimuli	_____
6. Excessive involvement in pleasurable activities with a high potential for negative consequence	_____
7. Decreased need for sleep	_____
8. Inflated self-esteem or grandiosity	_____

Other Diagnostic Considerations

Bipolar I disorder (296.xx)
Cyclothymic disorder (301.13)
Bipolar disorder NOS (296.80)
Mood disorder due to a general medical condition (293.83)
Substance-induced mood disorder (293.83)
Mood disorder NOS (296.90)
Major depressive disorder (296.xx)
Dysthymia (300.4)
Psychotic disorders (298.xx)

TREATMENT PLAN
BIPOLAR II DISORDER

Client: _____ Date: _____

I. OBJECTIVES OF TREATMENT—Depressive Episode
    (*select one or more*)

    1. Reduce persistent depression.
    2. Restore interest in former pleasurable activities.
    3. Restore normal eating pattern.
    4. Restore normal sleep pattern.
    5. Eliminate feelings of worthlessness, guilt.
    6. Improve energy level.
    7. Eliminate or control suicidal ideations.

I. OBJECTIVES OF TREATMENT—Hypomanic Episode
    (*select one or more*)

    1. Control pressurized speech.
    2. Reduce psychomotor agitation.
    3. Increase ability to maintain concentration.
    4. Curtail potentially destructive activities.
    5. Restore normal sleep pattern.
    6. Reduce grandiosity.
    7. Increase ability to focus on a single thought or task.

II. SHORT-TERM BEHAVIORAL GOALS AND
    INTERVENTIONS
    (select goals and interventions appropriate for your client)

CLIENT'S SHORT-TERM BEHAVIORAL GOALS	THERAPIST'S INTERVENTIONS
Cooperate in confirming diagnosis.	Confirm diagnosis.

Join in collaborative effort.	Cultivate therapeutic alliance or collaborative relationship to build trust and enhance outcome.
Understand nature of bipolar II disorder.	Review nature of disorder with client.
Review treatment plan and agree on target problems for treatment.	Formulate treatment plan and review with client. Agree on target problems for treatment.
Confirm and define depression.	Refer for or administer the Beck Depression Inventory—II (BDI-II) to confirm existence of the disorder and level of intensity of the depression.
Be hospitalized to prevent any suicide attempts.	If client is actively suicidal, refer immediately for hospitalization. Call 911 or ambulance. Do not leave client unattended.
Clinically assess intent.	Refer for or administer the Beck Scale for Suicidal Ideation (BSS) to help evaluate intent.
Willingly enter into a "suicide pact" with the therapist to report all suicidal ideations and active plans. Agree to inform therapist of your intent before taking action.	If client is not actively suicidal but has ideations, suggest and implement a "suicide pact" in which the client agrees to inform you of suicidal ideations and active plans, and promises to inform you before taking action.
Undergo medical evaluation.	Refer client for medical evaluation.
Be treated for physical problems.	Confirm or revise diagnosis. Rule out disorder due to a general medical condition.

Undergo substance abuse evaluation, and if positive attend twelve-step program.	Investigate and rule out substance abuse. Revise diagnosis and treat if necessary. See appropriate treatment plan.
Follow through with referral for psychiatric evaluation to assess need for medication and possible antisuicide measures.	Refer client for psychiatric evaluation and follow-up to confirm he/she kept appointment.
Maintain regular medication schedule and report urges to ignore or discontinue meds.	If medication is prescribed, confirm that prescription is filled and meds are taken on schedule.
Provide prompt feedback on the effectiveness of the medication and possible side effects.	Refer client to psychiatrist for possible dosage adjustment and feedback on side effects.
Confirm or rule out sexual abuse.	Evaluate for and rule out sexual abuse. Treat if necessary. See appropriate treatment plan.
Understand possible need for hospitalization.	Explain to client possible need for hospitalization and resolve any anxiety.
Accept hospitalization as necessary to protect self or others.	Hospitalize client when advisable to prevent suicide or harm to others.
Alienation is reduced.	Conduct or refer for family counseling.
Family learns to deal with client in a more effective way.	Act as consultant to educate family about the disorder.
Report to therapist all destructive self-talk and thoughts of harm to self or others.	Explain self-talk to client. Closely monitor destructive thoughts and urges.

Replace destructive self-talk with positive affirmations of self-worth and the ability to cope successfully with ADLs.	Replace destructive thoughts and urges with positive affirmations drawing on past successes with ADLs.
Become aware of underlying feelings and learn to stop and think before acting.	Explore and clarify underlying feelings that cause client to act pathologically.
Accept that he/she has a chronic disorder.	Educate client about chronicity of disorder to reduce anger and denial.
Learn technique to help slow down when manic.	Teach client diaphragmatic breathing to slow down pressurized speech or flight of ideas (see Homework, Chapter 23).
Build new assertiveness skills.	Teach client principles of assertiveness—equal respect for self and others.
Responsibly complete homework assignments designed to affirm self-worth.	Discuss with client positive premorbid experiences with ADL and feelings of self-worth. Provide trigger to reframe negative thoughts and feelings.
Diminish need to "hide out" because of guilt or anger over having this disorder.	Gradually build client's confidence to a level where avoidance behavior is no longer a rational response.
Realize that he/she is more than the disorder and uses unique skills to deal with problems.	Empower client by further reinforcing strengths and new skills.
Recognize grandiosity and reframes thinking and behavior.	Investigate client's grandiose thinking and behavior.

Become more aware of behavioral triggers and how to control actions.	Discuss psychomotor agitation and its triggers.
Gradually become aware of the negative consequences of acting out.	Explore excessive involvement in pleasurable activities that have negative consequences.
Participate in recreational activities with others.	Review with client past interests in recreational activities (sports, exercise, chess, cards, etc.) and urge client to join external exercise or recreational group to renew pattern of contact and communication with others.
Maintain a daily journal to record continuing depressive feelings and situations that trigger them. Record success in overcoming these feelings. Discuss with therapist.	Assign client to keep a daily journal to record feelings of depression and successes in overcoming those feelings.
Begin to listen to others and reduce pressurized speech.	Teach client active listening skills.
Improve sleep pattern. Symptoms of sleep deprivation are diminished.	Investigate sleep disorder and see that client gets appropriate treatment if required.
Identify triggers for dreams or nightmares that disturb sleep.	Explore dreams or nightmares that may interfere with sleep.
Renew personal contact with relatives, friends, and neighbors.	Urge client to reach out and renew contacts with relatives and former friends and neighbors.

Review termination plan. Investigate with therapist issues of termination, including separation anxiety and dependency.	Review termination plan. Discuss with client issues of termination, specifically separation anxiety and dependency.
Regularly attend and actively participate in recommended self-help groups or group therapy sessions.	Recommend to client active participation in an appropriate self-help group or group therapy.

BIPOLAR DISORDER NOS (296.80)

Bipolar disorder not otherwise specified include those disorders with bipolar features that do not meet the specifications for other specific bipolar disorders. Bipolar disorder NOS is characterized by quick alternating manic and depressive symptoms, usually over a matter of days, that do not meet the duration requirements for a manic episode (one week), or a major depressive episode (two weeks). The symptoms cause major impairment in functioning.

The objectives of treatment, goals, and interventions are identical to those of cyclothymic disorder (see Chapter 7).

Other Diagnostic Considerations

Bipolar I disorder (296.xx)
Bipolar II disorder (296.89)
Cyclothymic disorder (301.13)

7

Depressive Disorders

MAJOR DEPRESSIVE DISORDER (296.xx)

Specify:

Single episode (296.2x)
Recurrent episode (296.3x)

Specifiers coded in the fifth digit:

1—Mild
2—Moderate
3—Severe without psychotic features
4—Severe with psychotic features
5—In partial remission
6—In full remission

Major depressive disorder is characterized by one or more major depressive episodes without a history of manic, mixed, or hypomanic episodes. If manic, mixed, or hypomanic episodes occur, the diagnosis should be revised to a bipolar disorder.

As many as 15 percent of individuals diagnosed with severe major depressive disorder die by suicide. Persons with the disorder over 55 years of age are particularly vulnerable. The disorder may be preceded by dysthymic disorder. Other disorders may also coexist with major depressive disorder.

Behavioral Symptoms—Single Episode
(severity index: 1, mild; 2, moderate; 3, intense)

Five or more of the following occurring within a two-week period. The symptoms occur almost all day, almost every day:

<u>Severity</u>

1. Depressed mood reported by client or observed by others _____
2. Diminished interest or pleasure in almost all activities _____
3. Significant weight loss or gain or increase or decrease in appetite _____
4. Insomnia or hypersomnia _____
5. Psychomotor agitation or retardation _____
6. Fatigue or loss of energy _____
7. Feelings of worthlessness or excessive guilt _____
8. Diminished ability to think or concentrate _____
9. Recurrent thoughts of death _____
10. Recurrent suicidal ideations with or without a plan _____
11. Attempted suicide _____

Behavioral Symptoms—Recurrent Episode
(severity index: 1, mild; 2, moderate; 3, intense)

Characterized by two or more major depressive episodes with an interval of at least two consecutive months between them. See above symptoms.

Other Diagnostic Considerations

Dysthymic disorder (300.4)
Depressive disorder NOS (311)
Bipolar I disorder (296.0x)
Bipolar II disorder (296.89)

TREATMENT PLAN
MAJOR DEPRESSIVE DISORDER

Client: _____ Date: _____

I.   OBJECTIVES OF TREATMENT
     (*select one or more*)

      1. Reduce persistent depression.
      2. Restore interest in former pleasurable activities.
      3. Restore normal eating pattern.
      4. Restore normal sleep pattern.
      5. Eliminate feelings of worthlessness, guilt.
      6. Improve energy level.
      7. Eliminate or control suicidal ideations.

II. SHORT-TERM BEHAVIORAL GOALS AND
     INTERVENTIONS
     (*select goals and interventions appropriate for your client*)

CLIENT'S SHORT-TERM BEHAVIORAL GOALS	THERAPIST'S INTERVENTIONS
Assist in confirmation of diagnosis.	Confirm diagnosis.
Review treatment plan and agree on target problems for treatment.	Formulate treatment plan and review with client. Agree on target problems for treatment.
Join in collaborative treatment effort.	Cultivate therapeutic or collaborative alliance to build trust and enhance treatment outcome.

Confirm and define depression.	Refer for or administer the Beck Depression Inventory–II (BDI-II) to confirm existence of the disorder and level of intensity of the depression.
Understand possible need for hospitalization.	Explain to client possible need for hospitalization and resolve any anxiety.
Clinically assess intent.	Refer for or administer the Beck Scale for Suicidal Ideation (BSS) to help evaluate intent.
Be hospitalized to protect yourself from harm.	If client is actively suicidal, hospitalize immediately. Call 911 or ambulance. Do not leave client unattended.
Willingly enter into a "suicide pact" with the therapist to report all suicidal ideations and active plans. Agree to inform therapist of your intent before taking action.	If client is not actively suicidal, but has suicidal ideations, implement a "suicide pact" in which the client agrees to inform you of suicidal ideations and active plans, before taking action.
Undergo medical evaluation.	Refer client for medical evaluation.
Be treated for physical problems.	Confirm or revise diagnosis. Rule out disorder due to a general medical condition.
Undergo substance abuse evaluation, and if positive attend twelve-step program.	Investigate and rule out substance abuse. Revise diagnosis and treat if necessary. See treatment plan.

Follow through with referral for psychiatric evaluation to assess need for medication and possible antisuicide measures.	Refer client for psychiatric evaluation and follow-up to confirm he/she kept appointment.
Maintain regular medication schedule and report urges to ignore or discontinue meds.	If medication is prescribed, confirm that prescription is filled and meds are taken on schedule.
Provide prompt feedback on the effectiveness of the medication and possible side-effects.	Refer client to psychiatrist for possible dosage adjustment and feedback on side effects.
Confirm or rule out sexual abuse.	Evaluate for and rule out sexual abuse. Treat if necessary. See treatment plan.
Cooperate with genogram to understand family interactions.	Construct genogram to identify patterns of family interaction (see Chapter 22).
Family therapy improves interactions.	Conduct or refer for family therapy, if appropriate, to reduce anger at client, improve communications, and teach family members better coping skills.
Recognize existing triggers for depression.	Explore and clarify underlying feelings and issues that cause or contribute to depressive feelings.
Recognize and express feelings of rage and self-anger.	Encourage client to share rage and anger at self.
Report to therapist all destructive self-talk and thoughts of harm to self or others.	Explain self-talk to client. Closely monitor destructive thoughts and urges.

Maintain a daily journal to record continuing depressive feelings and situations that trigger them. Record success in overcoming these feelings. Discuss with therapist.	Assign client to keep a daily journal to record feelings of depression and successes in overcoming those feelings.
Replace destructive self-talk with positive affirmations of self-worth and the ability to cope successfully with ADLs.	Replace destructive thoughts and urges with positive affirmations drawing on past successes with ADLs.
Accept that he/she has a chronic disorder.	Educate client about chronicity of disorder to reduce anger and denial.
Learn technique to help slow down when manic.	Teach client diaphragmatic breathing to slow down pressurized speech or flight of ideas (see Homework, Chapter 23).
Build new assertiveness skills.	Teach client principles of assertiveness—equal respect for self and others.
Responsibly complete homework assignments designed to affirm self-worth.	Discuss with client positive premorbid experiences with ADL and feelings of self-worth. Provide trigger to reframe negative thoughts and feelings.
Receive increased family support.	If appropriate, conduct or refer for family counseling to reduce anger toward client.

Learn new techniques for handling depression.	Use hypnosis, visualization, relaxation technique, or biofeedback to coach client in new ways to handle triggers of depression. If appropriate, provide audiotape for home use and reinforcement.
Read self-help book to enhance new skills.	Assign client to read self-help book on depression to enhance understanding and coping skills (see Bibliotherapy, Chapter 24).
Diminish need to "hide out" because of guilt or anger over having this disorder.	Gradually build client's confidence to a level where avoidance behavior is no longer a rational response.
Realize that he/she is more than the disorder and uses unique skills to deal with problems.	Empower client by further reinforcing strengths and new skills.
Recognize grandiosity and reframe thinking and behavior.	Investigate client's grandiose thinking and behavior.
Become more aware of behavioral triggers and how to control actions.	Discuss psychomotor agitation and its triggers.
Gradually become aware of the negative consequences of acting out.	Explore excessive involvement in pleasurable activities that have negative consequences.
Participate in recreational activities with others.	Review with client past interests in recreational activities (sports, exercise, chess, cards, etc.) and urge client to join external exercise or recreational group to renew pattern of contact and communication with others.

Begin to listen to others and reduce pressurized speech.	Teach client active listening skills.
Improve sleep pattern. Symptoms of sleep deprivation are diminished.	Investigate sleep disorder and see that client gets appropriate treatment if required.
Identify triggers for dreams or nightmares that disturb sleep.	Explore dreams or nightmares that may interfere with sleep.
Renew personal contact with relatives, friends, and neighbors.	Urge client to reach out and renew contacts with relatives and former friends and neighbors.
Review termination plan. Investigate with therapist issues of termination, including separation anxiety and dependency.	Review termination plan. Discuss with client issues of termination, specifically separation anxiety and dependency.
Regularly attend and actively participate in recommended self-help groups or group therapy sessions.	Recommend to client active participation in an appropriate self-help group or group therapy focused on depression.

CYCLOTHYMIC DISORDER (301.13)

Cyclothymic disorder is a chronic fluctuating mood disturbance persisting for at least two years and characterized by periods of hypomanic and periods of depressive symptoms. The individual is not without symptoms for more than two months out of the twenty-four. The symptoms cause significant distress or impairment in social or occupational functioning. The hypomanic symptoms are insufficient to meet the criteria for a manic episode and the depressive symptoms are insufficient to meet those for a major depressive episode. The diagnosis is contingent upon the absence of major depressive, manic, or mixed episodes over the initial two-year period. After the initial period, manic or mixed episodes (bipolar I disorder) and major depressive episodes (bipolar II disorder) can be superimposed on the cyclothymic disorder in a dual diagnosis.

Note: cyclothymic disorder should not fully meet the following criteria sets for hypomanic or depressive symptoms:

Behavioral Symptoms—Hypomanic
(severity index: 1, mild; 2, moderate; 3, intense)

Three or more of the following, but not severe enough to cause impairment in social or occupational functioning or to require hospitalization. No psychotic features are present:

	Severity
1. Grandiosity, inflated self-esteem	_____
2. Diminished need for sleep	_____
3. Talkative, pressurized speech	_____
4. Flight of ideas, feels that thoughts are racing	_____
5. Easily distracted by external stimuli	_____
6. Psychomotor agitation	_____
7. Increase in goal-directed activity	_____
8. Excessive involvement in pleasurable activities that have a high destructive potential	_____

9. Symptoms cause distress or impairment in social
   or occupational functioning   _____

Behavioral Symptoms—Depressive

Five or more of the following present in a two-week period. One
symptom must be depressed mood or loss of interest.

		Severity
1.	Depressed mood	_____
2.	Diminished pleasure or interest in all or most activities	_____
3.	Significant weight change (± 5 percent)	_____
4.	Insomnia or hypersomnia	_____
5.	Psychomotor agitation or retardation	_____
6.	Fatigue or loss of energy	_____
7.	Feelings of worthlessness or excessive guilt	_____
8.	Indecisiveness, inability to concentrate	_____
9.	Recurrent thoughts of death	_____
10.	Suicidal ideations with or without a plan	_____
11.	Attempted suicide	_____
12.	Symptoms cause major distress or impairment in social or occupational functioning	_____

Other Diagnostic Considerations

Mood disorder due to a general medical condition (293.9)
Substance-induced mood disorder (see specific substance)
Bipolar I disorder with rapid cycling (296.xx)
Bipolar II disorder with rapid cycling (296.89)
Borderline personality disorder (301.83)

TREATMENT PLAN
CYCLOMANIC DISORDER

Client: _____   Date: _____

I.   OBJECTIVES OF TREATMENT

1. Diminish grandiosity.
2. Restore normal sleep pattern.
3. Reduce pressurized speech.
4. Control flight of ideas.
5. Increase ability to concentrate.
6. Ease psychomotor agitation.
7. Eliminate pleasurable activities with negative consequences.
8. Ease depression.
9. Restore interest in activities.
10. Restore normal eating patterns, weight.
11. Restore normal sleep patterns.
12. Reduce fatigue.
13. Increase self-esteem.
14. Diminish guilt feelings.
15. Control suicidal ideations.
16. Prevent suicide.
17. Prevent relapse.

II.   SHORT-TERM BEHAVIORAL GOALS AND INTERVENTIONS
(select goals and interventions appropriate for your client)

CLIENT'S SHORT-TERM BEHAVIORAL GOALS	THERAPIST'S INTERVENTIONS
Cooperate in confirming diagnosis of cyclothymic disorder.	Confirm diagnosis.

Review treatment plan and agree on target problems for treatment.	Formulate treatment plan and review with client. Agree on target problems for treatment.
Enter into collaborative treatment relationship.	Cultivate therapeutic alliance or collaborative relationship to build trust and enhance treatment outcome.
Confirm and define depression.	Refer for or administer the Beck Depression Inventory—II (BDI-II) to confirm existence of the disorder and level of intensity of the depression.
Understand nature of cyclothymic disorder.	Review nature of disorder with client.
Clinically assess intent.	Refer for or administer the Beck Scale for Suicidal Ideation (BSS) to help evaluate intent.
Enter hospital to prevent self-harm.	If client is actively suicidal, refer immediately for hospitalization. Call 911 or ambulance. Do not leave client unattended.
Willingly enter into a "suicide pact" with the therapist to report all suicidal ideations and active plans. Agree to inform therapist of your intent before taking action.	If client has suicidal ideations, but is not actively suicidal, implement a "suicide pact" in which the client agrees to inform you of suicidal ideations and active plans, and promises to inform you before taking action.
Undergo medical evaluation.	Refer client for medical evaluation.
Be treated for physical problems.	Confirm or revise diagnosis. Rule out disorder due to a general medical condition.

Undergo substance abuse evaluation, and if positive attend twelve-step program.	Investigate and rule out substance abuse. Revise diagnosis and treat if necessary. See appropriate treatment plan.
Follow through with referral for psychiatric evaluation to assess need for medication and possible antisuicide measures.	Refer client for psychiatric evaluation and follow-up to confirm he/she kept appointment.
Maintain regular medication schedule and report urges to ignore or discontinue meds.	If medication is prescribed, confirm that prescription is filled and meds are taken on schedule.
Provide prompt feedback on the effectiveness of the medication and possible side effects.	Refer client to psychiatrist for possible dosage adjustment and feedback on side effects.
Confirm or rule out sexual abuse.	Evaluate for and rule out sexual abuse. Treat if necessary. See appropriate treatment plan.
Understand possible need for hospitalization.	Explain to client possible need for future hospitalization and resolve any anxiety.
Accept hospitalization as necessary to protect self or others.	Hospitalize client when advisable to prevent suicide or harm to others.
Report to therapist all destructive self-talk and thoughts of harm to self or others.	Explain self-talk to client. Closely monitor destructive thoughts and urges.
Replace destructive self-talk with positive affirmations of self-worth and the ability to cope successfully with ADLs.	Replace destructive thoughts and urges with positive affirmations drawing on past successes with ADLs.

Learn to impose thought between the ideation and the action.	Explore and clarify underlying feelings that lead to destructive behavior.
Anger and denial are reduced.	Educate client about chronicity of disorder to reduce anger and denial.
Learn technique to help slow down when manic.	Teach client diaphragmatic breathing to slow down pressurized speech or flight of ideas (see Behavioral Techniques, Chapter 22).
Build new assertiveness skills.	Teach client principles of assertiveness—equal respect for self and others.
Responsibly complete homework assignments designed to affirm self-worth.	Discuss with client positive premorbid experiences with ADLs and feelings of self-worth. Provide trigger to reframe negative thoughts and feelings.
Alienation is reduced.	Conduct or refer for family counseling.
Family learns to deal with client in a more effective way.	Act as consultant to educate family about the disorder.
Diminish need to "hide out" because of guilt or anger over having this disorder.	Gradually build client's confidence to a level where avoidance behavior is no longer a rational response.
Realize that you are more than the disorder and use unique skills to deal with problems.	Empower client by further reinforcing strengths and new skills.
Recognize grandiosity and reframe thinking and behavior.	Investigate client's grandiose thinking and behavior.

Become more aware of behavioral triggers and how to control actions.	Discuss psychomotor agitation and its triggers.
Gradually become aware of the negative consequences of acting out.	Explore excessive involvement in pleasurable activities that have negative consequences.
Participate in recreational activities with others.	Review with client past interests in recreational activities (sports, exercise, chess, cards, etc.) and urge client to join external exercise or recreational group to renew pattern of contact and communication with others.
Maintain a daily journal to record continuing depressive feelings and situations that trigger them. Record success in overcoming these feelings. Discuss with therapist.	Assign client to keep a daily journal to record feelings of depression and successes in overcoming those feelings.
Begin to listen to others and reduce pressurized speech.	Teach client active listening skills.
Improve sleep pattern. Symptoms of sleep deprivation are diminished.	Investigate sleep disorder and see that client gets appropriate treatment if required.
Identify triggers for dreams or nightmares that disturb sleep.	Explore dreams or nightmares that may interfere with sleep.
Renew personal contact with relatives, friends, and neighbors.	Urge client to reach out and renew contacts with relatives and former friends and neighbors.

Review termination plan. Investigate with therapist issues of termination, including separation anxiety and dependency.	Prepare termination plan. Discuss with client issues of termination, specifically separation anxiety and dependency.
Regularly attend and actively participate in recommended self-help groups or group therapy sessions.	Recommend to client active participation in an appropriate self-help group or group therapy.

DYSTHYMIC DISORDER (300.4)
(Specify: Early Onset < Age 21; Late Onset > Age 21)

Five to ten percent of all Americans suffer from major depression or dysthymia each year. Dysthymia has fewer symptoms and is less severe than major depression. Dysthymia is differentiated from a normal nonclinically depressed mood by the intensity and pervasiveness of the symptoms, which are in excess of those considered to be normal reactions to the difficulties of life. The client must have experienced depressed mood and at least two of the behavioral symptoms below for at least two consecutive years.

Clients with dysthymia are vulnerable to major depression. Studies have shown that psychotherapy may be effective in treating dysthymia. If no progress is apparent, the client should be reevaluated and the treatment plan adjusted to include viable alternatives.

Behavioral Symptoms
(severity index: 1, mild; 2, moderate; 3, intense)

	Severity
1. Pervasive depressed mood	_____
2. Generalized loss of interest	_____
3. Feelings of helplessness or hopelessness	_____
4. Fatigue	_____
5. Irritability or excessive anger	_____
6. Decreased activity—effectiveness or productivity	_____
7. Poor concentration	_____
8. Low self-esteem	_____
9. Insomnia or hypersomnia	_____
10. Difficulty making decisions	_____
11. Excessive or inappropriate guilt	_____
12. Social withdrawal	_____
13. Poor appetite	_____
14. Overeating	_____
15. Thoughts of death or suicide	_____

Other Diagnostic Considerations

Major depressive disorder (296.xx)
  Single episode (296.2x)
  Recurrent episode (296.3x)
Depressive disorder NOS (311)

TREATMENT PLAN
DYSTHYMIC DISORDER

Client: _____ Date: _____

I. OBJECTIVES OF TREATMENT
   (*select one or more*)

   1. Reduce the symptoms of depression.
   2. Restore client to former level of functioning.
   3. Prevent relapse.

II. SHORT-TERM BEHAVIORAL GOALS AND
   INTERVENTIONS
   (*select goals and interventions that are appropriate for your client*)

CLIENT'S SHORT-TERM TREATMENT GOALS	THERAPIST'S INTERVENTIONS
Review features of the disorder with therapist.	Confirm diagnosis.
Enter into collaborative treatment relationship.	Cultivate therapeutic alliance or collaborative relationship to build trust and enhance treatment outcome.
Review treatment plan and agree on target problems to be addressed.	Develop treatment plan, review with client, agree on target problems to be addressed.
Confirm and define depression.	Refer for or administer the Beck Depression Inventory–II (BDI-II) to confirm existence of the disorder and level of intensity of the depression.

Recognize and understand the symptoms of depression and their origin.	Investigate with client the symptoms of depression, determine when they first appeared and their possible triggers.
Clinically assess intent.	Refer for or administer the Beck Scale for Suicidal Ideation (BSS) to help evaluate intent.
Prevent harm by hospitalization.	If client is actively suicidal, hospitalize immediately to prevent harm to himself. Call 911 or an ambulance. Do not leave client unattended.
Willingly enter into a "suicide pact" with the therapist to report all suicidal ideations and active plans. Agree to inform therapist of your intent before taking action.	If client is not actively suicidal, but has suicidal ideations, implement a "suicide pact" in which the client agrees to inform you of suicidal ideations, and active plans, and promises to inform you before taking action.
Follow through with referral for psychiatric evaluation to assess need for medication and possible antisuicide measures.	Refer client for psychiatric evaluation and follow-up to confirm he/she kept appointment.
Maintain regular medication schedule and report urges to ignore or discontinue meds.	If medication is prescribed, confirm that prescription is filled and meds are taken on schedule.
Provide prompt feedback on the effectiveness of the medication and possible side effects.	Refer client to psychiatrist for possible dosage adjustment and feedback on side effects.
Report to therapist all destructive self-talk and thoughts of harm to self or others.	Explain self-talk to client. Monitor destructive thoughts and urges.

Assist in creating genogram to understand family interactions.	Construct genogram to understand family interactions and boundaries (see Chapter 22).
Start family therapy.	Conduct or refer for family therapy as appropriate to reduce anger at client, improve communications among family members, and teach better coping skills.
Identify underlying feelings that lead to depression.	Explore and clarify underlying feelings that lead to depression.
Share feelings of anger and rage at self.	Encourage client to share feelings such as rage, or anger at self.
Replace destructive self-talk with positive affirmations of self-worth and the ability to cope successfully with ADLs.	Replace destructive thoughts and urges with positive affirmations drawing on past successes with ADLs.
Maintain a daily journal to record continuing depressive feelings and situations that trigger them. Record success in overcoming these feelings. Discuss with therapist.	Assign client to keep a daily journal to record feelings of depression and successes in overcoming those feelings.
Improve personal hygiene and grooming.	Coach client on importance of good hygiene and grooming and encourage client to take an active interest in how he appears to others.
Responsibly complete homework assignments designed to affirm self-worth.	Discuss with client positive premorbid experiences with ADL and feelings of self-worth. Provide trigger to reframe negative thoughts and feelings.

Learn and practice new ways of dealing with triggers of depression.	Conduct relaxation technique, hypnosis, visualization, or biofeedback to practice improved ways of handling depression triggers. If appropriate, provide audiotape for home use.
Read self-help book to enhance coping skills.	Assign client to read self-help book to help deal with feelings and learn better ways of dealing with them (see Chapter 24).
Participate in recreational activities with others.	Review with client past interests in recreational activities (sports, exercise, chess, cards, etc.) and urge client to join external exercise or recreational group to renew pattern of contact and communication with others.
Renew personal contact with relatives, friends, and neighbors.	Urge client to reach out and renew contacts with relatives and former friends and neighbors.
Review termination plan. Investigate with therapist issues of termination, including separation anxiety and dependency.	Prepare treatment plan. Discuss with client issues of termination, specifically separation anxiety and dependency.
Regularly attend and actively participate in recommended self-help groups or group therapy sessions.	Recommend to client active participation in an appropriate self-help group or group therapy focused on depression.

8

Dissociative Disorders

Dissociative disorders usually are marked by a disruption in the functions of consciousness, perception, memory, or identity. The disorder can be gradual or sudden or transient or chronic. Included in the category of dissociative disorders are: dissociative amnesia, dissociative fugue, dissociative identity disorder, depersonalization disorder, and dissociative disorder NOS. Dissociative symptoms may also be found in acute stress disorder, posttraumatic stress disorder, and somatization disorder.

In some societies, dissociative states are an accepted expression of cultural activities or religious experience. They do not lead to significant impairment or distress, and are not considered pathological.

DISSOCIATIVE AMNESIA (300.12)

Behavioral Symptoms
(severity index: 1, mild; 2, moderate; 3, intense)

Severity

1. Excessive inability to recall important personal information not explainable as simple forgetfulness _____
2. Significant stress or impairment in the activities of daily living (ADLs) _____

The symptoms do not occur during the course of dissociative dissociative identity disorder, dissociative fugue, posttraumatic stress disorder, acute stress disorder, or somatization disorder, and are not due to a substance or medical condition.

DISSOCIATIVE FUGUE (300.13)

Behavioral Symptoms
(severity index: 1, mild; 2, moderate; 3, intense)

Severity

1. Sudden, unexpected travel away from home or work _____
2. Inability to recall past _____
3. Identity confusion or assumption of new identity _____
4. Significant stress or impairment in activities of daily living (ADLs) _____

The symptoms do not occur exclusively during the course of dissociative identity disorder, and are not due to a substance or general medical condition.

DISSOCIATIVE IDENTITY DISORDER (300.14)

Behavioral Symptoms
(formerly called multiple personality disorder)
(severity index: 1, mild; 2, moderate; 3, intense)

<u>Severity</u>

1. The existence of two or more distinct
   personalities each with their own pattern of
   thinking and relating to the environment, self,
   and others   _____
2. Each of the personalities recurrently take control
   of the person's behavior   _____
3. Inability to recall important personal information
   (not simple forgetfulness)   _____

The symptoms are not due to a substance or a general medical condition.

DEPERSONALIZATION DISORDER (300.6)

Behavioral Symptoms
(severity index: 1, mild; 2, moderate; 3, intense)

<u>Severity</u>

1. Persistent or recurrent feeling of being detached
   from one's mind or body   _____
2. Reality testing remains intact   _____
3. The symptoms cause significant distress or
   impairment in the activities of daily living
   (ADLs)   _____

The symptoms do not occur exclusively during the course of another mental disorder and are not the result of a substance or general medical condition.

DISSOCIATIVE DISORDER NOS (300.15)

Behavioral Symptoms
(severity index: 1, mild; 2, moderate; 3, intense)

Similar, but does not meet the full criteria for dissociative identity disorder.

	Severity
1. Derealization without depersonalization	_____
2. Dissociation in persons subjected to prolonged and extensive coercive persuasion	_____
3. Dissociative trance related to locations or cultures	_____
4. Possession trance, control by a new identity attributed to a spirit, diety, power, or person	_____
5. Loss of consciousness not the result of a general medical condition	_____

Other Diagnostic Considerations

Amnestic disorder due to a general medical condition (294.0)
Amnestic disorder due to brain injury (294.0)
Seizure disorders
Delirium (293.1)
Dementia (290.4)
Substance-induced persisting amnestic disorder (see Substance)
Substance intoxication (see Substance)
Posttraumatic stress disorder (309.81)
Acute stress disorder (308.3)
Somatization disorder (300.81)
Age-related cognitive decline (780.9)

TREATMENT PLAN
DISSOCIATIVE DISORDERS

Client: _____ Date: _____

I. OBJECTIVES OF TREATMENT
(select one or more)

    1. Reduce acute symptomatology.
    2. Encourage compliance with meds.
    3. Identify environmental stressors.
    4. Integrate primary personality and alters.
    5. Reduce associated depression.
    6. Reduce irrational beliefs.
    7. Promote socialization.
    8. Develop discharge plan for coping with everyday life.

II. SHORT-TERM BEHAVIORAL GOALS AND
INTERVENTIONS
(select goals and interventions appropriate for your client)

CLIENT'S SHORT-TERM BEHAVIORAL GOALS	THERAPIST'S INTERVENTIONS
Discuss treatment plan and agree on target problem.	Develop treatment plan, discuss with client, and agree on target problems.
Join with therapist in collaborative treatment relationship.	Cultivate a therapeutic alliance or collaborative relationship to build trust and enhance treatment outcome.
Follow-up and comply with medical and psychiatric recommendations.	Refer client for medical and psychiatric evaluations.

Understand need for hospitalization during crisis periods and resolve any fears of hospitalization.	Evaluate need for hospitalization, and resolve client fears of being hospitalized.
Maintain medication journal to help comply with regular meds schedule, and report any urges to ignore or overdose.	When medication is prescribed, confirm that prescription has been filled and meds are taken on a regular schedule. Assign client to keep journal.
Provide prompt feedback on effectiveness of medication and side effects. See psychiatrist for adjustment if necessary.	If necessary, refer to psychiatrist for dosage adjustment and control of side effects.
Understand dangers of mixing medication with other drugs.	Instruct client on dangers of mixing prescribed medication with other drugs.
Replace destructive thoughts and urges with self-talk drawing on past successes with the activities of daily living.	Teach client to counter destructive thoughts and urges with positive self-talk drawing on past successful experience with the activities of daily living.
Replace irrational beliefs and consequences with rational thought.	Explore and confront client's irrational belief system. Point out rational beliefs and consequences.
Agree with treatment goals and feel safer.	Set firm treatment goals.
Exhibit tolerance in sessions for negative emotions.	Increase client's tolerance for negative emotions.
Practice antiavoidance behavior outside of therapy.	Encourage client to test and develop confidence with antiavoidance behavior outside of therapy.

Become more exposed to splits in personality.	Use hypnosis or relaxation technique to help identify alter personalities.
Realize existence of alters.	Guide client to realization of the existence of alter personality/personalities.
Focus on integration of personalities. Develop tolerance for the splits.	Establish a therapeutic relationship with each personality and work toward integration.
Realize reasons for dissociation and abandon this avoidance behavior.	Investigate core reasons for dissociation, including possible sexual abuse. Treat if necessary. See treatment plan.
Improve personal hygiene and grooming.	Coach client in taking an active interest in his appearance. Teach client the importance of grooming and hygiene.
Cooperate in constructing genogram to identify interactive patterns, alliances, triangles, and changing emotional currents.	Construct genogram to better identify interactions (see Behavioral Techniques, Chapter 22).
Strengthen family support structure.	Involve client's family in treatment and act as family consultant to help them understand and deal with the client.
Family understanding improves. New skills developed for interaction with client.	Lessen family anxiety and teach them new skills for interaction with the client.
Experience support and reduce risk of being hurt.	Involve family to reduce need for risk factors such as wandering.

Expand daily journal to include thoughts, feelings, and behavior.	Assign client to expand daily journal to include thoughts, feelings, and behavior.
Review journal with therapist and help identify triggers that set off unacceptable behavior.	Regularly review journal with client and identify triggers that result in aberrant behavior.
Learn new skills for coping with trigger points and controlling behavior.	Teach client stress reduction or relaxation technique to control trigger points.
Expand understanding by reading self-help book.	Assign client to read self-help book (see Chapter 24).
Improve socialization skills at self-help group.	Refer to self-help group to relearn socialization.
Enter structured environment such as group home or residential treatment center.	If client is severely disturbed, refer to residential treatment center or group home.
Learn marketable vocational skills.	Refer client for vocational training.
Spend more time in real world.	Do reality testing and encourage client to focus on real world rather than fantasies.
Recognize symptoms of depression, anger, and anxiety as they contribute to the disorder. Ease feelings of inadequacy.	Explore underlying feelings of depression, anger, and anxiety. Lessen feelings of inadequacy.
Recognize and understand the dynamics of anxiety and panic.	Teach client laws of anxiety— not dangerous, not permanent, avoidance increases anxiety.
Reduce aggression; learn principles of assertiveness— equal respect for yourself and others.	Explain principles of assertiveness to replace aggression.

Accept diagnosis and use available resources to live more comfortably with it.	Help client overcome denial and fully accept illness.
Become more aware of time lapses in your experience.	Explore time lapses for which client cannot account.
Review termination plan. Resolve issues of separation anxiety and dependence.	Discuss termination plan and resolve termination issues.

9

Eating Disorders

ANOREXIA NERVOSA (307.1)

Anorexia nervosa is characterized by an abnormal drive toward thinness and perfection, an intense fear of gaining weight or becoming fat, and a refusal to maintain a normal body weight. The onset usually begins in adolescence with a disturbance in the way individuals think about the size and weight of their bodies. Females are twice as likely as males to be affected by this disorder. The norms of Western society, cognitive distortions, and family obsessions have been identified as contributing factors.

There are two subtypes of this disorder: restricting and purging. The restricting type reduces body weight by controlling calories, and is usually obsessed with one's food intake and feelings about superiority because of one's control. The binge-eating, purging type controls weight by vomiting and using laxatives and/or diuretics. Unlike bulimic clients, purging clients do not regularly overeat, but will purge even small amounts of food.

Behavioral Symptoms
(severity index: 1, mild; 2, moderate; 3, intense)

	Severity
1. Body weight is significantly below (85%) normal	_____
2. Intense fear of gaining weight or becoming fat	_____
3. Amenorrhea—absence of three consecutive menstrual cycles	_____
4. Denies seriousness of low body weight	_____
5. Restricts calorie intake; obsessed with low-calorie, low-fat foods	_____
6. Overeats and purges by vomiting, or use of laxatives, enemas, or diuretics	_____
7. Excessive exercise used to control weight	_____
8. Feels superior to others because of food control	_____
9. Extremely self-critical; needs to be perfect	_____

Other Diagnostic Considerations

Major depressive disorder (296.xx)
Schizophrenia (295.xx)
Social phobia (300.23)
Obsessive-compulsive disorder (301.4)
Body dysmorphic disorder (300.7)
Bulimia nervosa (307.51)
Narcissistic personality disorder (301.81)

TREATMENT PLAN
ANOREXIA NERVOSA

Client: _____ Date: _____

I. OBJECTIVES OF TREATMENT
   (*select one or more*)

   1. Promote weight gain.
   2. Reduce preoccupation with food.
   3. Eliminate stressors that cause client to undereat or overeat.
   4. Develop healthy coping styles with family and others.
   5. Eliminate irrational fears of fat.
   6. Eliminate purging.
   7. Restore normal eating patterns.

II. SHORT-TERM BEHAVIORAL GOALS AND INTERVENTIONS
   (*select goals and interventions appropriate for your client*)

CLIENT'S SHORT-TERM BEHAVIORAL GOALS	THERAPIST'S INTERVENTIONS
Agree with therapist on target problems.	Create treatment plan and agree on target problems.
Join in treatment relationship.	Cultivate a therapeutic alliance or collaborative relationship to build trust and enhance treatment outcome.
Discuss underlying dynamics and possible causes of disorder.	Encourage client to discuss feelings about self and clarify underlying dynamics that have created or contributed to eating disorder.

Follow-up on referral and comply with medical and psychiatric recommendations.	Refer client for medical and psychiatric evaluation.
Eliminate existence of other medical conditions that may mimic the effects of anorexia.	Request medical evaluation for disorders which mimic anorexia (Crohn's disease, irritable bowel disease, colitis).
Follow-up on dental evaluation and undergo treatment if necessary.	Refer client to dentist for evaluation of deterioration caused by vomiting.
Explore possible mood disorders that may exacerbate anorexia.	Evaluate possible mood disorders that may contribute significantly to anorexia; see appropriate treatment plan.
Maintain daily journal of eating patterns, feelings, triggers, and reactions. Discuss with therapist.	Assign client to keep daily journal of eating patterns and reactions. Discuss with client.
Explore irrational beliefs about becoming fat.	Examine client's beliefs about fatness and its consequences.
Replace distorted beliefs with rational thinking about weight and appropriate body size.	Provide rational thoughts about weight and body size.
Cooperate in constructing genogram to identify interactive patterns, alliances, triangles, and changing emotional currents.	Construct genogram to better identify interactions (see Behavioral Techniques, Chapter 22).
Identify societal and family obsessions with thinness.	Investigate family issues that reinforce pathological eating pattern.
Recognize and replace distortions and explore issue in family therapy if required.	Correct distortions, and if necessary refer client for family therapy with self or others.

Explore fears of becoming an adult and wanting to remain childlike. (In females, fear of sex, menstruation.)	Explore client's desire to remain childlike and associated fears of growing up.
Discuss and resolve fear of hospitalization.	Explain need for hospitalization, and refer client for inpatient treatment if necessary.
In hypnosis or creative visualization, experience self at normal weight.	Using hypnosis or creative visualization, instruct client to visualize self at normal weight.
Use audiotape at home to build self-esteem.	Assign use of audiotape as homework to reinforce new self-image.
Read assigned self-help book and discuss with therapist to determine your specific fears and how they started.	Assign reading of self-help book as homework (see Chapter 24).
Replace abnormal weight goals with realistic ones.	Urge client to discard irrational weight goals.
Recognize an underlying need for perfection and how it started.	Address with client the need for perfection and its origins.
Accept lower expectations of self as good enough. Live more comfortably within self.	Teach client that "good enough" is acceptable.
Recognize secondary gains (control, attention, feelings of superiority, avoidance of adulthood) and replace them with new coping skills.	Point out to client the secondary gains of food control and replace them with new coping skills.
Diminish and eliminate purging behavior.	Evaluate purging behavior and replace with new coping skills.

Build confidence in relating to others; reduce pathological interactions.	Teach client more appropriate ways of interacting with others at home, school, and work.
Confront and eliminate need to control family and others by passive-aggressive behavior, e.g., refusing to eat.	Point out passive-aggressive need to control family and others, and correct the pattern.
Discuss and resolve separation anxiety and dependency issues with therapist.	Prepare termination plan. Discuss and resolve separation issues with client.
Regularly attend recommended support group to interact with others who have similar problems.	Refer to appropriate support group. (Note: Overeaters Anonymous is inappropriate for this disorder.)

BULIMIA NERVOSA (307.51)

Bulimia nervosa is marked by binge eating followed by inappropriate compensatory methods to prevent weight gain such as purging, excessive exercise, and use of laxatives, enemas, or diuretics. Body size and weight excessively influence self-esteem. The disorder typically begins in adolescence or early adulthood, predominantly in females. Binge eating usually occurs in secrecy and is accompanied by feeling a lack of control. Binge eating is usually triggered by dysmorphic mood, interpersonal stressors, or intense hunger following a prolonged period of dieting. Clients are typically reluctant to discuss symptoms as the result of embarrassment or ambivalence toward binging. Some evidence of pathology in the family of origin exists, and it is possible that the disorder is linked to sexual abuse. There are two subtypes of bulimia nervosa: purging and nonpurging. The latter relies on fasting and overexercising to control weight.

Behavioral Symptoms
(severity index: 1, mild; 2, moderate; 3, intense)

	Severity
1. Recurrent binge eating	_____
2. Feeling of loss of control during binge	_____
3. Inappropriate use of vomiting, laxatives, enemas, diuretics	_____
4. Overexercising	_____
5. Exhibits low self-esteem	_____
6. Over-concern with body weight and fatness	_____
7. Extremely self-critical	_____
8. Depressed and/or anxious	_____
9. Difficulties with family of origin	_____
10. Poor interpersonal skills	_____

Other Diagnostic Considerations

Anorexia nervosa (307.1)
Major depressive disorder (296.xx)
Borderline personality disorder (301.83)

TREATMENT PLAN
BULIMIA NERVOSA

Client: _____ Date: _____

I. OBJECTIVES OF TREATMENT
(select one or more)

1. Restore healthy eating patterns.
2. Eliminate preoccupation with weight and body size.
3. Eliminate purging and other compensatory actions.
4. Reduce need to be perfect.
5. Develop new coping styles and improve interpersonal relationships.
6. If relevant, resolve sexual abuse issues.

II. SHORT-TERM BEHAVIORAL GOALS AND INTERVENTIONS
(select goals and interventions appropriate for your client)

CLIENT'S SHORT-TERM BEHAVIORAL GOALS	THERAPIST'S INTERVENTIONS
Discuss with therapist and agree with treatment plan and target problem.	Formulate treatment plan and discuss with client.
Join in collaborative treatment relationship.	Cultivate therapeutic alliance or collaborative relationship to build trust and enhance treatment outcome.
Comply with psychiatric, medical, and dental recommendations.	Refer client for psychiatric, medical, and dental evaluation.
Maintain daily journal of eating patterns, binging, triggers, and emotional reactions.	Instruct client to keep daily log of eating patterns and reactions. Discuss with client.

Identify factors that trigger or contribute to bulimia.	Identify people, places, and things that exacerbate bulimic behaviors.
Cooperate in constructing genogram to identify interactive patterns, alliances, triangles, and changing emotional currents.	Construct genogram to better identify interactions (see Behavioral Techniques, Chapter 22).
Talk about your feelings about self.	Encourage client to share feelings about self.
Recognize and reevaluate irrational beliefs about food and weight.	Examine irrational beliefs about food, body size, and weight.
Reframe beliefs and consequences.	Replace irrational beliefs with positive thinking.
Investigate possible mood disorders and their impact on your eating patterns and quality of life.	Explore possible mood disorders that may contribute to binge-eating.
Read and discuss "Fear of Fat," and discuss with therapist.	Assign client to read and discuss "Fear of Fat," or other self-help book (see Chapter 24).
Control purging behaviors.	Eliminate need for purging behaviors.
Learn and apply healthy dietary controls to restrict weight.	Teach client healthy dietary food intake to control weight.
Develop new coping skills to deal with family of origin.	Explore family issues that promote or reinforce pathological eating.
Improve interpersonal skills.	Assist client in developing new interpersonal skills.

Family therapy develops new coping skills.	Conduct or refer for family treatment, if appropriate, to reduce anger at client, improve family communication, and develop improved coping skills.
Discuss and eliminate fear of hospitalization.	Discuss and eliminate fears associated with possible hospitalization, if it becomes necessary.
Understand need for and comply with temporary hospitalization if required.	Refer client for inpatient treatment if required.
Use hypnosis or creative visualization to practice control of binge eating and improve self-esteem. Use tape at home during critical periods.	Use hypnosis or creative visualization to help control impulsive binging and raise self-esteem. Provide audiotape for home use.
Frankly examine early family history, including sexual abuse.	If appropriate, investigate early family history and possible sexual abuse.
If appropriate, explore and resolve anger, self-blame, and other self-defeating feelings associated with sexual abuse.	Work through sexual abuse issues, if necessary.
Reframe need for perfection with a "good enough" approach to life.	Explore client's need for perfection and its origins.
Completely eliminate overeating and purging behavior.	Reevaluate and eliminate client's overeating/purging behavior.
Use self-rewards to reinforce success in normal eating patterns and interpersonal relationships.	Teach client self-reward schema for successes in practicing new life skills.

Explore with therapist and resolve termination issues of separation and dependency.	Develop termination plan. Discuss and resolve termination issues.
Regularly attend self-help group to reinforce success.	Refer client to self-help group for bulimics. (Note: Overeaters Anonymous is inappropriate for this disorder.)

10

Factitious Disorders

Predominantly psychological (300.16)
Predominantly physical (300.19)
Combined (300.19)
Not otherwise specified (300.19)

Individuals with factitious disorder feign psychological or physical symptoms, or both, in order to play the "sick role." The disorders differ from malingering in which there are secondary gains such as avoiding conscription or jury duty. In factitious disorders, clients may even take medications to produce symptoms of illness, but deny intentionality. Some may even have surgical intervention. These clients are pathological, usually liars with a dramatic flair and more than a little knowledge of medical terminology.

Since individuals with factitious disorder may use many different doctors or hospitals, there has a been little success in collecting prevalence data. The onset of the disorder is usually in early childhood and develops into a lifelong pattern. Most individuals with this disorder have poor family ties and bad employment records. Denial and pathological lying combine to make the disorder difficult to treat.

Factitious disorder NOS is a diagnosis reserved for people who act out the behavior by proxy, for example, a child may feign illness for his or her parent.

These disorders are differentiated essentially by the type of predominant symptoms feigned, and are covered by a single treatment plan. Rule out malingering for personal or economic gain.

Behavioral Symptoms
(severity index: 1, mild; 2, moderate; 3, intense)

	Severity
1. Feigns physical or psychological symptoms	_____
2. Behaviors aimed at seeking hospitalization	_____
3. Motivated to assume "sick role"	_____
4. Chronic complaints of illness	_____
5. Feelings of helplessness/hopelessness	_____
6. Pathological lying	_____
7. Exaggerates illness	_____
8. Excessive worry about self	_____
9. Indirect assumption of "sick role" by feigning illness in another person	_____

Other Diagnostic Considerations

Somatization (300.81)
Malingering (V65.2) AXIS II

TREATMENT PLAN
FACTITIOUS DISORDERS

Client: _____   Date: _____

I.   OBJECTIVES OF TREATMENT
(*select one or more*)

     1. Make client aware of fictitious nature of symptoms.
     2. Eliminate need for hospitalization.
     3. Acknowledge need for "sick role."
     4. Reduce pathological behaviors.
     5. Restore client to optimum level of functioning.
     6. Prevent relapse.

II.   SHORT-TERM BEHAVIORAL GOALS AND
      INTERVENTIONS
(*select goals and interventions appropriate for your client*)

CLIENT'S SHORT-TERM BEHAVIORAL GOALS	THERAPIST'S INTERVENTIONS
Join in collaborative treatment relationship.	Cultivate collaborative relationship or therapeutic alliance to build trust and enhance treatment outcome.
Cooperate in revealing past patterns of sickness behavior.	Explore history of hospitalization and physicians and treatment.
Sign releases.	Request necessary release to collect client records from all sources.
Review records with therapist and confirm.	Review records with client and confirm diagnosis.

Assist in constructing treatment plan and agree on target problems.	Formulate treatment plan and select target problems to address.
Confirm or deny secondary gains.	Investigate secondary gains of sick role behavior. Revise diagnosis or rule out malingering.
Acknowledge and understand self-defeating sick roles.	Assess client's understanding of pathological behaviors and their interference with his/her functioning.
Become aware of underlying emotions that contribute to behavior. Learn to think before acting.	Clarify underlying emotions that lead toward factitious behavior. Learn to insert thought between urge and action.
Follow through with evaluations and maintain medication regimen as required.	Refer client for medical and psychiatric evaluations, possible medication.
Stabilize any possible medical conditions.	See that medical problems are treated.
Keep medication log and review with therapist.	Assign client to keep medication log and monitor notations regularly.
Look realistically at causes of sick role behavior.	Explore with client underlying fears and triggers of sick role behavior.
Get treated for underlying depression and/or anxiety.	Evaluate for dual diagnosis, e.g., depression and anxiety, and treat. See appropriate treatment plan.

Learn new coping skills to better handle anxiety.	Teach client self-hypnosis, relaxation technique, or creative visualization to cope with anxieties that may lead to factitious behavior. Provide audiotape for home use.
Assist in building genogram to identify and understand family interactions and stressors.	Prepare genogram to identify interactive patterns and stressors (see Behavioral Techniques, Chapter 22).
Reduce family system tension.	Initiate family sessions to reduce the conflicts that may produce pathological behavior.
Feel more secure in stronger family environment.	Instruct family about this disorder and outline other resources available.
Learn new coping skills as alternative to sick role.	Teach client new coping skills in everyday life to preclude need for sick role.
Attend self-help group to reinforce new skills.	Refer to self-help group.
Become more aware of denial and pathological lying.	Gently confront pathological lying.
Confront need for sick role.	Urge client to confront and challenge the need for sick-role behaviors.
Follow up on homework reading. Outlook is improved.	Assign reading of self-help book (see Chapter 24).
Review termination plan. Resolve remaining separation anxiety and dependence issues.	Prepare termination plan. Address separation anxiety and dependence issues.

11

Gambling—Pathological (312.31)

Pathological gambling is characterized by persistent and recurrent maladaptive gambling that disrupts the client's occupational and interpersonal activities. These clients are preoccupied with gambling, either reliving past experiences or anticipating new ones. They often claim to be motivated by the "action" and not the money, and cannot cut back or control the behavior. They will lie to family and therapist or resort to antisocial actions to conceal their gambling. Distortions in thinking are commonplace, including denial, superstition, and over-confidence.

Data on the prevalence of gambling is limited since gamblers only enter therapy when forced to by negative circumstances. However, it is suggested that a reasonable estimate of prevalence is 1 to 3 percent of the population. Women are underrepresented, probably as a result of the stigma attached to female gamblers. There are familial gambling patterns, and gamblers usually have parents who are or were gamblers.

Behavioral Symptoms
(severity index: 1, mild; 2, moderate; 3, intense)

<u>Severity</u>

1. Preoccupied with gambling or getting money to gamble   _____
2. Needs to increase the stakes to maintain the excitement   _____
3. Unsuccessful in repeated efforts to stop or cut back   _____
4. Becomes restless/irritable when trying to stop   _____
5. Chases losses by doubling up on bets or other methods   _____
6. Relies on superstition and magical thinking   _____
7. Lies to family and therapist about gambling   _____
8. Resorts to criminal acts to finance gambling   _____
9. Borrows from others to cover financial crisis caused by gambling   _____
10. Gambling has resulted in loss of job or important relationship   _____

Other Diagnostic Considerations

Antisocial personality disorder (301.7)
Narcissistic personality disorder (301.810
Borderline personality disorder (301.83)
Major depression (296.xx)
Dysthymia (300.4)
Generalized anxiety disorder (300.02)

TREATMENT PLAN
PATHOLOGICAL GAMBLING

Client: _____ Date: _____

I. OBJECTIVES OF TREATMENT
   (*select one or more*)

   1. Control anger and anxiety over idea of curtailing gambling.
   2. Reframe denial/magical thinking/superstition with reality.
   3. Determine family connections with gambling.
   4. Strengthen family support and improve interaction.
   5. Confront lying and criminal behavior.
   6. Confront destructive impact on all activities of daily living (ADLs).
   7. Prevent relapse.

II. SHORT-TERM BEHAVIORAL GOALS AND INTERVENTIONS
   (*select goals and interventions appropriate for your client*)

CLIENT'S SHORT-TERM BEHAVIORAL GOALS	THERAPIST'S INTERVENTIONS
Review treatment plan, agree on target problems.	Construct treatment plan, discuss with client, and agree on target problems.
Join in collaborative treatment relationship, feel less hopeless and more optimistic that the problem can be controlled.	Develop collaborative relationship to build trust and enhance treatment outcome.
Discuss anger and anxiety over curtailment of gambling.	Explore anger and anxiety over giving up gambling.

Start daily thought and feelings log.	Assign client to maintain daily thought and feelings log to record urges to gamble and reactions (see Homework Assignments, Chapter 23).
Learn new anger management techniques.	Teach client anger management techniques (see Anger Management, Chapter 23).
Learn about anxiety and how to deal with it.	Teach client dynamics of anxiety. See appropriate treatment plan.
Practice control of anger and anxiety using self-hypnosis.	Instruct client and practice relaxation techniques, hypnosis, creative visualization to deal with anger and anxiety over abstention. Provide audiotape for home use.
Reframe denial, magical thinking, and superstition with evidence-based thinking.	Explore, confront, and reframe denial, magical thinking, and superstition.
Discuss with therapist the history of gambling within family of origin.	Explore family involvement with gambling.
Help construct genogram.	Construct genogram to better understand family patterns and interactions (see Behavioral Techniques, Chapter 22).
Follow-up with psychiatric evaluation, conform with medication schedule.	If indicated, refer client for psychiatric evaluation and medication.
Maintain medication log to record reactions to medication and possible need for adjustment.	Assign client to keep a medication log to record reactions.

Comply with referral to family therapy.	Conduct family sessions and refer to family therapist to improve interactions.
Realize how family contributes to client need to gamble.	Act as family consultant to explore and control ways the family enables client's gambling.
Family members join self-help group.	If appropriate, refer family members to a self-help group to learn how to deal with a gambler in the family.
Experience abstention in role-playing sessions.	Conduct role-playing sessions with client to experience abstention.
Apply principles of mourning to gambling.	Explain mourning process as it applies to gambling.
Join Gamblers Anonymous for additional support, interaction with people dealing with the same problem.	Refer client to Gamblers Anonymous.
Recognize and confront need for ritualistic behaviors.	Investigate ritualistic nature of gambling behavior.
Identify triggers of need to gamble.	Identify people, places, and things associated with the urge to gamble.
Make commitment to someone else to refrain from gambling.	Urge client to sign contract to abstain from gambling.
Realize negative impact of gambling on other aspects of your life.	Explore destructive impact of gambling on interpersonal and occupational activities.
Take new skills into the real world. Learns to self-reward successes, correct failures, and try again.	Instruct client to externalize his new skills in the real world.

Explore shame and guilt with therapist as they diffuse attempts to stop gambling.	Review issues of shame and guilt that may inhibit client's attempts to give up gambling.
Identify factors that may cause relapse and how to avoid or control them.	Identify high-risk factors that could lead to relapse. Teach client avoidance, control, and alternate constructive behavior.
Discuss termination issues and agree on termination plan.	Discuss and resolve issues of separation anxiety and dependence. Agree on termination plan.

12

Mental Disorders Due to a General Medical Condition

When a medical condition is related to mental symptoms, the condition is diagnosed on both Axis III and Axis I. The medical condition may also impact Axis II codes. However, the impairments associated with personality disorders should be listed on Axis I to assure insurance reimbursement.

In these general medical conditions there is an organic problem that impacts the client's psychological functioning. The more chronic the condition or the longer the condition exists, the more severe is the psychological component. (See Appendix G in *DSM-IV* for ICD-10 Codes, pp. 813–828.)

The best prognosis for treatment involves a team of medical doctors and clinicians working collaboratively with both the patient and the family.

Behavioral Symptoms
(severity index: 1, mild; 2, moderate; 3, intense)

<u>Severity</u>

1. Client diagnosed with medical condition that impacts activities of daily living (ADLs)   _____

2. Pain causes impairments in all major areas of functioning (e.g., social, occupational)   _____

3. Psychological factors judged to have caused onset of medical condition (e.g., colitis, irritable bowel disease, gastro-intestinal problems, headache)   _____

4. Depression due to medical problems   _____

5. Anxiety over medical conditions (e.g., palpitations, shortness of breath, chest pains)   _____

Other Diagnostic Considerations

Note: Diagnostic considerations run the gamut of *DSM-IV* disorders and may include multiple diagnoses on every level.

Pain disorder associated with psychological factors (307.80)
Pain disorder—psychological and general medical (307.89)

TREATMENT PLAN
GENERAL MEDICAL CONDITION

Client: _____ Date: _____

I. OBJECTIVES OF TREATMENT
(*select one or more*)

1. Treat and stabilize general medical condition.
2. Accept chronicity of diagnosis.
3. Control pain associated with the condition.
4. Educate client on resources available to help deal with major illnesses.
5. Prevent relapse.
6. Restore client to optimal level of functioning.

II. SHORT-TERM BEHAVIORAL GOALS AND INTERVENTIONS
(*select goals and interventions appropriate for your client*)

CLIENT'S SHORT-TERM BEHAVIORAL GOALS	THERAPIST'S INTERVENTIONS
Discuss treatment plan with therapist and agree on target problem.	Confirm diagnosis, formulate treatment plan, agree with client on target problem.
Be aware of symptoms exacerbated by medical condition.	Evaluate for Axis I and Axis II impairments.
Feel less alienated, become more hopeful of a viable solution to your problem.	Develop a therapeutic or collaborative alliance to build trust and enhance treatment outcome.
Understand problem is being addressed medically and psychologically.	Collaborate with medical doctor to establish a collaborative approach to treatment.

Follow through with referral and takes meds if prescribed.	Refer client for psychiatric evaluation.
Follow-up with medication regimen. Maintain medication journal.	When meds are prescribed, confirm client follows through. Assign client to start medication journal.
Increase understanding of medical problem.	Explore client understanding of medical problem.
Get help with pain management.	Investigate pain associated with illness and refer to pain clinic if appropriate.
Receive appropriate level of care.	Assess severity of problem and refer to appropriate level of care.
Understand need for possible hospitalization and reduce anxieties.	Discuss possible need for hospitalization with client. Reduce anxiety and fear.
Accept hospitalization.	Refer to M.D. to hospitalize client as required.
Break through denial and deal more appropriately with illness.	Explore level of denial or "distressed thinking" about illness.
Identify possible origins of medical problems.	Review chronological history of client's medical problems.
Cooperate with evaluation.	Rule out factitious disorder or malingering. See appropriate treatment plan.
Recognize secondary gains of illness. Symptoms reduced.	Identify secondary gains derived from illness.
Learn new techniques for management of pain and other symptoms.	Teach client relaxation technique, self-hypnosis, or creative visualization to deal with pain and control other symptoms.

If substance abuse evaluation is positive, start appropriate treatment.	Evaluate for substance abuse (see appropriate treatment plan).
Become aware of underlying issues that influence your medical condition.	Explore underlying psychological issues that impact medical condition and treat (see appropriate treatment plan).
Verbalize about stressors and relieve anxiety, depression.	Urge client to ventilate about issues that have impacted on his/her life.
Help create genogram, to identify family patterns.	Produce genogram to identify interactive family patterns and stressors (see Behavioral Techniques, Chapter 22).
Family support structure is strengthened.	Involve client's family in treatment and, acting as family consultant, help them understand and deal with client problems.
Family learns and practices new interaction skills.	Lessen family anxiety. Teach new skills for interaction.
Understand the dynamics of anxiety usually associated with medical illness.	Instruct client and family on laws of anxiety: not dangerous, not permanent, avoidance makes it worse.
Replace irrational beliefs with rational thinking and new consequences.	Explore and confront client's irrational belief system. Reframe beliefs and revise consequences.
Maintain thought log to monitor cognitive distortions, and discuss with therapist.	Assign client to maintain thought log to facilitate identification of cognitive distortions (see Homework assignments, Chapter 23).

Replace negative self-talk with positive affirmations.	Instruct client to counter destructive thoughts and urges with positive self-talk.
Deepen understanding of condition and ways of dealing with it.	Assign homework reading of appropriate self-help book (see Chapter 24).
Weaken feelings of isolation.	Refer client to self-help group to encourage socialization and interact with others who have similar problems.
Improve occupational functioning.	If appropriate, refer for vocational counseling.
Make use of available community resources.	Make client aware of available community resources and refer to appropriate organization (e.g., Social Security Disability).
Discuss termination.	Discuss termination and develop plan.
Resolve termination issues.	Confront and resolve issues of dependence and separation anxiety.

13

Personality Disorders

Personality disorders pose a separate and distinct problem for most, if not all, major insurance companies. Axis II diagnoses are rooted in childhood development and tend to require longer treatment compared with other disorders. In addition, there is no body of evidence to suggest that behavioral management is an effective modality in the treatment of these disorders.

Clients with personality disorders usually do not come into treatment complaining of narcissistic, borderline, or other personalities disorders. They present with Axis I disturbances, such as anxiety, depression, or social phobia, which represent the tip of the iceberg. They historically respond poorly to medication and are difficult to treat medically as well as behaviorally. It is not easy to develop a therapeutic alliance or collaborative relationship with these clients.

Treating the Axis I behavioral problems of these clients offers a reasonable initial approach to the larger, deep-rooted disorder.

The difference between a personality trait and a personality disorder is a matter of degree. You can be narcissistic without necessarily having a narcissistic personality disorder. The same is true of all personality disorders. A personality trait is a consistent pattern of thinking, viewing, and relating to oneself and the social environment. When the trait is maladaptive or inflexible and the source of significant impairment in interpersonal or occupational functioning, it becomes a disorder. The behavioral characteristics usually emerge in adolescence or early adulthood and are not the transient response to situational distress. Treatment is often complicated by the fact that the traits are usually ego-systonic.

ANTISOCIAL PERSONALITY DISORDER (301.7)

Antisocial personality disorder is characterized by a maladaptive and persistent pattern of disregard for and violation of the rights of others, usually by use of deceit and manipulation. To justify this diagnosis, the individual must be at least 18 years old and must have a history of conduct disorder occurring before the age of 15 (see Conduct Disorder—312.82). In adulthood, individuals with this disorder fail to conform to the usual norms of social behavior. Because of the nature of this disorder, it may be helpful to supplement a clinical assessment with data from reliable outside sources when available.

Behavioral Symptoms
(severity index: 1, mild; 2, moderate; 3, intense)

Disregard or violation of the rights of others, and including three of the following:

	Severity
1. Repeatedly performs unlawful acts that are grounds for arrest	_____
2. Lies to or deceives others for fun or profit	_____
3. Acts on spur of the moment, fails to plan ahead	_____
4. Irritable and aggressive	_____
5. Reckless disregard for safety of self or others	_____
6. Consistently irresponsible	_____
7. Fails to sustain consistent work behavior	_____
8. Fails to honor financial commitments	_____

9. Indifference or lack of remorse over mistreating
   or harming others   _____

Other Diagnostic Considerations

Schizophrenia (295.xx)
Manic episode (296.2, 296.3x)
Narcissistic personality disorder (381.1)
Histrionic personality disorder (301.7)
Borderline personality disorder (301.83)
Paranoid personality disorder (301.0)
Adult antisocial behavior (V71.01)

TREATMENT PLAN
ANTISOCIAL PERSONALITY DISORDER

Client: _____ Date: _____

I. OBJECTIVES OF TREATMENT
    (*select one or more*)

    1. Curtail any unlawful activities.
    2. Confront need to lie and deceive others.
    3. Control impulsivity, learn to plan ahead.
    4. Treat depression and anxiety.
    5. Recognize importance of safety for self and others.
    6. Develop successful work habits.
    7. Recognize importance of financial responsibility.
    8. Develop remorse for mistreating or abusing others.

II. SHORT-TERM BEHAVIORAL GOALS AND
    INTERVENTIONS
    (*select goals and interventions appropriate for your client*)

CLIENT'S SHORT-TERM BEHAVIORAL GOALS	THERAPIST'S INTERVENTIONS
Discuss treatment plan and agree on target problems.	Confirm diagnosis and formulate treatment plan. Agree with client on target problems.
Join in collaborative treatment relationship.	Attempt to form collaborative relationship to build trust and enhance treatment outcome.
Explore underlying feelings that contribute to antisocial behavior.	Explore and clarify underlying feelings or anxieties that lead to antisocial behavior.
Comply with referral and maintain medication regimen if prescribed.	Refer for psychiatric evaluation and possible medication if appropriate.

Undergo treatment for depression.	Evaluate for underlying depression and treat. See appropriate treatment plan.
Understand confidentiality and its limits.	Assure client of confidential nature of therapy, and need to report certain criminal actions.
Admit questionable or unlawful behavior.	Explore unlawful behavior.
Recognize destructive consequences of unlawful behavior.	Review with client logical consequences of unlawful behavior.
Discuss irrational beliefs.	Investigate irrational belief system.
Replace negative behavior for positive consequences.	Reframe negative behavior and consequences.
Learn assertiveness to replace aggression.	Evaluate for aggressiveness and teach assertiveness as alternate behavior.
Admit lies.	Explore lies and other deceitful behavior.
Recognize negative consequences of lying.	Help client look at negative consequences of lying.
Learn basic respect for self and others.	Teach client to respect self and others.
Learn improved work habits and responsibilities.	Refer client to vocational counseling.
Cooperate in building genogram.	Construct genogram to identify family patterns and stressors (see Behavioral Techniques, Chapter 22).
Family therapy improves interactions.	Conduct or refer to family therapy to improve communications and family interactions.

Family learns new techniques for dealing with client.	Act as family consultant to help family deal with client.
Maintain thought log to monitor cognitive distortions.	Assign client to maintain thought log to facilitate identification of cognitive distortions (see Homework Assignments, Chapter 23).
Learn to deal with frustrating feelings.	Instruct client on laws of anxiety to reduce destructive behaviors.
Learn impulsive control techniques. Learns to plan and evaluate consequences.	Explore impulsivity; instruct client in planning fundamentals.
Learn remorse, make amends for those hurt or mistreated.	Urge expression of remorse for others mistreated or hurt by the client.
Interact with others who have similar problems.	Refer client to self-help group if possible.
Discuss and resolve separation anxiety and dependence issues; agree with termination plan.	Address terminal issues; draft termination plan.

AVOIDANT PERSONALITY DISORDER (301.82)

Social inhibition, feelings of inadequacy, and sensitivity to criticism characterize avoidant personality disorder. People with this disorder may avoid activities involving close interpersonal interaction, including work or school. They fear criticism, disapproval, or rejection and believe themselves to be socially inept and inferior to and unappealing to others. The lifestyle of these people is restricted by their low self-esteem. The disorder may coexist with panic disorder with agoraphobia.

Behavioral Symptoms
(severity index: 1, mild; 2, moderate; 3, intense)

At least four of the following:

	Severity
1. Avoids work-related interpersonal activity	_____
2. Fears criticism, disapproval, or rejection	_____
3. Gets involved with others only when assured of being liked	_____
4. Intimate relationships are inhibited by fear of shame or ridicule	_____
5. Preoccupied with being socially criticized or rejected	_____
6. Feelings of inadequacy in new social situations	_____
7. Views self as inferior, socially inept, and personally unappealing to others	_____
8. Avoids new activities as potentially embarrassing	_____

Other Diagnostic Considerations

Social phobia (300.23)
Antisocial personality disorder (301.7)
Panic disorder with agoraphobia (300.21)

Dependent personality disorder (301.6)
Schizoid personality disorder (301.20)
Schizotypal personality disorder (301.22)
Paranoid personality disorder (301.0)
Personality change due to a general medical condition (310.1)
Substance abuse—cocaine (305.60)

TREATMENT PLAN
AVOIDANT PERSONALITY DISORDER

Client: _____ Date: _____

I. OBJECTIVES OF TREATMENT
    (*select one or more*)

    1. Reduce fear of criticism, disapproval, or rejection.
    2. Eliminate interpersonal fears in the workplace.
    3. Control fear of shame or ridicule in close relationships.
    4. End preoccupation with shame or ridicule.
    5. Strengthen self-esteem.
    6. Develop feelings of adequacy in social situations.
    7. Meet new activities with optimistic anticipation.
    8. Recognizes self on equal footing with others.

II. SHORT-TERM BEHAVIORAL GOALS AND
    INTERVENTIONS
    (*select goals and interventions appropriate for your client*)

CLIENT'S SHORT-TERM BEHAVIORAL GOALS	THERAPIST'S INTERVENTIONS
Review treatment plan and agree on target problems.	Confirm diagnosis. Formulate treatment plan. Select target problems.
Collaborate with therapist in implementing treatment plan.	Attempt to establish a collaborative treatment relationship to build trust and enhance treatment outcome.
Cooperate in building genogram.	Construct genogram to identify family patterns and stressors (see Behavioral Techniques, Chapter 22).

Comply with referral, medication regimen.	Refer client for psychiatric evaluation and medication if indicated.
Learn about anxiety, its origins and triggers, and how to control it.	Explore underlying anxiety and treat as appropriate. See appropriate treatment plan.
Maintain thought log to record reactions to anxiety triggers. Discuss with therapist.	Instruct client to maintain thought log to record anxiety triggers and reactions (see Homework Assignments, Chapter 23).
Become aware of underlying feelings that lead to avoidant behavior and realize you do not have to act on them.	Explore underlying feelings that lead to avoidant behavior.
Start to improve self-esteem.	Using relaxation technique or hypnosis, put client in touch with past successes in interpersonal interactions.
Experience interpersonal interactions in role-playing sessions.	Conduct role-playing sessions to provide forum for interactive practice.
Weigh fears of criticism, rejection, and disapproval against evidence. Reframe irrational beliefs.	Evaluate client's negative feelings of self against evidence-based reality.
Learn that avoidance is ineffective in dealing with anxiety.	Teach client laws of anxiety in order to reduce avoidant behavior—not dangerous, time limited, avoidance increases anxiety.

Improve interaction with family.	Involve family members in therapy. Teach them new techniques for interacting with client.
Learn new techniques for dealing with interpersonal activities on the job. Investigate possible changes that would limit interpersonal activities at work.	Refer client for vocational counseling as necessary.
Read self-help book as homework.	Instruct client to read self-help book as homework (see Chapter 24).
Take newfound skills into the real world and reinforce successful interactions with self-rewards. Correct failures and retry.	Encourage client to expose his new skills to the outside world.
Interact with others in self-help group.	Refer client to self-help group for interaction with people who have similar problems.
Discuss termination plan.	Address termination issues and draft termination plan.
Resolve remaining issues of separation anxiety and dependency.	Resolve client's separation anxiety and dependency.

BORDERLINE PERSONALITY DISORDER (301.83)

Borderline personality disorder is characterized by a pattern of instability in affect, self-image, and interpersonal relationships, including marked impulsivity. Individuals with this disorder go to great lengths to avoid real or imagined abandonment. The perception of rejection or separation results in significant changes in self-image, affect, behavior, and cognition. They may have an intense fear of being alone, and to avoid abandonment may resort to self-mutilation or even attempt suicide. They are known to switch quickly from idealizing others, including caregivers, to devaluing them, sometimes with surprising intensity. Impulsivity may include gambling, irresponsible spending, substance abuse, binge eating, reckless driving, and unsafe sexual activities. They are often bored, and may display extreme reactions to interpersonal stress. The disorder usually begins by early adulthood. It may be concurrent with mood disorders.

Behavioral Symptoms
(severity index: 1, mild; 2, moderate; 3, intense)

At least five of the following:

	Severity
1. Frantically tries to avoid real or imagined abandonment	_____
2. Unstable and intense interpersonal relationships	_____
3. Switches between extremes of idealization and devaluation	_____
4. Splits between right and wrong	_____
5. Has unstable self-image or sense of self	_____
6. Self-damaging impulsivity in two of the following areas: sex, spending, substance abuse, binge eating, reckless driving	_____
7. Self-mutilating behavior	_____
8. Suicidal ideations, threats, or attempts	_____

9. Short-term affective instability due to marked
   reactivity of mood: intense dysphoria, irritability,
   or anxiety   _____
10. Chronic feelings of emptiness, boredom   _____
11. Intense and inappropriate anger, displays of
    temper, fighting   _____
12. Stress-related paranoid ideations or severe
    dissociative symptoms   _____

Other Diagnostic Considerations

Mood disorder (296.xx)
Histrionic personality disorder (301.50)
Schizotypal personality disorder (301.22)
Paranoid personality disorder (301.0)
Narcissistic personality disorder (301.891)
Antisocial personality disorder (301.7)
Dependent personality disorder (301.6)
Personality change due to a general medical condition (310.1)

TREATMENT PLAN
BORDERLINE PERSONALITY DISORDER

Client: _____ Date: _____

I. OBJECTIVES OF TREATMENT
(*select one or more*)

1. Understand that fears of abandonment are unreal.
2. Control self-damaging impulsivity.
3. Eliminate self-mutilating behavior.
4. Control suicidal ideations, threats.
5. Stabilize sense of self.
6. Realize that all people are good and bad.
7. Control reactive depression and anxiety.
8. Learn improved reactions to stress.
9. Medicate and/or hospitalize as necessary.

II. SHORT-TERM BEHAVIORAL GOALS AND INTERVENTIONS
(*select goals and interventions appropriate for your client*)

CLIENT'S SHORT-TERM BEHAVIORAL GOALS	THERAPIST'S INTERVENTIONS
Discuss treatment plan and agree on target problems.	Confirm diagnosis. Draft treatment plan. Discuss with client. Agree on target problems.
Join in collaborative relationship. Diminish fears of abandonment.	Try to develop a collaborative relationship to build trust and enhance treatment outcome.
Explore underlying feelings related to depression or abandonment.	Explore and clarify underlying feelings that lead to depression or feelings of abandonment.

Explore possible negative consequences of impulsive behaviors.	Explore negative consequences of self-damaging impulsive behavior: unprotected sex, spending, binge-eating, substance abuse, reckless driving.
Reframe activities to assure positive consequences.	Revise future actions to assure positive consequences.
Understands that you are not bad or evil and that self-mutilation is extreme and uncalled for.	Discuss and eliminate need to mutilate self or attempt suicide.
Comply with referral and medication schedule.	Refer for psychiatric evaluation and medication if required.
Understand possible hospitalization and resolve fears.	Explain possible requirement for hospitalization and address associated fears.
Comply with need for hospitalization.	Hospitalize if and when necessary to prevent harm to self or others.
Enter hospital to prevent self-harm.	If actively suicidal, refer for immediate hospitalization. Call 911 or ambulance. Do not leave client unattended.
Enter into suicide pact with therapist.	If not actively suicidal, but has suicidal ideations, implement suicide pact in which client agrees to inform you of ideations and active plans, and agrees not to act without first notifying you.
Start daily thought and behavior log.	Assign client to maintain a log of thoughts and behaviors (see Homework Assignments, Chapter 23).

Recognize irrational beliefs and use evidence-based reality to change consequences.	Investigate irrational beliefs and reframe.
Cooperate in building genogram.	Construct genogram to identify family patterns and stressors (see Behavioral Techniques, Chapter 22).
Family therapy improves interactions and communication.	Conduct or refer to family therapy to relieve anger at client, improve communications, and repair interactions.
Family learns new techniques for dealing with client.	Acting as consultant, teach family improved techniques for dealing with client.
Learn new ways to interrupt negative reactions.	Conduct hypnosis, relaxation technique, or creative visualization to teach client how to interrupt negative reactions. Where possible, provide audiotape for home use and reinforcement.
Realize that all people, including self, are a mixture of good and bad, not all one or the other.	Teach client that all people have both good and bad features.
Explore attributes of your personality beyond the disorder.	Instruct client that he/she is not the disorder.
Enter treatment for depression.	Investigate underlying depression and treat (see appropriate treatment plan).
Enter treatment for anxiety.	Investigate underlying anxiety and treat (see appropriate treatment plan).

Learn new techniques for dealing with stress.	Teach client improved techniques for dealing with stress.
Join self-help group.	Refer client to self-help group.
Discuss termination.	Draft termination plan and discuss with client.
Address and resolve separation anxiety and dependency.	Resolve separation anxiety and dependency issues.

DEPENDENT PERSONALITY DISORDER (301.6)

Dependent personality disorder is characterized by the excessive need to be taken care of, as expressed by clinging and submissive behavior and fear of separation. People with this disorder believe they are unable to function adequately without help from others. They often have great difficulty making simple, everyday decisions without considerable advice and reassurance from others. They are usually passive and may allow another to take responsibility for all aspects of his or her life. This goes far beyond what could be considered appropriate assistance from others. They also have great difficulty disagreeing with people on whom they are dependent out of fear of losing support or approval. People with this disorder lack self-confidence and have difficulty initiating projects. They are convinced that they cannot function independently.

Behavioral Symptoms
(severity index: 1, mild; 2, moderate; 3, intense)

At least five of the following:

Severity

1. Has great difficulty making everyday decisions without help

_____

2. Needs others to be responsible for most major areas of life

_____

3. Difficulty disagreeing with others out of fear of losing support

_____

4. Lack of self-confidence in ability to act on one's own

_____

5. Goes to great lengths to obtain or maintain support

_____

6. Feels uncomfortable or helpless alone

_____

7. Fears not being able to fend for self

_____

Other Diagnostic Considerations

Mood disorders (2986.xx)
Panic disorder (300.21)
Agoraphobia (300.22)
Borderline personality disorder (301.83)
Histrionic personality disorder (301.50)
Avoidant personality disorder (301.82)
Personality change due to a general medical condition (310.1)
Substance abuse—cocaine (305.60)

TREATMENT PLAN
DEPENDENT PERSONALITY DISORDER

Client: _____ Date: _____

I. OBJECTIVES OF TREATMENT
(select one or more)

1. Teach client to make his/her own decisions.
2. Help client gradually take over responsibility for all major areas of life.
3. Build self-confidence in ability to act/live on own.
4. Develop tolerance for being alone.
5. Eliminate fear of disagreeing with others to protect support.
6. Dissolve need to do disagreeable things for continued support.

II. SHORT-TERM BEHAVIORAL GOALS AND INTERVENTIONS
(select goals and interventions appropriate for your client)

CLIENT'S SHORT-TERM BEHAVIORAL GOALS	THERAPIST'S INTERVENTIONS
Review treatment plan and agree on target problems.	Confirm diagnosis, formulate treatment plan, discuss target problems.
Join in responsibility for success of treatment.	Try to develop collaborative treatment relationship with client to build trust and enhance treatment outcome.
Comply with evaluation referral and medication if prescribed.	Refer client for psychiatric evaluation and medication if prescribed.

Discuss underlying anxiety and depression with therapist. Undergo treatment as required.	Explore underlying anxiety and depression. Treat as necessary. See appropriate treatment plan.
Learn anxiety control in hypnosis or relaxation technique. Use tape at home to reinforce skill.	In relaxation technique or hypnosis, teach client control of anxiety. Provide tape for home use.
Starts a daily thought and behavior log.	Instruct client to maintain thought and behavior log (see Homework Assignments, Chapter 23).
Evaluate rationality of thoughts and behaviors.	Confront irrational thoughts and behaviors.
Reframe irrational thoughts and behaviors with reality.	Urge client to use evidence-based reality to reframe irrational elements of thought and behavior.
Read referred self-help book.	Assign client to read self-help book (see Chapter 24).
Expand self-confidence.	Review progress made by client in acting on own.
Practice activities of daily living in role-playing sessions.	Conduct role-playing sessions to gain self-confidence in routine activities of living.
Practice new skills in daily life. Self-reward successes. Correct failures.	Instruct client to externalize role-playing skills.
Gain self-confidence in being able to say no.	As fears of being able to fend for self are dissipated, role-play disagreements with others.
Learn to make rational decisions on own in all phases of life. Stand on own feet.	Coach client in making rational decisions in everyday life.

Discuss termination plan.	Draft and discuss termination plan.
Resolve issues of separation from and dependency on therapist.	Resolve issues of separation anxiety and dependency.

HISTRIONIC PERSONALITY DISORDER (301.50)

Histrionic personality disorder is marked by a pattern of excessive emotionality and attention-seeking actions. People with this disorder feel uncomfortable if they are not the center of attention. They may appear lively, open, or flirtatious, and often may be inappropriately sexually provocative or seductive in dress or behavior. In therapy, they may present new physical or psychological symptoms each visit or make up stories to be the focus of the therapist's attention.

Behavioral Symptoms
(severity index: 1, mild; 2, moderate; 3, intense)

	Severity
1. Must be the center of attention	_____
2. Inappropriate sexually seductive or provocative dress or behavior	_____
3. Quickly changing, shallow expression of emotions	_____
4. Uses appearance to be focus of attention	_____
5. Uses impressionistic speech void of details	_____
6. Over-dramatic, exaggerated emotions	_____
7. Highly suggestible, easily influenced by others	_____
8. Sees relationships as more intimate than they really are	_____

Other Diagnostic Considerations

Borderline personality disorder (301.83)
Antisocial personality disorder (301.7)
Narcissistic personality disorder (301.81)
Dependent personality disorder (301.6)
Personality change due to a general medical condition (310.1)
Symptoms associated with chronic substance abuse (see substance)

TREATMENT PLAN
HISTRIONIC PERSONALITY DISORDER

Client: _____ Date: _____

I.   OBJECTIVES OF TREATMENT
     (*select one or more*)

1. Change dress habits to be less seductive.
2. Revise behavior patterns to be less provocative.
3. Reduce need to use appearance to gain attention.
4. Recognize emotional expression as superficial.
5. Reduce suggestibility.
6. Develop new detailed speech habits.
7. View relationships for what they are.
8. Reduce need to be the center of attention.

II. SHORT-TERM BEHAVIORAL GOALS AND
     INTERVENTIONS
     (*select goals and interventions appropriate for your client*)

CLIENT'S SHORT-TERM BEHAVIORAL GOALS	THERAPIST'S INTERVENTIONS
Discuss treatment plan and agree on target problems.	Confirm diagnosis, construct treatment plan, agree on target problems.
Join in collaborative effort to address target problems.	Attempt to develop collaborative treatment relationship to build trust and enhance outcome of treatment.
Become aware of distorted messages.	Explore cognitive messages that are translated into histrionic behaviors.

Comply with referral and start medication. Report reaction to meds.	Refer client for psychiatric evaluation and possible medication. Adjust as required.
Look at other sources of provocative behaviors.	Explore origins of other provocative behavior patterns.
Cooperate in building genogram.	Construct genogram to identify family patterns and stressors (see Behavioral Techniques, Chapter 22).
Receive feedback from family members about your role in the family.	Conduct or refer for family sessions to improve communications and help client gain further feedback about relationship.
Family reduces anger toward client; communication is improved.	Act as family consultant to reduce anger at client and improve communication among family members.
Reframe attitudes toward attention by others.	Explore use of appearance to be center of attention.
Review current relationships and adjust view of levels of intimacy based on reality.	Review level of intimacy of existing relationships. Adjust view of intimacy based on reality.
Have underlying disorders treated.	Explore underlying anxiety and depression, and treat as required (see appropriate treatment plan).
Learn that you have other significant attributes besides sexuality that should be the focus of attention.	Reinforce other important attributes of the client that should be recognized by others.

Learns new ways to deal with histrionic behavior.	Conduct hypnosis, relaxation techniques, or creative visualization to teach client how to interrupt histrionic behavior.
Learn to deal with anxiety rather than act out.	Teach client laws of anxiety— not dangerous, not permanent, increased by avoidance.
Develop healthy relationships, lessen need to be the center of attention.	Encourage client to develop new behaviors aimed at healthy relationships not based on being the center of attention.
Learn to express emotions in depth and detail.	Teach client to express emotions appropriately.
Ease suggestibility. Build confidence in self.	Urge client to rely on his/her own perceptions and cognitions and not on others.
Explore and resolve separation anxiety and dependence.	Address termination issues. Draft termination plan.

NARCISSISTIC PERSONALITY DISORDER (301.81)

Clients with narcissistic personality disorder may seek treatment for anger and depression after the loss of a spouse or a job. They feel the world has failed them. Confrontation, which often triggers a hardened defense and intense anger in these clients, is contraindicated. Clarification may offer a better technique. If you provide these clients with an Axis II diagnosis, treatable behavioral symptoms must be identified on Axis I as indicated above.

Behavioral Symptoms
(severity index: 1, mild; 2, moderate; 3, severe)

	Severity
1. Depression	_____
2. Generalized anxiety	_____
3. Grandiosity, self-important	_____
4. Sense of superiority, specialness	_____
5. Preoccupied with power, perfection, unlimited success	_____
6. Sense of entitlement	_____
7. Lack of empathy	_____
8. Exploits others	_____
9. Envious	_____
10. Arrogant, haughty	_____

Other Diagnostic Considerations

Histrionic personality disorder (301.50)
Antisocial personality disorder (301.7)
Borderline personality disorder (301.83)
Schizotypal personality disorder (301.22)
Paranoid personality disorder (301.0)
Personality change due to a general medical condition (310.1)

TREATMENT PLAN
NARCISSISTIC PERSONALITY DISORDER

Client: _____ Date: _____

I. OBJECTIVES OF TREATMENT
   (*select one or more*)

   1. Reduce overall intensity of anger and depression.
   2. Lower levels of expectation that are out of contact with reality.
   3. Develop less grandiose view of self.
   4. Eliminate need for perfection.
   5. Reduce arrogant/haughty behavior.
   6. Increase ability to empathize with others.

II. SHORT-TERM BEHAVIORAL GOALS AND INTERVENTIONS
   (*select goals and interventions appropriate for your client*)

CLIENT'S SHORT-TERM BEHAVIORAL GOALS	THERAPIST'S INTERVENTIONS
Discuss treatment plan and agree on target problem.	Develop treatment plan, discuss with client, and agree on target problem.
Attempt as much as possible to join in collaborative treatment relationship.	Attempt to cultivate therapeutic alliance or collaborative relationship with client.
Become hospitalized for your protection, or enter into a "suicide pact" with the therapist. Agree to report all ideations and active plans, and to inform therapist before taking action.	Evaluate client's suicide potential. If actively suicidal, hospitalize immediately. If not active and ideations exist, enter into a formal suicidal pact with client.

Examine evidence of irrational beliefs and consequences.	Assist client in examination of irrational beliefs dealing with perfection, grandiosity, arrogance, etc.
Develop and accept lower expectations of self and the world.	Guide client in reframing beliefs to reduce stressors and accept lower expectations of self and the world.
Maintain a daily thought log to track automatic thoughts, feelings.	Assign client to maintain a thought log (see Homework Assignments, Chapter 23).
Revise cognitive distortions with more rational responses.	Using log, investigate cognitive distortions and replace with rational responses.
Increase awareness of behaviors that result in anger and/or depression.	Explore triggers of anger and depression with client.
Reduce chronic stress and burnout.	Identify client "musts" and "should dos."
Understand problems of faulty communication in vivo.	Practice role playing with client.
Learn new techniques for dealing with problem situations in the future.	Explore events that prompt problems and alternative ways of dealing with them.
Understand problem behavior and how to change it.	Provide chain analysis of problem behavior. Assign homework. Discuss in session.
Become aware of how you often feel victimized.	Identify how client feels victimized.
Undergo treatment for anxiety or depression.	Explore symptoms of anxiety and depression and their origins. See appropriate treatment plan.

Follow through on referral for psychiatric evaluation and take medication as prescribed.	Refer client for psychiatric evaluation. Follow-up to confirm appointment was kept.
Maintain meds regimen and provide feedback on reactions, noncompliance, and/or required dosage adjustment.	Instruct client on importance of medication feedback.
Become aware of emotions that lead toward problematic behaviors and be less likely to act without thinking.	Clarify underlying emotions that lead to narcissistic behaviors.
Begin to listen to others; reduce pressurized speech.	Teach client active listening skills.
Report and discuss with therapist all destructive or grandiose self-talk.	Explain to client the nature of self-talk, and monitor grandiose and destructive thoughts and urges.
Lessen anger and aggression.	Help client to release anger and aggression against self and others.
Reduce feelings of grandiosity and superiority.	Identify grandiose expectations and help client to release them.
Become aware of negative or ambivalent feelings toward others.	Identify ways client lacks empathy for others.
Discuss issues of separation anxiety and dependence with therapist and resolve as a prelude to termination.	Discuss termination plan/issues with client.
Attend recommended self-help group to reinforce gains in therapy.	Refer client to a self-help group.

PARANOID PERSONALITY DISORDER (301.0)

Paranoid personality disorder is characterized by a pattern of suspiciousness and mistrust that perceives the motives of others as malevolent.

Behavioral Symptoms
(severity index: 1, mild; 2, moderate; 3, intense)

Distrust and suspicion of others, including at least four of the following:

Severity

1. Unsubstantiated suspicion of exploitation, deception, or harm by others   _____
2. Unjustified preoccupation with the loyalty or trustworthiness of friends and others   _____
3. Unjustified fear that others will maliciously betray confidences   _____
4. Interprets hidden or threatening meanings into benign remarks or events   _____
5. Persistently fails to forgive slights, insults, or injuries by others   _____
6. Imagines attacks on character or reputation not apparent to others and is quick to react in anger _____

Other Diagnostic Considerations

Psychotic disorders (295.xx)
Anxiety disorders (300.xx)
Mood disorders (296.xx)
Posttraumatic stress disorder (309.81)
Substance-related disorder (see substance)
Personality change due to a general medical condition (310.1)

TREATMENT PLAN
PARANOID PERSONALITY DISORDER

Client: _____ Date: _____

I. OBJECTIVES OF TREATMENT
    (*select one or more*)

> 1. Test and resolve unsubstantiated suspicions of exploita-
>   tion, deception, or harm by others.
> 2. Recognize feelings of distrust or disloyalty as unjustified.
> 3. Recognize as unjustified feelings that friends will betray
>   confidences.
> 4. Realize that routine remarks and events are benign.
> 5. Learn to forgive and forget imagined slights and insults.
> 6. Test and resolve perceived attacks on character or repu-
>   tation.
> 7. Control urge to retaliate in anger.

II. SHORT-TERM BEHAVIORAL GOALS AND
    INTERVENTIONS
    (*select goals and interventions appropriate for your client*)

CLIENT'S SHORT-TERM BEHAVIORAL GOALS	THERAPIST'S INTERVENTIONS
Review treatment plan and agree on target problems.	Confirm diagnosis, formulate treatment plan, agree with client on target problems.
Gain hope that problems can be solved. Feels less alienated.	Attempt to develop therapeutic alliance or collaborative relationship to build trust and enhance treatment outcome.
Comply with referral and maintain medication schedule if meds are prescribed.	Refer client for psychiatric evaluation and possible medication.

Be treated for underlying disorder.	Explore for underlying disorders, e.g., anxiety and depression, and treat. See appropriate treatment plan.
Recognize possible need for more structured environment; resolve fears of hospitalization.	Discuss possible need for hospitalization and resolve associated fears.
Enter hospital as necessary.	Hospitalize client as required.
Keep medication log to help determine need for meds adjustment.	Instruct client to maintain a medication log to record reactions.
Monitor thoughts and feelings. Discuss periodically with therapist.	Instruct client to maintain a thought and feelings log to monitor routine reactions to interactions with others.
Test suspicions of exploitation, deception, or harm against reality. Discard unjustified suspicions.	Identify suspicions of exploitation, deception, and harm by others and test against evidence-based reality.
Test feelings of distrust and disloyalty by others against reality and discard if unjustified.	Identify perceptions of distrust and disloyalty by others and test against evidence-based reality.
Review fear of betrayal and test against reality.	Explore feelings of possible betrayal of confidences by friends.
Recognize and accept as benign the random remarks and actions of others.	Investigate nature of remarks and events regarded as malevolent and evaluate against reality.
Recognize and forgive past slights, insults, and injuries attributed to others.	Explore past slights, insults, and injuries, and guide client to regard them as unreal or meaningless.

Realize overreaction to remarks by others as attacks on character.	Teach client that not all remarks are character attacks.
Explore underlying feelings that lead or contribute to paranoid thoughts.	Identify and clarify underlying dynamics that lead to paranoid thinking.
Improve communication among family members in order to reduce alienation.	Conduct or refer for family therapy.
Improve family interactions. Family works with client to reduce and control paranoid thinking.	Act as consultant to improve family interactions.
Rework any remaining unsubstantiated suspicions to reframe with positive cognitions.	Review and confirm reframing of all unsubstantiated suspicions with evidence-based cognition. Rework any remaining inappropriate feelings.
Learn and apply new ways to handle anger and control impulsivity.	Instruct client on principles of anger management.
Use hypnosis or relaxation techniques to practice better ways to handle anger, control impulsive reaction.	Use relaxation technique or hypnosis to teach new constructive ways of dealing with anger. Provide audiotape for home use.
Practice anger management in role-playing sessions.	Conduct role-playing sessions to practice anger management.
Use anger management techniques in the real world. Self-reward success. Correct failures and retry techniques.	Urge client to externalize new anger management skills.
Interact with others. Learn you are not alone. Practice new skills.	Refer client to self-help group (see Chapter 25).

| Review termination plan and resolve remaining issues of separation anxiety and dependence. | Discuss separation anxiety and dependence. Formulate treatment plan. |

SCHIZOID PERSONALITY DISORDER (301.20)

Schizoid personality disorder is characterized by a pattern of detachment from social relationships and restricted expression of emotions in interpersonal relations. Clients with this disorder are often characterized as "loners" who seem indifferent to possible close relationships or a desire for intimacy. They usually prefer spending time by themselves and appear to get little if any satisfaction from being part of a family or social group. They may also exhibit reduced pleasure from sensory, bodily, or interpersonal experiences, including sex. They seem also to be indifferent to approval or criticism by others.

Behavioral Symptoms
(severity index: 1, mild; 2, moderate; 3, intense)

At least four of the following:

	Severity
1. Neither enjoys nor desires close relationships, including family relationships	_____
2. Usually prefers solitary activities	_____
3. Little or no interest in sexual activities	_____
4. Finds no pleasure in most, if not all, activities	_____
5. No close friends outside of close relatives	_____
6. Indifferent to approval or criticism of others	_____
7. Flat affect, emotionally cold, detached	_____

Other Diagnostic Considerations

Delusional disorder (297.1)
Schizophrenia (295.xx)
Mood disorder with psychotic features (296.xx)
Autistic disorder (299.00)
Asperger's disorder (299.80)

Schizotypal personality disorder (301.22)
Paranoid personality disorder (301.0)
Avoidant personality disorder (301.82)
Obsessive-compulsive personality disorder (301.40)

TREATMENT PLAN
SCHIZOID PERSONALITY DISORDER

Client: _____ Date: _____

I. OBJECTIVES OF TREATMENT
(*select one or more*)

1. Evaluate psychiatrically for medication and monitor compliance.
2. Adopt alternate means to deal effectively with anger.
3. Learn appropriate reactions to the routine events of life.
4. Learn improved methods for dealing with stress.
5. Provide vocational counseling as necessary.
6. Improve interactions with others.
7. Reduce maladaptive functioning.
8. Achieve moderate behavior.
9. Increase overall quality of life.

II. SHORT-TERM BEHAVIORAL GOALS AND INTERVENTIONS
(*select goals and interventions appropriate for your client*)

CLIENT'S SHORT-TERM BEHAVIORAL GOALS	THERAPIST'S INTERVENTIONS
Review treatment plan and agree on target problems.	Confirm diagnosis, formulate treatment plan, agree with client on target problems.
Join in treatment effort. Gain hope that problems can be solved.	Attempt to develop therapeutic alliance or collaborative relationship to build trust and enhance treatment outcome.
Comply with referral and maintain medication schedule if meds are prescribed.	Refer client for psychiatric evaluation and possible medication.

Recognize possible need for more structured environment. Resolve fears of hospitalization.	Discuss possible need for hospitalization and resolve associated fears.
Be hospitalized as necessary.	Hospitalize client as required.
Cooperate in building genogram.	Construct genogram to identify family patterns and stressors (see Behavioral Techniques, Chapter 22).
Keep medication log to help determine need for meds adjustment.	Instruct client to maintain a medication log to record reactions.
Monitors thoughts and feelings. Discuss periodically with therapist.	Instruct client to maintain a thought and feelings log to monitor routine reactions to interactions with others.
Begin to realize the ego-syntonic nature of established behavior patterns.	Review client's behavioral patterns and discuss the maladaptive nature of his/her interactions.
Recognize alternate behaviors that offer significant personal benefits.	Point out alternate positive behaviors and the potential benefits.
Learn and apply new ways to handle anger and control impulsivity.	Instruct client on principles of anger management.
Use hypnosis or relaxation techniques to practice better ways to handle anger, control impulsive reaction.	Use relaxation technique or hypnosis to teach new constructive ways of dealing with anger. Provide audiotape for home use.
Practice anger management in role-playing sessions.	Conduct role-playing sessions to practice anger management.

Use anger management techniques in the real world. Self-reward success. Correct failure and retry techniques.	Urge client to externalize new anger management skills.
Begin to seek interpersonal relationships.	Encourage client to reach out to others, develop new relationships.
Establish new interest and improved relationships with family.	Urge client to establish new relationships with family members.
Improve family communications.	Conduct or refer for family therapy.
Family reduces anger toward client. Interactions with client are substantially improved.	Act as family consultant to improve interactions, reduce anger, and improve dealings with client.
Understand patterns of emotional interaction.	Use family sessions to determine emotional bonding and distancing patterns.
Family increases understanding of emotional relationships among members.	Have family create a family sculpture to demonstrate relationships, e.g., alliances, misalliances, triangles (see Chapter 22).
Undergo retraining in job functions. Expand opportunities.	Refer client for vocational training.
Seek people to date.	As socialization improves, urge client to date.
Start to interact with others. Learn you are not alone. Practice new skills.	Refer client to self-help group.
Recognize significant gains achieved.	Review newfound enjoyment in interactive relationships to reinforce improvements.

Expand interests.	Urge expansion of pleasurable activities.
Review termination plan and resolve remaining issues of separation anxiety and dependence.	Discuss separation anxiety and dependence. Formulate treatment plan.

SCHIZOTYPAL PERSONALITY DISORDER (301.22)

Schizotypal personality disorder is characterized by deficits in interpersonal functioning, acute discomfort in close relationships, cognitive or perceptive distortions, and eccentric behavior. These clients often tend to misinterpret casual events as having specific and unusual meaning. They may be superstitious or preoccupied with paranormal phenomena, and often believe they can sense events before they happen or read people's minds. They typically believe they have magical control over the actions of others. Their speech can be vague or digressive without being incoherent. Individuals with this disorder are usually suspicious of others and exhibit paranoid ideations. Their mannerisms and dress are often eccentric. They may experience psychotic episodes in response to stress. People with this disorder may also have a concurrent diagnosis of major depressive disorder or schizoid, paranoid, avoidant, or borderline personality disorders.

Behavioral Symptoms
(severity index: 1, mild; 2, moderate; 3, intense)

	Severity
1. Misinterprets casual events as having special meanings	_____
2. Magical thinking, superstitions, clairvoyance, telepathy	_____
3. Unusual perceptual experiences	_____
4. Odd thinking and speech	_____
5. Suspiciousness, paranoid ideations	_____
6. Inappropriate affect	_____
7. Eccentric appearance or behavior	_____
8. No close friends besides immediate family	_____
9. Acute social anxiety is not eased by familiarity	_____

Other Diagnostic Considerations

Delusional disorder (297.1)
Schizophrenia (295.xx)
Paranoid personality disorder (301.0)
Schizoid personality disorder (301.20)
Avoidant personality disorder (301.82)
Narcissistic personality disorder (301.81)
Borderline personality disorder (301.83)
Communication disorders (315.xx)
Autistic disorder (299.00)
Asperger's disorder (299.80)

TREATMENT PLAN
SCHIZOTYPAL PERSONALITY DISORDER

Client: _____ Date: _____

I. OBJECTIVES OF TREATMENT
   (*select one or more*)

   1. Evaluate for concurrent mental disorders and treat as appropriate.
   2. Refer for psychiatric evaluation and medication.
   3. Reframe magical thinking, superstition, and other maladaptive beliefs with evidence-based reality.
   4. Investigate unusual perceptual experiences and evaluate against reality.
   5. Correct odd thinking and bizarre speech patterns.
   6. Explore and treat underlying anxiety and depression.
   7. Improve eccentric appearance.
   8. Point out and correct other eccentric behavior.
   9. Encourage socialization.

II. SHORT-TERM BEHAVIORAL GOALS AND INTERVENTIONS
    (*select goals and interventions appropriate for your client*)

CLIENT'S SHORT-TERM BEHAVIORAL GOALS	THERAPIST'S INTERVENTIONS
Confirm or revise diagnosis.	Confirm or revise diagnosis. Evaluate possible dual diagnoses.
Discuss treatment plan and agree on target problems.	Create appropriate treatment plan and agree with client on target problems.

Join in collaborative relationship as much as possible.	Attempt to establish collaborative relationship to build trust and enhance outcome of treatment.
Comply with referral and medication regimen if prescribed.	Refer client for psychiatric evaluation and medication if necessary.
Cooperate in building genogram.	Construct genogram to identify family patterns and stressors (see Behavioral Techniques, Chapter 22).
Family reduces anger toward client. Communications are improved.	Conduct or refer for family therapy to reduce anger toward client and improve family communications.
Improve family interactions. Be less detached as support is increased.	Acting as consultant in family sessions, improve interaction among members.
Relate examples of magical thinking and other distorted beliefs.	Explore magical thinking, superstition, and other cognitive distortions.
Evaluate beliefs against evidence-based reality.	Evaluate distortions against evidence-based reality.
Replace distorted beliefs with reality.	Reframe cognitive distortions.
Be evaluated for underlying anxiety and treated if necessary.	Evaluate and treat underlying anxiety. See appropriate treatment plan.
Be evaluated for underlying depression and treated.	Evaluate for underlying depression and treat (see appropriate treatment plan).
Explore odd thinking patterns and unusual speech patterns. Correct if possible.	Address odd thinking and speech patterns and correct.

Learn more appropriate dress and grooming.	Point out eccentric appearance and instruct client in appropriate attire and grooming.
Improve interactional skills.	Conduct role playing to improve client's interactional skills with others.
Become aware of underlying causes of distorted thinking.	Explore and clarify underlying feelings that lead toward distorted thinking.
Join with others who have similar problems.	Refer client to self-help group or group therapy.
Learn to interact with others.	Encourage socialization.
Replace remaining eccentric behavior with more positive alternates.	Evaluate and provide alternates for remaining eccentric behaviors.
Discuss separation anxiety and dependency.	Address separation anxiety and dependence issues.
Discuss termination plan.	Create and agree on termination plan.

14

Psychological Factors Affecting Medical Condition (316)*

The essential feature of this diagnosis is the presence of a behavioral or psychological factor that adversely affects an existing medical condition. These factors may be found in Axis I and Axis II disorders, personality traits that do not fully meet the established criteria for these diagnoses, and social and environmental stressors. They should be coded on Axis I with the accompanying medical ICD-10 code on Axis III (see *DSM-IV* Appendix G). If more than one behavioral or psychological factor exists, the most prominent should be coded.

In addition to psychological factors affecting medical conditions, there can also be physical symptoms caused by a temporal situation such as substance abuse or somatoform disorder. Pain is not diagnosed as a psychological factor causing medical symptoms, but as pain disorder with psychological factors or medical conditions.

---

*Coded on AXIS III

Behavioral Symptoms
(severity index: 1, mild; 2, moderate; 3, intense)

Note: General medical condition (Axis III) exists

Severity

1. Substance use/dependence interferes with medical treatment _____
2. Mental disorder affects general medical condition _____
3. Psychological factor affects development of, exacerbates, or delays recovery from general medical condition _____
4. Personality or coping style affects general medical condition _____
5. Negative health behavior affects general medical condition _____
6. Stress-related responses exacerbate medical symptoms _____
7. Psychological factor increases health risk _____
8. Major impairment in occupational, social, and other areas of living _____

Other Diagnostic Considerations

Substance use/dependence (303.xx)
Factitious disorder (300.xx)
Pain disorders (307.80)
Hypochondriasis (300.7)
Generalized anxiety disorder (300.02)
Major depression (296.xx)
Dysthymia (300.4)
Personality disorders (301.xx)
Eating disorders (307.xx)
Relational problems (V61.xx)

TREATMENT PLAN
PSYCHOLOGICAL FACTORS AFFECTING
MEDICAL CONDITION

Client: _____ Date: _____

I. OBJECTIVES OF TREATMENT
   (*select one or more*)

   1. Treat for substance use/dependence if necessary.
   2. Treat indicated mental disorder.
   3. Teach client how psychological problems affect medical condition.
   4. Teach client new coping styles to replace problematic behavior.
   5. Discontinue negative health behavior.
   6. Control stressors that impact medical problem.
   7. Foster realization of increased health risks.
   8. Optimize treatment and stabilize medical condition.
   9. Restore client to optimal level of functioning in activities of daily living.

II. SHORT-TERM BEHAVIORAL GOALS AND INTERVENTIONS
   (*select goals and interventions appropriate for your client*)

CLIENT'S SHORT-TERM BEHAVIORAL GOALS	THERAPIST'S INTERVENTIONS
Discuss treatment plan and agree on target problem.	Confirm diagnosis, assess impairments, and formulate treatment plan. Discuss target problems with client.
Feel less hopeless.	Establish therapeutic or collaborative alliance.

Understand interaction of medical and psychological problems.	Make client aware of relationship between medical problem and psychological factors.
Follow up on evaluation referrals and comply with medication schedule if meds are prescribed.	Refer for medical and psychiatric evaluations.
Start medication log.	Instruct client to maintain a medication log to monitor regimen and need for adjustment.
Have mental disorder treated.	Identify underlying mental disorder and treat (see appropriate treatment plan).
Address other psychological problems.	Identify other psychological problems and treat as appropriate.
Be treated for substance use/ dependence if indicated.	Evaluate for substance use/dependence and treat. See appropriate treatment plan.
Help create genogram.	Create genogram to identify family interactions and stressors (see Behavioral Techniques, Chapter 22).
Recognize family origins of psychological factors.	Explore family history relating to this problem.
Realize possible need for hospitalization.	Discuss possible hospitalization and eliminate fear/anxieties.
Undergo hospitalization to stabilize your condition.	Hospitalize client as required.
Identify impact of pain.	Assess severity of pain and its impact on psychological and medical problems.

Learn new pain management techniques.	Teach client how to deal effectively with pain.
Attend pain clinic.	If pain persists, refer to pain clinic.
Reduce pain or anxiety.	Introduce client to relaxation technique or self-hypnosis to handle pain or other side effects that exacerbate medical condition. Provide audiocassette for home use (see Chapter 23).
Start thought journal, discuss entries periodically with therapist.	Instruct client to maintain a thought journal.
Reframe irrational belief system with rational thinking and improved consequences.	Discuss irrational beliefs and reframe for new consequences.
Family strengthens support for client.	Involve family in treatment and act as consultant to help them understand and deal with client.
Improve family interactions.	Ease family anxiety and teach them new skills for interacting with client.
Realize you are more than just a disorder.	Help client to see he/she is a whole person and not just a disorder.
Meet and interact with others who have similar problems. Realize you are not alone.	Refer client to self-help group.
Read self-help book. Increase understanding.	Assign reading of self-help book as homework (see Chapter 24).

Accept medical condition and cooperate fully with medical treatment.	Help client overcome denial and accept medical condition.
Discuss termination.	Discuss termination and agree on termination plan.
Discuss and resolve remaining issues.	Resolve remaining issues of dependence and separation anxiety.

15

Psychotic Disorders

SCHIZOPHRENIA

Psychosis is characterized by delusions or hallucinations and other disorganized behaviors that significantly impair the individual's ability to function in daily life. Although the prevalence rate is only 1 percent, the societal costs are high. Schizophrenics occupy one-quarter of the beds in the nation's mental hospitals, and the course of this illness is chronic. Although it is doubtful that individuals with psychotic disorders can be cured by psychotherapy alone, it is possible, using psychotherapy and medication, to ameliorate their symptoms and improve their general level of functioning and quality of life. Subtypes of schizophrenia include paranoid, disorganized, catatonic, undifferentiated, and residual.

Behavioral Symptoms
(severity index: 1, mild; 2, moderate; 3, intense)

	Severity
1. Delusions	_____
2. Hallucinations	_____
3. Bizarre behavior	_____
4. Incoherent speech	_____
5. Disorganized or catatonic behavior	_____
6. Withdrawal from society	_____
7. Inappropriate affect	_____
8. Occupational dysfunction	_____
9. Loss of sense of self	_____
10. Paranoia	_____
11. Abnormal psychomotor activities	_____

SCHIZOPHRENIA—PARANOID TYPE (295.30)

This disorder is marked by a preoccupation with delusions and auditory hallucinations, catatonic behavior, disorganized speech, and inappropriate affect.

Behavioral Symptoms
(severity index: 1, mild; 2, moderate; 3, intense)

	Severity
1. Preoccupation with delusions	_____
2. Frequent auditory hallucinations	_____
3. Withdrawal from society	_____
4. Occupational dysfunction	_____
5. Loss of sense of self	_____
6. Paranoia	_____

(Note: symptoms of schizophrenia are present, but disorganized speech, disorganized or catatonic behavior, or inappropriate affect are not prominent features.)

SCHIZOPHRENIA—DISORGANIZED TYPE (295.10)

This disorder is marked by inappropriate affect and disorganized speech and/or behavior.

Behavioral Symptoms
(severity index: 1, mild; 2, moderate; 3, intense)

All of the following:

	Severity
1. Disorganized speech	_____
2. Disorganized behavior	_____
3. Flat or inappropriate affect	_____

(Note: catatonic type features are not present.)

SCHIZOPHRENIA—CATATONIC TYPE (295.20)

This disorder is marked by two or more of the following symptoms: motoric inability, catalepsy including stupor or waxy flexibility, excessive motor activity, extreme negativism, posturing, alogia (restricted thought and speech), and avolition (lack of goal-directed behavior).

Behavioral Symptoms
(severity index: 1, mild; 2, moderate; 3, intense)

At least two of the following:

	Severity
1. Motor immobility, catalepsy, stupor	_____
2. Excessive and purposeless motor activity	_____
3. Extreme negativism, mute	_____

4. Posturing, stereotyped movements, preeminent
   mannerisms/grimacing _____
5. Echolalia or echopraxia _____

SCHIZOPHRENIA—UNDIFFERENTIATED TYPE (295.90)

In this disorder, the symptoms of schizophrenia are present, but do not meet the criteria for paranoid, disorganized, or catatonic type.

Behavioral Symptoms
(severity index: 1, mild; 2, moderate; 3, intense)

(Note: symptoms for schizophrenia are present, but criteria for paranoid, catatonic, or disorganized types are missing.)

Severity

1. Withdrawal from society _____
2. Occupational dysfunction _____
3. Loss of sense of self _____
4. Paranoia _____

SCHIZOPHRENIA—RESIDUAL TYPE (295.60)

This disorder is marked by the absence of delusions, hallucinations, or catatonic behavior, but includes flat affect, poverty of speech, avolition, plus more attenuated schizophrenic symptoms such as odd beliefs and unusual perceptive experiences.

Behavioral Symptoms
(severity index: 1, mild; 2, moderate; 3, intense)

(Note: symptoms of schizophrenia are present, but not delusions, hallucinations, disorganized speech, or disorganized or catatonic behavior.)

Two or more of the following in attenuated form:

	Severity
1. Withdrawal from society	_____
2. Inappropriate affect	_____
3. Occupational dysfunction	_____
4. Loss of sense of self	_____
5. Paranoia	_____

Other Diagnostic Considerations

Delirium (293.0).
Dementia (290.xx)
Substance-induced psychotic disorder (see substance)
Substance-related disorders (see substance)
Schizoaffective disorder (295.70)
Schizophreniform disorder (295.40)
Delusional disorder (297.1)
Pervasive development disorders (298.80)
Schizotypal personality disorder (301.22)
Schizoid personality disorder (301.20)
Paranoid personality disorder (301.0)

TREATMENT PLAN
PSYCHOTIC DISORDERS

Client: _____ Date: _____

I. OBJECTIVES OF TREATMENT
   (*select one or more*)

   1. Reduce acute symptomatology.
   2. Encourage compliance with medications.
   3. Encourage client to understand and accept that meds may not always be able to control symptoms.
   4. Help client lower expectations of quality of life.
   5. Reduce irrational beliefs.
   6. Help client develop better coping skills.
   7. Develop discharge plan for coping with everyday life, including living arrangements, work, etc.
   8. Promote socialization.

II. SHORT-TERM BEHAVIORAL GOALS AND INTERVENTIONS
   (*select goals and interventions appropriate for your client*)

CLIENT'S SHORT-TERM BEHAVIORAL GOALS	THERAPIST'S INTERVENTIONS
Discuss treatment plan and agree on target problem.	Develop treatment plan, discuss with client, and agree on target problem.
Follow up and comply with medical and psychiatric recommendations.	Refer client for medical and psychiatric evaluations.
Understand need for hospitalization during crisis periods and resolve any fears of hospitalization.	Evaluate need for hospitalization, and resolve client fears of being hospitalized.

Maintain medication journal to help comply with regular meds schedule, and report any urges to ignore or overdose.	When medication is prescribed, confirm that prescription has been filled and meds are taken on a regular schedule. Assign client to keep journal.
Provide prompt feedback on effectiveness of medication and side effects. See psychiatrist for adjustment if necessary.	If necessary, refer to psychiatrist for dosage adjustment and control of side effects.
Understand dangers of mixing medication with other drugs.	Instruct client on dangers of mixing prescribed medication with other drugs.
Replace destructive thoughts and urges with self-talk drawing on past successes with the activities of daily living.	Teach client to counter destructive thoughts and urges with positive self-talk drawing on past successful experience with the activities of daily living.
Replace irrational beliefs and consequences with rational thought.	Explore and confront client's irrational belief system. Point out rational beliefs and consequences.
Improve personal hygiene and grooming.	Coach client in taking an active interest in his appearance. Teach client the importance of grooming and hygiene.
Help create genogram.	Produce genogram to help understand family interactions and stressors (see Behavioral Techniques, Chapter 22).
Family support structure is strengthened.	Involve client's family in treatment and act as family consultant to help them understand and deal with the client.

Family improves understanding. New skills developed for interaction with client.	Lessen family anxiety and teach new skills for interaction with the client.
Expand daily journal to include thoughts, feelings, and behavior.	Assign client to expand daily journal to include thoughts, feelings, and behavior.
Review journal with therapist and help identify triggers that set off unacceptable behavior.	Regularly review journal with client and identify triggers that result in aberrant behavior.
Learn new skills for coping with trigger points and controlling behavior.	Teach client stress reduction or relaxation technique to control trigger points.
Improve socialization skills at self-help group.	Refer to self-help group to learn and practice socialization.
Enter structured environment such as group home or residential treatment center.	If client is severely disturbed, refer to residential treatment center or group home.
Learn marketable vocational skills.	Refer client for vocational training.
Spend more time in real world.	Do reality testing and encourage client to focus on real world rather than fantasies.
Recognize symptoms of depression, anger, and anxiety as they contribute to the disorder. Ease feelings of inadequacy.	Explore underlying feelings of depression, anger, and anxiety. Lessen feelings of inadequacy.
Recognize and understand the dynamics of anxiety and panic.	Teach client laws of anxiety— not dangerous, not permanent, avoidance increases anxiety.
Reduce aggression; learn principles of assertiveness— equal respect for yourself and others.	Explain principles of assertiveness to replace aggression.

Accept diagnosis and use available resources to live more comfortably with it.	Help client to overcome denial and fully accept illness.
Deal effectively with termination.	Develop termination plan and discuss issues associated with termination, e.g., dependency and separation.

SCHIZOPHRENIFORM DISORDER (295.40)

This disorder includes the features of schizophrenia but with a duration of at least one month and less than six months and the absence of flat affect. Impairment of social and occupational functioning is not required, but may exist. The diagnosis is considered "provisional" if the symptoms exist for less than six months. If the symptoms exist for more than six months, the diagnosis should be changed to schizophrenia; specify with or without good prognosis features.

Behavioral Symptoms
(severity index: 1, mild; 2, moderate; 3, intense)

	Severity
1. The symptoms of schizophrenia for more than one month and less than six months	_____
2. Onset of psychotic symptoms within four weeks of change in behavior	_____
3. Confusion at height of the psychotic episode	_____
4. Good social and occupational functioning	_____
5. Absence of flat affect	_____

Other Diagnostic Considerations

Brief psychotic disorder (298.8)

TREATMENT PLAN
SCHIZOPHRENIFORM DISORDER

Client: _____ Date: _____

I. OBJECTIVES OF TREATMENT
    (*select one or more*)

    1. Reduce and control delusions and hallucinations.
    2. Encourage compliance with medication.
    3. Understand and accept that meds may not always be able to control symptoms.
    4. Lower expectations of quality of life.
    5. Reduce irrational beliefs.
    6. Develop improved coping skills.
    7. Encourage socialization.
    8. Maintain normal affect.
    9. Maintain social and occupational functioning.

II. SHORT-TERM BEHAVIORAL GOALS AND INTERVENTIONS
    (*select goals and interventions appropriate for your client*)

CLIENT'S SHORT-TERM BEHAVIORAL GOALS	THERAPIST'S INTERVENTIONS
Discuss treatment plan and agree on target problem.	Develop treatment plan, discuss with client, and agree on target problem.
Try as much as possible to join in collaborative treatment effort. Feel less alienated.	Attempt to establish collaborate relationship or therapeutic alliance to build trust and enhance treatment outcome.
Follow up and comply with medical and psychiatric recommendations.	Refer client for medical and psychiatric evaluations.

Understand need for hospitalization during crisis periods and resolve any fears of hospitalization.	Evaluate need for hospitalization, and resolve client fears of being hospitalized.
Maintain medication journal to help comply with regular meds schedule, and report any urges to ignore or overdose.	When medication is prescribed, confirm that prescription has been filled and meds are taken on a regular schedule. Assign client to keep journal.
Provide prompt feedback on effectiveness of medication and side effects. See psychiatrist for adjustment if necessary.	If necessary, refer to psychiatrist for dosage adjustment and control of side effects.
Understand dangers of mixing medication with other drugs.	Instruct client on dangers of mixing prescribed medication with other drugs.
Understand that persistent symptoms require revised diagnosis.	If symptoms persist for six months, review and update diagnosis to schizophrenia.
Replace destructive thoughts and urges with self-talk drawing on past successes with the activities of daily living.	Teach client to counter destructive thoughts and urges with positive self-talk drawing on past successful experience with the activities of daily living.
Cooperate in constructing genogam.	Prepare genogram to identify family interactions (see Behavioral Techniques, Chapter 22).
Anger at client is reduced. Communication improves.	Conduct or refer for family therapy to reduce anger at client and improve family communications.

Improve family interactions.	Act as consultant and coach family members in ways to improve interactions.
Relate past and present feelings, gain increased awareness of his/her problem.	Explore client's emotional history.
Replace irrational beliefs and consequences with rational thought.	Explore and confront client's irrational belief system. Point out rational beliefs and consequences.
Improve personal hygiene and grooming.	Coach client in taking an active interest in his appearance. Teach client the importance of grooming and hygiene.
Family strengthens support structure for client.	Involve client's family in treatment and act as family consultant to help family understand and deal with the client.
Family understanding improves. New skills developed for interaction with client.	Lessen family anxiety and teach them new skills for interaction with the client.
Expand daily journal to include thoughts, feelings, and behavior.	Assign client to expand daily journal to include thoughts, feelings, and behavior.
Review journal with therapist and help identify triggers that set off unacceptable behavior.	Regularly review journal with client and identify triggers that result in aberrant behavior.
Learn new skills for coping with trigger points and controlling behavior.	Teach client stress reduction or relaxation technique to control trigger points.
Improve socialization skills at self-help group.	Refer to self-help group to relearn socialization.

Enter structured environment such as group home or residential treatment center.	If client is severely disturbed, refer to residential treatment center or group home.
Spend more time in real world.	Do reality testing and encourage client to focus on real world rather than fantasies.
Recognize symptoms of depression, anger, and anxiety as they contribute to the disorder. Ease feelings of inadequacy.	Explore underlying feelings of depression, anger, and anxiety, and treat (see appropriate treatment plan).
Recognize and understand the dynamics of anxiety and panic.	Teach client laws of anxiety— not dangerous, not permanent, avoidance increases anxiety.
Reduce aggression; learn principles of assertiveness— equal respect for yourself and others.	Explain principles of assertiveness to replace aggression.
Accept diagnosis and use available resources to live more comfortably with it.	Help client overcome denial and fully accept illness.
Understand that termination may bring up other issues and work them through with therapist.	Develop termination plan. Discuss issues of dependency and separation anxiety.

16

Relational Problems

PARENT–CHILD RELATIONAL PROBLEM (V61.20)

If the focus of attention is on the parents and child or children, it is necessary to use the correct current procedural terminology (CPT) code and an Axis I diagnosis to get reimbursed by an insurance company. Axis II disorders usually have symptoms that should be treated under an Axis I diagnosis.

Behavioral Symptoms
(severity index: 1, mild; 2, moderate; 3, intense)

	Severity
1. Impaired communication	_____
2. Inadequate discipline	_____
3. Underprotective-overprotective	_____
4. Quarrelling among family members	_____
5. Poor parenting skills	_____
6. Mental disorders among family members	_____
7. Medical problems	_____
8. Isolation of one or more family members	_____
9. Irrational expectation of parent–child roles	_____

Other Diagnostic Considerations

Adjustment disorders (309.xx)
Anxiety disorders (300.xx)
Attention deficit and disruptive behavior disorder (214.xx)
Depressive disorders (296..xx)
Dissociative disorders (300.xx)
Eating disorders (307.xx)
Factitious disorders (300.xx)
Pathological gambling (312.31)
Impulse control disorder (312.xx)
Obsessive-compulsive disorder (301.4)
Personality disorders (301.xx)
Sexual abuse disorders (V61.21) Axis IV

TREATMENT PLAN
PARENT–CHILD RELATIONAL PROBLEM

Client: _____   Date: _____

I. OBJECTIVES OF TREATMENT
    (*select one or more*)

      1. Reduce overall intensity of quarreling.
      2. Develop better parenting skills.
      3. Investigate and resolve medical problems.
      4. Improve communication skills.
      5. Restore rational discipline.
      6. Increase ability to empathize with each other.
      7. Establish rational expectations of parent–child roles.

II. SHORT-TERM BEHAVIORAL GOALS AND
     INTERVENTIONS
     (*select goals and interventions appropriate for your client*)

CLIENT'S SHORT-TERM BEHAVIORAL GOALS	THERAPIST'S INTERVENTIONS
Discuss treatment plan and agree on target problems.	Formulate treatment plan and discuss with clients in family session. Agree on target problems.
Improve treatment outlook. Diminish feelings of anger and isolation.	Develop therapeutic alliance or collaborative relationship with client to instill trust and enhance treatment outcomes.
Cooperate in completion of a family genogram. Begin to understand historical communication patterns and contributions of ancestors as "Ghosts in the Nursery."	Prepare complete genogram to uncover and display family actions, interactions, patterns, rules, roles, and secrets (see Behavioral Techniques, Chapter 22).

Follow up with evaluation referrals.	As appropriate, refer clients for medical and psychiatric evaluations.
Treat uncovered medical problem.	Resolve medical problems uncovered.
Start and maintain medication log to monitor medication schedule. Record reactions for adjustment if necessary.	If medications prescribed, assure compliance with regimen. Identify need for adjustment.
Maintain thought and feelings log. Discuss with therapist.	Instruct each client to maintain a thought and feelings log to record events and reactions between visits.
Be evaluated for other disorders; individual treatment is initiated as appropriate.	Evaluate each client for other Axis I and Axis II disorders and treat as appropriate (see appropriate treatment plan).
Cooperate with therapist in exploration of family dynamics. Family begins working on issues together.	Identify if there is a designated "patient" in the family.
Reframe problem as a family problem and not an individual problem.	Help family realize the relationship problem is a system problem and not a person problem.
Receive feedback and support from peers; develop understanding and control.	Explore substance abuse, and if required, refer to twelve-step or alternative rational recovery program.
Attend group to work on sexual addictions.	Explore sexual abuse, and if needed, refer to sexual offenders group.
Attend parenting group to improve parenting skills.	Refer client to parenting group to improve parenting skills.

Identify triggers that cause family conflicts.	Make client aware of triggers that touch off family conflicts.
Receive insights from instant feedback on your behavior as a family member.	Conduct role-playing sessions for each client to act out the other client's behaviors.
Examine evidence of irrational beliefs and realize their consequences.	Help client examine his irrational beliefs dealing with perfection, grandiosity, or arrogance.
Reframe irrational beliefs to improve consequences.	Help client reframe his beliefs to change the consequences.
Understand where you stand emotionally in the other's life using another medium besides language.	Perform family sculpturing in office to demonstrate the emotional relationships among and between family members.
Be made aware of your disruptive relational patterns in family.	Identify disruptive relational patterns.
Help develop family solution and become part of the solution rather than the problem.	Preclude a "search for the guilty" by helping clients to stay solution-focused.
Realize that anxiety and feelings of awkwardness are normal accompaniments to family change.	Instruct clients on difficulties of, and resistances to, change.
Learn to listen to one another and ask for clarification when necessary.	Teach clients active listening and clarification skills.
Learn new techniques to handle anxiety and control impulses.	Teach relaxation technique or self-hypnosis to counteract anxieties of change.
Learn new rational perspective of the other.	Further clarify irrational distortions in client's perceptions.

Gain new knowledge and insights into your problem.	Assign self-help books (see Chapter 24).
Address and resolve issues of termination and dependency.	Develop termination plan and resolve termination issues.

PARTNER RELATIONAL PROBLEM (V61.1)

Couples may request family therapy or marriage counseling, which could logically be coded under V61.1. Although most insurance companies cover family/couples therapy, they do not recognize V codes for reimbursement. The answer is to find an Axis I disorder that fits one or both clients and proceed from there. The usual CPT code for conjoint or family therapy is 90847.

In recent national studies, one in six couples reported acts of physical aggression over a twelve-month period. Violence represents a dangerous problem for any couple-focused treatment. Although conjoint therapy might be useful in such cases, the safer course might be to refer the violence perpetrator to a specialized treatment group dealing specifically with violence. Victims might be referred for individual or group therapy centered on support and empowerment, or in more extreme cases, referred to a shelter.

Behavioral Symptoms
(severity index: 1, mild; 2, moderate; 3, intense)

<u>Severity</u>

Partner A:

1. Lack of pleasing behaviors	_____
2. Excess of displeasing behaviors	_____
3. Distorted expectations of marriage	_____
4. Unrealistic marital standards	_____
5. Lacks communication skills	_____
6. Deficient in problem-solving skills	_____
7. Engaged in extra-marital affair	_____
8. Destructive expressions of anger	_____

Severity

Partner B:

1. Lack of pleasing behaviors	_____
2. Excess of displeasing behaviors	_____
3. Distorted expectations of marriage	_____
4. Unrealistic marital standards	_____
5. Lacks communication skills	_____
6. Deficient in problem-solving skills	_____
7. Engaged in extra-marital affair	_____
8. Destructive expressions of anger	_____

Other Diagnostic Considerations

Anxiety disorders (300.xx)
Depressive disorders (296.xx)
Substance dependence (304.00)
Personality disorders (301.xx) Axis II
Eating disorders (307.xx)
Sexual dysfunctions (302.xx)
Attention-deficit/hyperactivity disorder (314.9)
Conduct disorder (312.18)
Disruptive behavior disorder (3112.9)
Antisocial personality disorders (301.7)

TREATMENT PLAN
PARTNER RELATIONAL PROBLEM

Client: _____ Date: _____

I.   OBJECTIVES OF TREATMENT
(*select one or more*)

1. Improve ratio of pleasing to displeasing behaviors.
2. Replace global complaints with behaviorally specific statements.
3. Build expressive and receptive communication skills.
4. Replace character assaults with "I" statements.
5. Improve problem-solving skills.
6. Ease financial stressors.
7. Improve child-rearing skills.
8. Reframe cognitive distortions.
9. Learn effective anger management.

II. SHORT-TERM BEHAVIORAL GOALS AND INTERVENTIONS
(*select goals and interventions appropriate for your client*)

CLIENTS' SHORT-TERM BEHAVIORAL GOALS	THERAPIST'S INTERVENTIONS
Join in collaborative relationship with therapist.	Retaining a neutral stance, cultivate a collaborative relationship or therapeutic alliance with both partners to build trust and enhance outcome.
Open up communication in a safe, controlled environment.	Conduct conjoint session and discuss marital distress.

Attend violence/abuse-oriented group or individual psychotherapy.	If relationship is violent, refer clients to appropriate treatment groups or individual treatment to avoid violent behavior triggered by conjoint sessions.
Cooperate in completing comprehensive assessment.	Complete comprehensive assessment of perceptions, attributions, expectations, assumptions, and standards for each partner.
Discontinue affair or enter individual psychotherapy.	If active affair uncovered, cease treatment unless affair is abandoned, or refer clients for individual psychotherapy.
Start individual treatment as required.	If substance abuse uncovered, perform individual therapy or refer client to appropriate group for treatment. See appropriate treatment plan.
Review treatment plan. Agree on target problems.	Develop treatment plan. Discuss and agree on target problems.
Follow-up with medical and psychiatric evaluations. Stabilize medical condition. Start medication regimen if prescribed.	Refer clients for separate medical and psychiatric evaluations and follow-up to confirm clients have kept appointments.
Help construct accurate and complete genogram.	Construct genogram of family relationships, e.g., actions, interactions, patterns, rules, roles, and secrets (see Behavioral Techniques, Chapter 22).

Maintain behavior logs.	Assign clients to maintain behavior log to monitor positive or negative reinforcing behavior of the other partner (see Homework Assignments, Chapter 23).
Learn to stay solution-focused.	Guide clients in staying solution-focused rather than problem-focused.
Observe your behavior and the reactions to it.	Conduct role-playing with partner A acting out partner B's behaviors and then vice versa.
Learn new communication skills and shared understanding.	Teach clients expressive and receptive skills.
Learn new problem-solving skills; increase mutual validation and trust.	Teach clients new problem-solving skills.
Practice new skills—define problem, brainstorm, agree on trial solution, implement, evaluate, and revise. Increase intimacy.	Assign techniques to tackle problem.
Maintain thought/belief log and discuss with therapist.	Assign each client to maintain a thought/belief log.
Reframe cognitive distortions.	Monitor thought/belief log entries for cognitive distortions and reframe.
Understand how underlying depression and/or anxiety disrupts couple or family functioning.	Investigate issues of anxiety and depression that may interfere with couples or family functioning. See appropriate treatment plan.
Become more aware of cycle of abuse.	Instruct clients on victimization and abuse cycle.

Discuss abuse openly without as much fear of retaliation.	Develop escape plan for suspected abuse victim with 800 telephone number if necessary.
Talk openly about abuse problem.	Evaluate for physical or sexual abuse and if suspected, perform individual therapy.
Attend self-help groups for support and increased understanding.	Refer to separate self-help groups, abuser and victim.
Develop parenting skills.	Refer to parenting group if required.
Complete assigned homework.	Assign clients to complete appropriate assignments from Brief Couples Homework Planner (see Homework Assignments, Chapter 23).
Realize that change may cause uncomfortable but normal feelings.	Teach clients about resistances and other difficulties associated with change. New behaviors sometimes feel awkward and create anxiety.
Recognize triggers and refrain from taking automatic action.	Urge clients to confront triggers that touch off family conflicts.
Learn "time-out" response.	Teach clients "time-out" response to anger.
Learn alternate methods for control of impulses.	Instruct each client in relaxation techniques or self-hypnosis as an alternate response to anger.
Do assigned reading.	Assign reading of "Stop Blaming," "Start Loving," or "Getting the Love You Want" (see Bibliotherapy, Chapter 24).

Discuss termination plan.	Prepare termination plan and discuss with clients.
Resolve remaining issues of separation anxiety and dependence.	Address and resolve issues of separation anxiety and dependence.

OCCUPATIONAL PROBLEM (V62.2)

Although occupational problems can be quite serious, both financially and interpersonally, V-codes cannot be listed as a treatable Axis I disorder. They must be coded as an Axis IV explanation of a disorder listed on Axis I. However, major impairments caused by the occupational problems can be treated under the appropriate Axis I mental disorder. Unemployment is a major problem and can exacerbate many disorders that otherwise might remain under control, triggering multiple impairments across most of the *DSM-IV* categories.

Behavioral Symptoms
(severity index: 1, mild; 2, moderate; 3, intense)

	Severity
1. Pervasive depressed mood	_____
2. Feelings of helplessness, hopelessness	_____
3. Irritability, excessive anxiety	_____
4. Decreased effectiveness, productivity	_____
5. Low self-esteem	_____
6. Insomnia, hypersomnia	_____
7. Social withdrawal	_____
8. Poor appetite/overeating	_____
9. Substance abuse	_____
10. Homicidal or suicidal thoughts	_____
11. Anxiety attacks	_____
12. Dissociation	_____
13. Marital problems	_____
14. Housing problems	_____

Other Diagnostic Considerations

Adjustment disorders (309.xx)
Anxiety disorders (300.xx)
Body dysmorphic disorder (300.7)

Bipolar disorders (296.xx)
Depressive disorders (296.xx)
Dissociative disorders (300.1x)
Factitious disorders (300.xx)
Gambling (312.31)
Impulse control disorders (312.xx)
Sexual disorders (302.xx)
Substance abuse disorders (see substance)
Personality disorders (Axis II coded) (301.xx)

TREATMENT PLAN
OCCUPATIONAL PROBLEM

Client: _____ Date: _____

I. OBJECTIVES OF TREATMENT
   (*select one or more*)

   1. Decrease anxiety and/or depression.
   2. Develop plan to deal with unemployment, and find suitable new employment.
   3. Lower level of job expectations that are out of contact with reality.
   4. Restore normal eating and sleeping patterns.
   5. Relieve feelings of helplessness.
   6. Raise self-esteem.
   7. Restore social contacts.
   8. Control homicidal/suicidal thoughts.
   9. Reinforce family support system.
   10. Restore to optimum level of functioning.

II. SHORT-TERM BEHAVIORAL GOALS AND
    INTERVENTIONS
    (*select goals and interventions appropriate for your client*)

CLIENT'S SHORT-TERM BEHAVIORAL GOALS	THERAPIST'S INTERVENTIONS
Discuss treatment plan with therapist and agree on target problems.	Develop treatment plan with client and agree on target problems.
Join with therapist, feel less alienated, more hopeful of working out problems.	Develop a therapeutic or collaborative alliance to build trust and enhance outcome of treatment.

Be more aware of symptoms triggered by unemployment. Impairments are addressed in treatment.	Evaluate for Axis I and II impairments. Treat as required (see appropriate treatment plan).
Use all resources available to deal with problem; feel less hopeless.	Investigate with client available resources to deal with occupational and/or financial problems.
Agree to suicide pact with therapist. Agree not to take action without first informing therapist. If actively suicidal or homicidal, agree to hospitalization to protect self and others.	Explore for active homicidal/ suicidal ideations and take appropriate actions, including immediate hospitalization. If only suicidal ideations are present, enter into suicide pact with client.
Follow through with psychiatric evaluation and prescribed medication.	Refer for psychiatric evaluation and follow-up to confirm appointment is kept, medications are taken if prescribed.
Keep daily journal for periodic review with therapist.	Assign client to maintain a daily journal to record thoughts, feelings, and reactions to medication. Adjust meds if needed.
Cooperate with assessment of gambling/substance abuse.	Investigate for possible gambling and/or substance abuse. If positive, see appropriate treatment plan.
Replace negative self-talk with positive affirmations.	Teach client to counter negative thoughts and urges with positive self-talk.
Add structure back into your life, relieve feelings of helplessness, aimlessness.	Review client's activities of daily living (ADLs). Help client structure his/her life.

Feel you are in a safe environment and can work things out step by step.	Set firm attainable goals. First things first.
Cooperate with therapist in exploring the possibilities of other disorders that might interfere with employment.	Investigate for personality disorders or other impairments that interfere with suitable employment. (See appropriate treatment plan.)
Cooperate in producing genogram.	Create genogram to identify family interactions and stressors (see Behavioral Techniques, Chapter 22).
Improve family understanding. Crisis can provide an awareness of need for new skills to deal with interactions.	Involve client's family in treatment and act as consultant to help them understand and better deal with client's problem.
Reduce family's anger and blame toward client.	Teach family how to empathize with client and provide support.
Understand familial patterns relating to money matters.	Conduct role playing to better understand family attitudes toward money and skill in money management.
Develop renewed confidence to deal with future job interviews.	Expand role-playing to cover job interviews.
Create an emergency budget. Record spending in special notebook. Eliminate unnecessary expenses.	Help client develop an emergency budget to control finances. Carry notebook to record spending.
Learn new ideas about possible future employment.	Refer client for career counseling.
Replace irrational beliefs and consequences with rational thought.	Explore and confront client's irrational belief system. Point out rational beliefs and consequences.

Use relaxation techniques to visualize new, positive ways of dealing with your problem and open new possibilities.	Use relaxation technique to boost client's self-esteem and create positive expectations. Provide audiotape.
Recognize the dynamics of depression and anxiety and their contribution to your problem.	Explore underlying feelings of depression, anger, and anxiety. Ameliorate feelings of inadequacy.
Meet with others who have similar problems.	Send client to self-help group.
Feel supported by a strong social network.	Encourage client to overcome shame and humiliation in reaching out to friends and family for support.
Read self-help books and gleans new ideas for dealing with problems.	Assign client to read self-help books as homework assignment (see Chapter 24).
Agree with therapist on termination plan. Address and resolve issues of separation anxiety and dependence.	Develop termination plan, discuss and resolve termination issues.

17

Sexual Dysfunctions

Sexual dysfunctions are characterized by disturbances in sexual desire and in the psychophysiological changes that characterize the sexual response cycle and by pain associated with sexual intercourse. The sexual response cycle is separated into four phases: desire, excitement, orgasm, and resolution. Dysfunction can occur in one or more of the phases simultaneously. The sexual disorders may be further characterized by subtypes specifying onset (lifelong or acquired), context (generalized or situational), or etiology (due to psychological factors or due to combined factors).

Age, gender, culture, ethnicity as well as social and religious background may have a great deal of influence on sexual desire, expectations, and attitudes about performance and should be considered in assessing all sexual disorders. Prevalence of the disorders remains undetermined due the lack of reliable studies and taboos surrounding the subject of sex.

The sexual dysfunctions are organized by the four phases of the sexual cycle:

1. Desire:

    Hypoactive sexual desire disorder (302.71)

    Sexual aversion disorder (302.79)

2. Arousal:

    Female sexual arousal disorder (302.72)

    Male erectile disorder (302.72)

3. Orgasm:

    Female orgasmic disorder (302.73)

    Male orgasmic disorder (302.74)

    Premature ejaculation (302.75)

4. Resolution:

    Dyspareunia (302.76) not due to a general medical condition

    Vaginismus (306.51) not due to a general medical condition

HYPOACTIVE SEXUAL DESIRE DISORDER (302.71)

Behavioral Symptoms
(severity index: 1, mild; 2, moderate; 3, intense)

Specify: lifelong, acquired, generalized, or situational.

Consider other factors that affect sexual functioning such as age and life context; rule out substance-induced disorder, general medical condition, and other Axis I disorders except another sexual dysfunction.

	Severity
1. Persistent or recurrent lack of sexual fantasies and desire for sexual activity	_____
2. Disorder causes marked distress or interpersonal difficulty	_____

SEXUAL AVERSION DISORDER (302.79)

Behavioral Symptoms
(severity index: 1, mild; 2, moderate; 3, intense)

Specify: lifelong, acquired, generalized, or situational.

Consider other factors that affect sexual functioning such as age and life context; rule out substance-induced disorder, general medical condition, and other Axis I disorders except another sexual dysfunction.

Severity

1. Persistent or recurrent extreme aversion to or avoidance of genital sexual contact with a sexual partner _____
2. Disorder causes marked distress or interpersonal difficulty _____

FEMALE SEXUAL AROUSAL DISORDER (302.72)

Behavioral Symptoms
(severity index: 1, mild; 2, moderate; 3, intense)

Specify: lifelong, acquired, generalized, or situational.

Consider other factors that affect sexual functioning such as age and life context; rule out substance-induced disorder, general medical condition, and other Axis I disorders except another sexual dysfunction.

Severity

1. Recurrent or persistent inability to maintain until completion of sexual activity an adequate lubrication-swelling response of sexual excitement _____

2. The disorder causes marked distress or
   interpersonal problems   _____

MALE ERECTILE DISORDER (302.72)

Behavioral Symptoms
(severity index: 1, mild; 2, moderate; 3, intense)

Specify: lifelong, acquired, generalized, or situational.

Consider other factors that affect sexual functioning such as age and
life context; rule out substance-induced disorder, general medical
condition, and other Axis I disorders except another sexual dysfunction.

Severity

1. Persistent or recurrent inability to attain or
   maintain an adequate erection until completion
   of sexual activity   _____
2. The disorder causes marked distress or
   interpersonal difficulty   _____

FEMALE ORGASMIC DISORDER (302.73)

Behavioral Symptoms
(severity index: 1, mild; 2, moderate; 3, intense)

Specify: lifelong, acquired, generalized, or situational.

Consider other factors that affect sexual functioning such as age and
life context; rule out substance-induced disorder, general medical
condition, and other Axis I disorders except another sexual dysfunction.

Severity

1. Persistent or recurrent delay in or absence of orgasm following a normal sexual excitement phase _____

2. The disorder causes marked distress or interpersonal difficulty _____

MALE ORGASMIC DISORDER (302.74)

Behavioral Symptoms
(severity index: 1, mild; 2, moderate; 3, intense)

Specify: lifelong, acquired, generalized, or situational.

Consider other factors that affect sexual functioning such as age and life context; rule out substance-induced disorder, general medical conditions, and other Axis I disorders.

Severity

1. Persistent or recurrent delay in or absence of organism following a normal excitement phase _____

2. The disorder causes marked distress or interpersonal difficulty _____

PREMATURE EJACULATION (302.75)

Behavioral Symptoms
(severity index: 1, mild; 2, moderate; 3, intense)

Specify: lifelong, acquired, generalized, or situational.

Consider other factors that affect sexual functioning such as age and life context; rule out substance-induced disorder, general medical condition, and other Axis I disorders.

Severity

1. Persistent or recurrent onset of orgasm and ejaculation with minimal sexual stimulation, shortly after penetration or before one wishes it _____

2. The disorder causes marked distress or interpersonal difficulties _____

DYSPAREUNIA (302.76)

Specify: lifelong, acquired, generalized, or situational.

Dyspareunia involves genital pain in males or females before, during, or after sexual intercourse. The symptoms may range from mild discomfort to sharp pain and may cause distress or interpersonal problems. The disorder is not caused by vaginismus or lack of lubrication.

Behavioral Symptoms
(severity index: 1, mild; 2, moderate; 3, intense)

Consider other factors that affect sexual functioning such as age and life context; rule out substance-induced disorder, general medical condition, and other Axis I disorders.

Severity

1. Genital pain before, during, or after sexual intercourse _____

2. Disorder causes marked distress or interpersonal problems _____

VAGINISMUS (306.51)

Persistent or recurrent involuntary contraction of the perineal muscles upon attempted vaginal penetration.

Specify: lifelong, acquired, generalized, or situational.

Behavioral Symptoms
(severity index: 1, mild; 2, moderate; 3, intense)

Consider other factors that affect sexual functioning such as age and life context; rule out substance-induced disorder, general medical condition, and other Axis I disorders.

<u>Severity</u>

1. Involuntary contraction of perineal muscles when vaginal penetration is attempted   _____
2. Anticipation of penetration causes muscle spasms   _____
3. Condition causes marked distress or interpersonal problems   _____

TREATMENT PLAN
SEXUAL DYSFUNCTION

Client: _____ Date: _____

I. OBJECTIVES OF TREATMENT
(select one or more)

Female:

1. Restore sexual desire.
2. Reverse failure in sexual arousal—swelling, lubrication.
3. Enhance ability to achieve orgasm.
4. Eliminate pain before, during, or after intercourse.
5. Diminish distress or interpersonal impairment.

Male:

1. Restore sexual desire.
2. Increase ability to achieve and maintain erection.
3. Control premature ejaculation.
4. Eliminate pain before, during, or after intercourse.
5. Diminish distress or interpersonal impairment.

II. SHORT-TERM GOALS AND INTERVENTIONS
(select goals and interventions appropriate for your client)

CLIENT'S SHORT-TERM BEHAVIORAL GOALS	THERAPIST'S INTERVENTIONS
Review treatment plan with therapist and agree on target problems.	Develop treatment plan and select target problems with client.
Review problem with therapist.	Explore nature of problem.

Cooperate with treatment. Feel you can be helped and are not alone.	Establish therapeutic or collaborative alliance to build trust and enhance treatment outcome.
Follow through with medical tests and comply with recommendations or medications to stabilize condition.	Refer client or partner for medical evaluation, including diabetes and cardiovascular tests.
Follow through with medical referral. Stabilize.	If couples therapy, repeat medical evaluation with partner.
Discuss anger, communications, and differences in problem-solving ability with therapist.	Explore issues of anger, ineffective problem solving, and communications between partners.
Undergo therapy to resolve contributing nonsexual problems.	Put sexual therapy on hold and treat interpersonal problems uncovered. See appropriate treatment plans.
Address sexual disorder with therapist.	Address sexual disorders if they persist.
Follow through with individual or conjoint sex therapy.	Determine whether problem is an independent sexual disorder in one partner or a couple's sex problem.
Cooperate with construction of genograms.	Complete genograms to identify family interactions for both partners if applicable (see Behavioral Techniques, Chapter 22).
Understand the etiology of the disorder.	Assess mixed biogenic-psychogenic etiology of disorder and factors that originally contributed to the pathology.

Work on sexual abuse issue.	Explore possibility that client was sexually abused earlier.
Understand origin of inhibitors, source of fears, guilt, anxieties.	Assess causes of inhibitors: fears, guilt, anxieties.
Learn more about sexual disorders and their origins.	Give homework assignment in *Enhancing Sexuality: A Problem-Solving Approach* client workbook (see Homework, Chapter 23).
Work with therapist in formulating viable treatment strategies and trouble-shooting problems.	Review workbook with client.
Partners work together on disorder rather than blame.	Initiate couples therapy.
Explore underlying problems that may cause dysfunction.	Explore underlying anxieties, depression, substance abuse, or posttraumatic stress disorder.
Work on interpersonal relationships to decrease their effect on sexual desire.	Investigate factors in interpersonal relationships that may impinge on sexual desire, e.g., anger, distrust, attraction, negative feelings, lack of communication skills.
Recognize effects of impotency to be better able to deal with the issue.	Explore effects of impotency on relationship.
Reframe irrational attitudes toward sexual issues and myths, and replace with evidence-based reality.	Investigate irrational attitudes toward sexual issues.
Diminish sexual inhibitions.	Assign pleasuring exercises to reduce inhibitions. Practice sensate focus.

Improve sexual communication and heighten desires.	Teach client that it is okay to ask for what you like and want during sexual activity.
Improve control over orgasms.	With premature ejaculation, teach client how to slow down sensations of approaching orgasm.
Revitalize couple's sexual life.	Help couples explore each other's sexual preferences.
Feel more secure while having sex.	Investigate ways to increase feelings of security and improve arousal and satisfaction.
Help formulate relapse prevention plan. Use new skills learned.	Discuss relapse prevention and formulate plan to reinforce successful therapy, use new skills.
Review termination plan.	Formulate termination plan. Discuss with client.
Resolve remaining termination issues.	Resolve dependency and separation anxiety.

18

Adult Gender Identity Disorder (302.85)

Specify: sexually attracted to males, females, both, or neither.

Note: Rule out physical intersex condition (androgen insensitivity syndrome or congenital adrenal hypophasia).

Gender identity disorder includes the strong and persistent insistence that the individual is or desires to be of the other sex. The cross-gender identification must go beyond the perceived cultural advantages of being the other sex, and must include persistent discomfort with one's sex or a sense of inappropriateness in the gender role of that sex. In adults, the disorder is marked by preoccupation with the desire to be a member of the other sex. The desire may focus on adopting the gender role of the other sex or obtaining the physical appearance of the other sex by hormonal and/or surgical intervention. Adults with this disorder are uncomfortable being regarded by others or functioning socially as a member of their designated sex. They may adopt the behaviorisms, dress, and manner of the opposite sex. The preoccupation with cross-gender desires may seriously interfere with normal everyday activities at home and work.

Behavioral Symptoms
(severity index: 1, mild; 2, moderate; 3, intense)

	Severity
1. Strong, persistent cross-gender identification	_____
2. Insistence that one is of the other sex	_____
3. Desire to live or be treated as the other sex	_____
4. Frequently passes as the other sex.	_____
5. Conviction that has feelings and reactions more typical of the other sex	_____
6. Persistent discomfort with designated sex	_____
7. Significant distress or interpersonal impairment	_____

GENDER IDENTITY NOS (302.6)

Gender identity not otherwise specified includes those sexual disorders that are neither a specific sexual dysfunction nor paraphilia as listed in Chapters 17 and 19.

Behavioral Symptoms
(severity index: 1, mild; 2, moderate; 3, intense)

	Severity
1. Strong feelings of inadequacy regarding sexual performance	_____
2. Strong feelings of inadequacy regarding traits related to self-imposed standards of gender	_____
3. Distress over a string of lovers experienced only as things to be used	_____
4. Persistent strong distress over sexual orientation	_____

TREATMENT PLAN
ADULT GENDER IDENTITY DISORDER

Client: _____ Date: _____

I. OBJECTIVES OF TREATMENT
    (*select one or more*)

1. Reduce/control cross-gender identification.
2. Confront insistence that client is of the other sex.
3. Explore and confront underlying desire to be treated as the other sex.
4. Identify and control need to pass as the other sex.
5. Confront conviction that feelings and reactions are typical of the other sex.
6. Increase comfort with assigned sex.
7. Increase self-esteem.
8. Reduce gender distress to acceptable level.
9. Eliminate social and economic impairments.

II. SHORT-TERM GOALS AND INTERVENTIONS
     (select goals and interventions appropriate for your client)

CLIENT'S SHORT-TERM BEHAVIORAL GOALS	THERAPIST'S INTERVENTIONS
Review problem in a nonpunitive environment.	Explore nature of the problem in a non-punitive manner.
Assist in formulation of treatment plan and agree on target problems to be addressed.	Formulate treatment plan and agree on target problems.
Enter into collaborative relationship with therapist aimed at successful treatment. Feel less isolated.	Establish collaborative relationship or therapeutic alliance to build trust and enhance treatment outcome.

Follow through with medical and psychiatric evaluations. Comply with medication regimen if prescribed.	Refer client for medical and psychiatric evaluations and medication if indicated.
Be referred for psychological testing.	Refer client for psychological testing to further qualify gender identity disorder.
Confirm or deny transvestic fetishism.	Determine possible existence of transvestic fetishism.
Be evaluated for substance abuse and treated if required.	Evaluate for substance abuse and treat if positive. See appropriate treatment plan.
Be evaluated for suicide potential and hospitalized if necessary. If you have ideations but no active plan, agree to inform therapist of active plans and intentions before acting.	Evaluate for suicide. If actively suicidal, hospitalize immediately. If client has suicidal ideations, but no active plan, enter into suicide pact to inform you of plans and intentions.
Assist in construction of genogram.	Build genogram to display and understand family relationships (see Behavioral Techniques, Chapter 22).
Improve family interaction.	Refer for or conduct family sessions to improve family interaction with client.
Cooperate with family sculpturing procedure.	Conduct family sculpturing to determine client's relationships with family members and the patterns of interaction (see Chapter 22).
Understand the origins of the disorder in early family life.	Explore with client the early family origins of the disorder.

Reduce cross-dressing behavior.	Investigate with client the need for cross-dressing. Reduce and eliminate bizarre behavior.
Realize your sexual attributes and start to build self-esteem.	Determine and review with client his/her existing positive sexual characteristics.
Recognize your distorted cognitions regarding gender and reframe them with realistic thinking.	Explore client's distorted attitude toward gender and evaluate against evidence-based reality.
Recognize secondary gains of being of the other sex.	Investigate secondary gains associated with being of the other sex.
Weigh benefits of given gender against secondary gains.	Point out benefits of accepting given gender orientation.
Understand that sensitivity of feelings and reactions are not limited to one gender.	Help client understand that sensitive feelings and reactions are common to both men and women.
Lessen social and occupational distress.	Urge acceptance of given gender to eliminate social isolation and occupational distress.
Role-play given gender role and become more comfortable at it.	Conduct role-playing exercises in which client learns to function effectively in his/her given gender role.
Test your newfound confidence with friends and relatives outside of therapy.	Urge client to test his/her newfound role confidence in public interactions.
Record reactions and discuss them with therapist.	Instruct client to maintain a thought and behavior log to record reactions.
Reinforce successes.	Reinforce success with self-rewards.

Resolve termination issues.	Investigate underlying anxiety and depression associated with inevitable termination.
Discuss and implement termination plan.	Discuss and implement termination plan.

19

Paraphilias

Paraphilias include recurrent intense sexual fastasies, urges, or behaviors over a six-month period involving inanimate objects, the humiliation or suffering of self or partner, or children or other nonconsenting persons. For some, paraphiliac stimuli are essential for erotic arousal and are always included in sexual activity. In other cases, the need for such stimuli may arise only under specific conditions. In all cases, the condition causes marked distress or impairment in interpersonal functioning.

Paraphilia may be acted out with a nonconsenting partner (sexual sadism, pedophilia) and may be injurious to the partner. The offender may be subject to arrest, prosecution, and incarceration. Individuals with pedophilia, exhibitionism, and voyeurism constitute the majority of apprehended sexual offenders. In some cases, the paraphilia may result in self-injury (sexual masochism).

Persons with paraphilia disorders rarely, if ever, seek therapy voluntarily and are usually referred by the justice system. Individuals may have more than one paraphilia.

Included in this category are exhibitionism (exposure of the genitals), fetishism (use of inanimate objects), frotteurism (touching and rubbing against a nonconsenting person), pedophilia (centered on prepubescent children), sexual masochism (self-humiliation or suffering), sexual sadism (humiliation or suffering inflicted on another), transvestic fetishism (cross-dressing), and voyeurism (observing sexual activity).

EXHIBITIONISM (302.4)

Behavioral Symptoms
(severity index: 1, mild; 2, moderate; 3, intense)

	Severity
1. Recurrent fantasies, urges, or behavior over a six-month period involving the exposure of one's genitals to a nonsuspecting stranger	_____
2. The disorder causes significant distress or interpersonal impairment	_____

FETISHISM (302.81)

Behavioral Symptoms
(severity index: 1, mild; 2, moderate; 3, intense)

Note: The fetish objects are not limited to female clothing used in cross-dressing or devices designed specifically for genital stimulation.

	Severity
1. Recurrent fantasies, urges, or behaviors over a six-month period involving nonliving objects	_____
2. The disorder causes significant distress or interpersonal impairment	_____

FROTTEURISM (302.89)

Behavioral Symptoms
(severity index: 1, mild; 2, moderate; 3, intense)

<u>Severity</u>

1. Recurrent fantasies, urges, or behaviors over a
   six-month period involving the touching and
   rubbing against a nonconsenting person   _____
2. The disorder causes significant distress or
   impairment in interpersonal functioning   _____

PEDOPHILIA (302.2)

Behavioral Symptoms
(severity index: 1, mild; 2, moderate; 3, intense)

Note: The individual must be at least 16 years old and at least five years older than the other child. Do not include a late adolescent involved in an ongoing sexual relationship with a 12- or 13-year-old.

Specify:

 Sexually attracted to males
 Sexually attracted to females
 Sexually attracted to both sexes
 Limited to incest
 Exclusive (children only)
 Nonexclusive

<u>Severity</u>

1. Recurrent fantasies, urges, or behavior over a
   six-month period involving sexual activity with a
   child or children age 13 or younger   _____

2. Marked distress or impairment in interpersonal functioning   _____

SEXUAL MASOCHISM (302.83)

Sexual masochism includes sexual fantasies, urges, or behavior involving being humiliated, beaten, bound, or otherwise made to suffer. Some people experience masochistic fantasies during intercourse or masturbation, while others may act out their sexual urges on themselves or with a partner. A particularly dangerous form of sexual masochism is hypoxyphilia, or sexual arousal by oxygen deprivation alone or with a partner usually by means of a noose, mask, plastic bag, or inhalation of certain chemicals (nitrites). Such activities may result in accidental death.

Behavioral Symptoms
(severity index: 1, mild; 2, moderate; 3, intense)

Severity

1. Recurrent sexual fantasies, urges, or behavior involving being humiliated or made to suffer   _____
2. Significant distress or interpersonal impairment   _____

SEXUAL SADISM (302.3)

Sexual sadism involves acts in which an individual is sexually excited by the physical or psychological suffering or humiliation of another. In some cases, the fantasies are invoked during sexual intercourse. Sexual urges may be acted out with a partner or with a nonconsenting victim. It is the suffering of the victim that is sexually arousing. Typically, the sadistic acts increase in severity over time ending in injury or death of the victim.

Behavioral Symptoms
(severity index: 1, mild; 2, moderate; 3, intense)

Severity

1. Recurrent sexual fantasies, urges, or behaviors
   over a six-month period involving the physical or
   psychological suffering of a victim   _____
2. Significant distress or interpersonal impairment   _____

TRANSVESTIC FETISHISM (302.3)

Specify if with gender dysphoria.

This disorder involves cross-dressing. The male transvestite usually maintains a wardrobe of women's clothing to accommodate the urge to cross-dress and masturbate while imagining himself as both the subject and the object of the sexual fantasy. The disorder is usually found only in heterosexual males, and is not diagnosed when occurring exclusively with gender identity disorder. The symptoms may range from the occasional wearing of a female garment under masculine clothes to the complete dressing up as a female, including makeup.

Behavioral Symptoms
(severity index: 1, mild; 2, moderate; 3, intense)

Severity

1. Recurrent sexual fantasies, urges, or behaviors by
   a heterosexual male over a six-month period
   involving cross-dressing   _____
2. Significant distress or impairment in interpersonal
   functioning   _____

VOYEURISM (302.82)

This paraphilia involves the act of observing unsuspecting individuals while naked, in the act of disrobing, or engaging in a sexual act. Masturbation either accompanies the act of observation or may occur later in response to the memory of the witnessed scene. The individual may or may not have the fantasy of sexual contact with the person observed.

Behavioral Symptoms
(severity index: 1, mild; 2, moderate; 3, intense)

Severity

1. Recurrent sexual fantasies, urges, or behaviors over a six-month period involving the observation of an unsuspecting person who is naked, in the act of disrobing, or engaged in sexual activity   _____

2. Significant distress or interpersonal impairment   _____

PARAPHILIA NOS (302.82)

Paraphilias not otherwise specified is a category of those sexual disorders that do not meet the specifications for the other listed disorders. These include telephone scatologia (obscene phone calls), necrophilia (corpses), partialism (specific body parts), zoophilia (animals), coprophilia (feces), klismaphilia (enemas), and urophilia (urine).

Behavioral Symptoms
(severity index: 1, mild; 2, moderate; 3, intense)

Recurrent fantasies, urges, or behaviors over a six-month period, involving:

	Severity
1. Exposure of genitals to nonsuspecting strangers	_____
2. Touching or rubbing against a non-consenting person	_____
3. Sexual activity with a non-living object	_____
4. Sexual activity with a child/children under 13 years of age	_____
5. Sexual excitement over being humiliated or made to suffer	_____
6. Sexual excitement over the physical or psychological suffering of a victim	_____
7. Cross-dressing	_____
8. Observing unsuspecting persons naked, while disrobing, or during sexual activity	_____
9. Strong cross-gender identification	_____
10. Desire to live or be treated as the other sex	_____
11. Feelings/reactions more typical of the other sex	_____
12. Significant distress or interpersonal impairment	_____

TREATMENT PLAN
PARAPHILIAS

Client: _____ Date: _____

I. OBJECTIVES OF TREATMENT
(select one or more)

1. Diminish aberrant behaviors.
2. Eliminate need to act out.
3. Reduce pathological sexual fantasies.
4. Increase normal interactions with others.
5. Reduce underlying anxieties and depression.
6. Restore client to optimal levels of functioning.
7. Separate client from harmful sexual behaviors.
8. Prevent relapse.

II. SHORT-TERM GOALS AND INTERVENTIONS
(select goals and interventions appropriate for your client)

CLIENT'S SHORT-TERM BEHAVIORAL GOALS	THERAPIST'S INTERVENTIONS
Review problem in a nonpunative environment.	Explore nature of the problem in a nonpunative manner.
Assist in formulation of treatment plan and agree on target problems to be addressed.	Formulate treatment plan and agree on target problems.
Enter into collaborative relationship with therapist aimed at successful treatment. Feel less isolated.	Establish collaborative relationship or therapeutic alliance to build trust and enhance treatment outcome.
Follow through with medical and psychiatric evaluations. Comply with medication regimen if prescribed.	Refer client for medical and psychiatric evaluations and medication if indicated.

Recognize etiology of the disorder.	Assess mixed biogenic and psychogenic etiology and identify factors that originally established the pathology or contributed to it.
Understand that hospitalization is temporary but necessary, and be less afraid.	Refer to temporary hospital in-patient program to monitor behaviors and protect from abundance of sexual images.
Understand requirement for therapist to report certain incidents.	Discuss your obligation to report deviant behavior if and when mandated by law.
Start and maintain a daily behavior log to track triggers of recurrent sexual behavior.	Urge client to maintain a daily behavior log to monitor his/her behavior and effectiveness of treatment.
Confront issue of previous sexual abuse.	Evaluate client for previous sexual abuse.
Cooperate in construction and evaluation of genogram.	Construct genogram and evaluate client's sexual history. Explore for sexual abuse (see Chapter 22).
Recognize underlying shame, guilt, or depression.	Explore underlying shame, guilt, and depression that may trigger negative behavior.
Resolve underlying problem(s).	Explore for underlying anxiety, depression, or other disorders and treat. See appropriate treatment plan.
Undergo treatment for substance abuse.	Evaluate client for substance abuse, and treat if necessary (see Chapter 20).
Attend 90-day program to help deal with behaviors.	Refer to appropriate twelve-step program.

Become more aware of the addictive nature of the disorder.	Assign homework quiz: "Am I Addicted to Sex?" (see Homework Assignments, Chapter 23).
Recognize cues that stimulate addictive sexual behaviors.	Discuss 90-day self-imposed abstinence to reveal and understand emotional cues.
Take responsibility for behavior.	Gently confront client denial.
Increase self-awareness.	Coach client in improving the ability to observe self.
Recognize the negative consequences of your behavior.	Have client list negative consequences of deviant sexual behavior.
Feel better in improved family environment. No longer avoid healthy relationships.	Initiate family treatment. Increase understanding, reduce anger and shame. Break through the denial. Develop a therapeutic alliance with family.
Increase awareness of health and legal risks of certain sexual behaviors.	Make client fully aware of the health and legal risks associated with certain sexual addictions.
Attend group with other sex offenders and feel less isolated.	If appropriate, assign client to attend sex offenders group.
Learn new technique for dealing with deviant sexual urges.	Teach client self-hypnosis to deal effectively with triggers of deviant sexual urges.
Return to work force with an improved prognosis for a new or revitalized career.	Explore client work history and refer for retraining in area approved by client.
Discuss termination with therapist and resolve existing separation and dependency issues.	Review termination plan and resolve termination issues.

20

Substance-Use Disorders

Substance-use disorders include those related to the use of a drug of abuse, the side effects of a prescribed or over-the-counter medication, and toxin exposure. They are divided into two general groups: substance-use disorders (dependence and abuse) and substance-induced disorders (intoxication and withdrawal).

This book discusses only substance-use disorders since substance intoxification and substance withdrawal are typically treated by immediate hospitalization to ensure the safety of the client. Many hospitals are equipped with treatment programs ranging from inpatient detoxification to outpatient treatment programs and support groups focused on abstinence. There are four levels of treatment: (1) outpatient, (2) intensive outpatient with partial hospitalization and structured programs, (3) around-the-clock inpatient care, and (4) acute inpatient care with 24-hour monitoring.

SUBSTANCE DEPENDENCE

Substance dependence disorders are coded by substance:

Alcohol dependence (303.90)
Amphetamine dependence (304.40)
Cannabis dependence (304.30)
Cocaine dependence (304.20)
Hallucinogen dependence (304.50)
Inhalant dependence (304.60)
Nicotine dependence (305.10)
Opioid dependence (304.00)
Phencyclidine dependence (304.60)
Sedative, hypnotic, or anxiolytic dependence (304.10)
Polysubstance dependence (304.80)

A diagnosis of substance dependence can be applied to every class of substance except caffeine. The symptoms of dependence are generally similar across the classes, although in some instances the symptoms are less salient and, in a few instances, not all symptoms apply. Substance dependence is characterized by a cluster of physical, mental, and behavioral symptoms indicating that the individual continues use of the substance despite significant substance-related problems with three or more of the symptoms occurring at any time in a twelve-month period. Impairment is clinically significant.

Behavioral Symptoms
(severity index: 1, mild; 2, moderate; 3, intensive)

Specify:

With physiological dependence
Without physiological dependence
Early full remission
Early partial remission
Sustained full remission

On agonist therapy
In controlled environment

Three or more of the following at any time in a twelve-month period:

	Severity
1. Need for increased amounts of the substance to reach desired effect	_____
2. Diminished effect with continued use of same amount of substance	_____
3. Characteristic withdrawal syndrome	_____
4. Same or related substance taken to avoid withdrawal symptoms	_____
5. Substance taken in larger amounts or over a longer period of time	_____
6. Persistent desire or unsuccessful effort to reduce or control use of substance	_____
7. Inordinate amount of time spent to obtain, use, or recover from substance	_____
8. Important social, occupational, or recreational activities are abandoned or reduced	_____
9. Substance use continues despite knowledge of a persistent related physical or psychological problem	_____

SUBSTANCE ABUSE

Substance abuse disorders are coded by substance:

Alcohol abuse (305.00)
Amphetamine abuse (305.20)
Cannabis abuse (305.20)
Cocaine abuse (305.60)
Hallucinogen abuse (305.30)
Inhalant abuse (305.90)
Opioid abuse (305.50)

Phencyclidine abuse (305.90)
Sedative hypnotic or anxiolytic abuse (305.40)

In contrast to substance dependence, a diagnosis of substance abuse covers a maladaptive pattern of substance use resulting in clinically significant impairment as manifested by only one symptom over a twelve-month period. Substance abuse does not apply to caffeine or nicotine.

Behavioral Symptoms
(severity index: 1, mild; 2, moderate; 3, intensive)

One or more of the following over a twelve-month period:

	Severity
1. Repeated substance use leading to failure to fulfill major work, home, or school obligations	_____
2. Repeated substance use in physically dangerous situations	_____
3. Recurrent substance-related legal problems	_____
4. Continued substance use despite resulting social or interpersonal problems	_____

TREATMENT PLAN
SUBSTANCE-USE DISORDERS—(_____)
Substance

Client: _____ Date: _____

I. OBJECTIVES OF TREATMENT—Dependence or Abuse
   (*select one or more*)

    1. Confront denial of substance abuse.
    2. Recognize and accept abuse as a disease.
    3. Refer to AA, NA, or rational recovery group.
    4. Sustain sobriety.
    5. Increase quality of life.
    6. Understand self-sabotaging behavior.
    7. Reduce/eliminate shame/guilt.
    8. Identify people, places, and things that trigger abuse.
    9. Prevent relapse.

II. SHORT-TERM TREATMENT GOALS AND
    INTERVENTIONS
    (*select goals and interventions appropriate for your client*)

CLIENT'S SHORT-TERM BEHAVIORAL GOALS	THERAPIST'S INTERVENTIONS
Discuss treatment plan with therapist and agree on target problems.	Discuss treatment plan and agree on target problems.
Join in treatment. Treatment outlook is improved as feelings of anger and isolation are diminished.	Cultivate therapeutic alliance or collaborative relationship with client to instill trust and enhance outcome of treatment.
Understand and accept possible need for hospitalization. Resolve fear of hospitalization.	Explain possible need for hospitalization.

Confirm or deny substance abuse.	Refer for or administer the Substance Abuse Subtle Screening Inventory (SASSI) to accurately identify chemical dependency.
As appropriate, be hospitalized or enter into suicide pact agreeing to inform therapist of ideations and plans, and to provide prior notification before any action.	Assess possible homicidal or suicidal effects of substance dependence. If homicidal, notify authorities. If actively suicidal, hospitalize immediately. If client has suicidal ideations, but no plan, enter into suicide pact.
Follow through with psychiatric evaluation and accepts hospitalization and detoxification if necessary.	Refer client for psychiatric evaluation and/or hospitalization if required.
Follow up on medical referral. Understand existing and potential physical problems related to substance.	Refer client for medical evaluation to identify physical problems caused by or exacerbated by substance use.
Help construct genogram. Describe family interactions.	Create genogram to better understand interactions of family members (see Behavioral Techniques, Chapter 22).
Identify potential genesis of substance abuse in family of origin.	Investigate chronological history of client and family substance use.
Confront denial and understand contributing factors.	Explore level of distressed thinking or denial, and assess client's level of cognitive and intellectual functioning that contributes to substance use.

Be freed to work on the problems rather than deny you have problems.	Help client overcome denial by looking at the facts of substance use and the problems they have caused.
Maintain a strict meds schedule.	Discuss importance of medication regimen.
Work on underlying issues that contribute to substance dependence.	Evaluate client for possible dual diagnosis and treat other symptoms, e.g., anxiety, depression, social phobia, etc. See appropriate treatment plan.
Comply with referral.	Refer for acupuncture if appropriate.
Understand patterns of stress that lead to substance use.	Explore past patterns of substance use in relation to life stressors.
Attend NA or AA and obtain a sponsor, or attend rational recovery group.	Refer client to twelve-step program (NA or AA) or to rational recovery group if NA/AA is rejected.
Understand process you must undergo to get clean.	Explain mourning process and help client mourn substance of choice.
Recognize and avoid potential triggers for relapse.	Identify person, place, and thing triggers that may cause backsliding or relapse.
Maintain a daily journal to monitor feelings rather than act them out.	Assign client to maintain a daily journal of his/her feelings and reactions.
Learn new techniques for dealing with destructive urges.	Teach client relaxation techniques, hypnosis, or creative visualization to cope with feelings. Provide audiotape for home use.

Recognize family triggers and avoid enablers.	Investigate family conflicts and identify enablers that aid in client's substance use.
Replace ritualistic behavior with more rational response.	Investigate ritualistic behaviors related to substance use and teach client more rational behaviors.
Realize destructive effects of substance on your quality of life.	Explore and identify the effects of substance use on the client's social, family, occupational, and other relations.
Improve family relations.	Conduct family sessions or refer to family therapist.
Family discovers better ways of dealing with client.	Refer family to Alanon for support.
Become more knowledgeable about the disorder.	Assign books on substance disorders as homework (see Chapter 24).
Develop understanding that disorder is not your fault, but must be constantly worked on to control.	Review issues of shame and guilt that may cause or contribute to substance use and dependence.
Make commitment to someone else for sobriety.	Obtain a contract or commitment for abstinence.
Develop alternate behaviors to substance use.	Discuss alternate behaviors to substance use, e.g., exercise, sports, hobbies, etc.
Diminish anger and aggression toward self and others.	Guide client in releasing anger and aggression toward self and others.
Make use of support systems when you feel substance use triggers are being activated.	Help client create support systems and resources in environment to maintain sobriety.

Gain confidence in role-playing sessions.	Conduct role-playing exercises to help client deal with persons, places, and things that trigger substance use.
Apply role-playing experience in external environment.	Guide client in practicing his new skills in the real world.
Reinforce success and improve skills as needed.	Retrain as necessary and reinforce successes.
Become aware of your negative or ambivalent feelings toward others.	If appropriate, identify client's lack of empathy for others.
Be armed with alternate behaviors to prevent relapse.	Teach client alternative constructive behaviors to prevent relapse.
Discuss and resolve termination issues with therapist. Discuss termination plan.	Discuss and resolve issues of separation anxiety and dependence with client. Develop termination plan.
Attend support group.	Refer client to active support group.

21

Sleep Disorders

There are two types of sleep disorder: dyssomnias and parasomnias. Dyssomnias include disturbance in the amount of sleep, falling asleep, and staying asleep. In primary insomnia, the problem is maintaining sleep, compared with hypersomnia, which is marked by excessive sleepiness. Narcolepsy includes the presence of cataplexy or daily uncomfortable attacks of sleep. Breathing-related disorders feature excessive sleep or insomnia apnea or circadian rhythm sleep disorder, caused by an environmentally imposed sleep–wake schedule.

Parasomnias include nightmares, sleep terror, and sleepwalking, in which abnormal events occur during sleep. These may be characterized by repeated awakenings, frightening dreams, abrupt awakenings, or sleepwalking. Sleepwalking usually occurs during the first third of major sleep episodes. Parasomnias cause inappropriate activation of cognitive processes in the nervous and motor systems.

All dyssomnias and parasomnias can cause significant distress or impairment in occupational and other major areas of functioning. Sleep disorders can be related to other Axis I and Axis II mental disorders.

There is a surprising one-year prevalence of insomnia of about 30 to 40 percent of the adult population. Sleep clinics report 15 to 25 percent of clients with chronic insomnia, with the prevalence increasing in the elderly and in women. Characteristically, young adults have trouble falling asleep, while the elderly have difficulty staying asleep. Although formal studies are lacking, there appears to be a familial disposition associated with sleep problems.

There are five distinct stages of sleep that can be measured by polysomnography (electrooculography and electromyography). These stages include REM (rapid eye movement) sleep, and four stages of non-REM sleep. Non-REM stage 1 sleep is the transition from wakefulness to sleep. Stage 2 is characterized by distinct waveforms. Stages 3 and 4, or slow-wave sleep, represent the deepest sleep level. REM sleep is the dream stage.

Age should be considered in all cases of sleep disorder. Sleep continuity and depth deteriorate with age. Wakefulness and stage 1 sleep increase, while stages 3 and 4 sleep decrease. Stage 1 sleep normally occupies about 5 percent of the total sleep period, while stages 3 and 4 occupy 10 to 20 percent of the total.

Systematic assessment of sleep disorders includes evaluation for other comorbid mental disorders, general medical conditions, and substance use, including medications.

DYSSOMNIA

Primary insomnia (307.42)
Primary hyposomnia (307.44)
Narcolepsy (347)
Breathing-related sleep disorder (780.59)
Circadian rhythm sleep disorder (307.45)

Behavioral Symptoms
(severity index: 1, mild; 2, moderate; 3, intense)

	Severity
1. Difficulty falling asleep	_____
2. Difficulty staying asleep	_____
3. Narcolepsy–irresistibile attacks of refreshing sleep	_____
4. Daytime fatigue	_____
5. Excessive sleepiness	_____
6. Uncontrollable attacks of sleep	_____
7. Cataplexy–sudden loss of muscle tone	_____
8. Intrusions in REM sleep	_____
9. Apnea—breathing-related sleep problems	_____
10. Mismatch in sleep and work or personal environment schedule	_____
11. Restless leg syndrome	_____

PARASOMNIA

Nightmare disorder (307.47)
Sleep terror disorder (307.46)
Sleep-walking disorder (307.46)
Parasomnia NOS (307.47)
Insomnia related to an Axis I or Axis II disorder (307.42)
Hypersomnia related to an Axis I or Axis II disorder (307.44)
Sleep disorder due to a general medical condition (780.xx)

Behavioral Symptoms
(severity index: 1, mild; 2, moderate; 3, intense)

	Severity
1. Nightmares	_____
2. Recurrent, abrupt awakenings due to night terrors	_____
3. Signs of autonomic arousal	_____
4. Terror about unrecalled dream	_____
5. Sleepwalking	_____

6. Sleepwalking with blank staring face, can be awakened only with great difficulty   _____
7. Amnesia of sleepwalking event   _____

Other Diagnostic Considerations

Adjustment disorder with anxiety (309.24)
Adjustment disorder with depressed mood (309.0)
Adjustment disorder mixed (309.28)
Major depressive disorder (296.31)
Generalized anxiety disorder (300.02)
Substance abuse (296.xx)
Dysthymic disorder (300.4)
Posttraumatic stress disorder (309.81)
Eating disorders (307.xx)
Personality disorders (301.xx)
Bipolar disorders (296.xx)
Schizophrenia (295.xx)

TREATMENT PLAN
SLEEP DISORDER

Client: _____ Date: _____

I. OBJECTIVES OF TREATMENT
(*select one or more*)

1. Identify and treat associated medical problems.
2. Identify and treat associated psychological problems.
3. Reduce nightmares and/or sleep terrors.
4. Terminate sleepwalking episodes.
5. Restore healthy sleep patterns.
6. Develop regular sleep routine.
7. Restore client to optimal level of functioning.
8. Prevent relapse.

Note: Rule out other mental disorders, general medical conditions, and drug abuse.

II. SHORT-TERM BEHAVIORAL GOALS AND INTERVENTIONS
(*select goals and interventions appropriate for your client*)

CLIENT'S SHORT-TERM BEHAVIORAL GOALS	THERAPIST'S INTERVENTIONS
Discuss treatment plan with therapist and agree on target sleep problems.	Develop treatment plan and agree with client on target sleep problems to address.
Improve treatment outlook; diminish feelings of isolation and fears.	Cultivate therapeutic alliance or collaborative working relationship with client to build trust and enhance treatment outcome.

Follow up with medical and psychiatric evaluations.	Refer client for medical and psychiatric evaluations.
Discuss evaluations with therapist. Follow through with recommended medical treatment or review revised diagnosis.	Discuss evaluations with client. If necessary, refer client for stabilization of medical disorder, revise diagnosis.
Discuss new treatment plan and agree on target problems to be addressed.	Revise treatment plan and target problems if necessary. See appropriate treatment plan.
Reconfirm original treatment plan.	Absent a general medical condition, another mental disorder, or substance abuse, reconfirm original treatment plan.
Understand need for evaluation.	Explain need for evaluation by sleep clinic and possible hospitalization to pinpoint sleep problem.
Report to sleep clinic for testing.	Refer client to sleep clinic for evaluation of sleep problems, i.e., polysomnography.
Discuss evaluation results with therapist.	Discuss with client the findings and recommendations of the clinic.
Identify pattern of sleep problems in family.	Construct genogram to explore familial history of sleep problems (see Behavioral Techniques, Chapter 22).
Understand and confront contributing factors.	Identify stressors that interfere with sleep.
Recognize normal sleep routine.	Discuss normal sleep patterns and amount of sleep time normally required.

Practice diaphragmatic breathing to relax and assist sleep.	Teach client diaphragmatic breathing for relaxation prior to sleep (see Chapter 22).
Develop more rational thoughts about sleep.	Explore cognitive distortions client may have about sleep.
Understand the importance of REM sleep.	Educate the client as to the role of REM sleep in healing the body physically and psychologically.
Learn about effects of stimulants on sleep patterns.	Advise client about use of caffeine-containing stimulants (coffee, coke, tea) on sleep and how they interfere with sleep.
Learn relaxation techniques. Use audiotape at home.	Teach client relaxation techniques. Provide relaxation audiotape for home use.
Use bed for sleep and sex only.	Educate client about using bed only for sleep and sex, not watching television, work, or other activities.
If necessary, undergo treatment for sexual abuse.	Investigate for possible sexual abuse and treat if necessary. See appropriate treatment plan.
Reduce anxiety toward nightmares or night terrors.	Explore night terrors or nightmares and their origins.
Relate and help interpret dreams.	Analyze dreams to reduce impact of nightmares on sleep.
Family understands problem and cooperates in support of the client.	Conduct family sessions and act as consultant to educate family on how to deal with sleepwalking problem.
Client or family takes necessary corrective actions to reduce dangerous situations.	Explore sleepwalking episodes and assess accompanying dangerous activities.

Reduce death anxiety.	Investigate death issues and associated anxiety.
Review termination plan. Resolve remaining separation anxiety and dependency issues.	Develop termination plan. Discuss and resolve issues of termination and separation anxiety.

PART III

TREATMENT AIDS

22

Behavioral Techniques

DIAPHRAGMATIC BREATHING
AND RELAXATION EXERCISE*

Commonly known as stomach or body breathing, diaphragmatic breathing can be used as an effective coping skill for anxiety. This exercise should be practiced at least once a day because the first step in developing a coping skill is getting your body acquainted with and used to it. After you feel comfortable with this exercise, your therapist can show you how a briefer version can be used to cope during public encounters.

Let's take a moment to think about breathing. Our lungs sit in our chest in a space that is surrounded on the top and sides by our rib cage and on the bottom by our diaphragm. The diaphragm is a sheet of

Adapted from *Specific Phobias: Clinical Applications of Evidence-Based Psychotherapy* by T. J. Bruce and W. C. Sanderson. Copyright © 1998 by Jason Aronson Inc., and used with permission.

muscle that bows upward like a dome beneath our lungs and separates the lung space from the abdominal cavity. As we breathe in, we must increase this lung space. Yet when we are anxious, the muscles of our shoulders and chest tighten and can make us feel that our breathing is labored, which in turn increases our feelings of anxiety. While there are several ways of increasing our lung space, diaphragmatic or stomach breathing requires the least effort and therefore can serve as the most effective coping skill for managing anxious situations.

While some people achieve diaphragmatic breathing naturally and with ease, others may need to practice for a while before they feel comfortable with the exercise. To see what it feels like to breathe diaphragmatically, lie on your stomach on a bed or on the floor and cross your arms beneath your head. You might even imagine that you are lying on the beach sunning your back as you look at the waves swell and crash at the shore. Now relax your stomach muscles and breathe normally, inhaling through your nose. In this position, you are most likely to breathe diaphragmatically. If you feel pressure from the floor or bed on your stomach as you inhale, you are breathing diaphragmatically. Try this for a few moments until you feel comfortable doing it without having to think about what you are doing so intensely. Now practice it as follows: sit in a comfortable chair with both feet on the floor. If you like, you can place one hand lightly on your chest and the other on your stomach just above your navel. Now breathe slowly through your nose, relaxing your stomach and using only your diaphragm. You might even feel as if you are inhaling with your stomach. Inhale as deeply as is comfortable and then exhale through pursed lips as if you were blowing through a straw. When you are breathing correctly, your stomach will rise as you breathe in, and slowly fall when you exhale. Now try to exhale for as long as it took you to inhale. This is called paced breathing.

When you feel comfortable with the paced diaphragmatic breathing, you can add one more component to this exercise. After you have taken a few breaths, mildly contract the muscles of your face and neck and then relax them again during the most convenient exhale. When you feel comfortable with this coordination component, try it with your neck and then back. This can be a great way to stretch and relax all of your major muscle groups! You may have to do some of the more tense muscle groups a few times before they fully unwind.

You should do this exercise at least once and preferably twice a day. Begin with five minutes of paced diaphragmatic breathing and then spend approximately 10 to 20 minutes combining it with the muscle stretching and relaxing followed by five more minutes of breathing. During those last five minutes allow your breathing to slow considerably and your muscles to feel heavy. Now indulge yourself in this quiet and calm place. You are finally fully relaxed!

A shorter version of this exercise can be used as a practical coping skill to manage anxiety before or during exposure. If you find yourself in such a situation, don't panic! You have all of the tools necessary to cope with your anxiety. Just take a deep diaphragmatic breath through your nose. Hold it for a second or so, then exhale slowly through pursed lips. Then pace your diaphragmatic breathing with the goal of slowing your rate of breathing. This may not seem so easy at first but just begin by extending your exhale and taking a deep breath when you can. You can even try holding your breath for a moment.

Eventually, you will be able to slow your breathing. As you are slowing your breathing rate, begin stretching and relaxing your major muscle groups. This will help you overcome the natural inclination to "freeze" when anxious, and to regroup and feel as if you can cope at your own pace. Remember that the goal is not to stop your feeling of anxiety, but rather to cope with the feelings that anxiety induces. Back at the beach, it would be like riding out an ocean wave, allowing it to pick you up and then set you back down. Your goal is not to stop it, but rather to flow with it and cope with it. You may also find it helpful to focus on your thoughts while you cope with your anxiety. Talk to your therapist about creating coping self-statements and other coping strategies that can be used with this exercise.

GENOGRAMS

A genogram (Figure 22–1) is a diagram that depicts the relationships between family members over three generations. The genogram uses symbols to illustrate the relationships with the units and major

Figure 22–1. Example of a genogram.

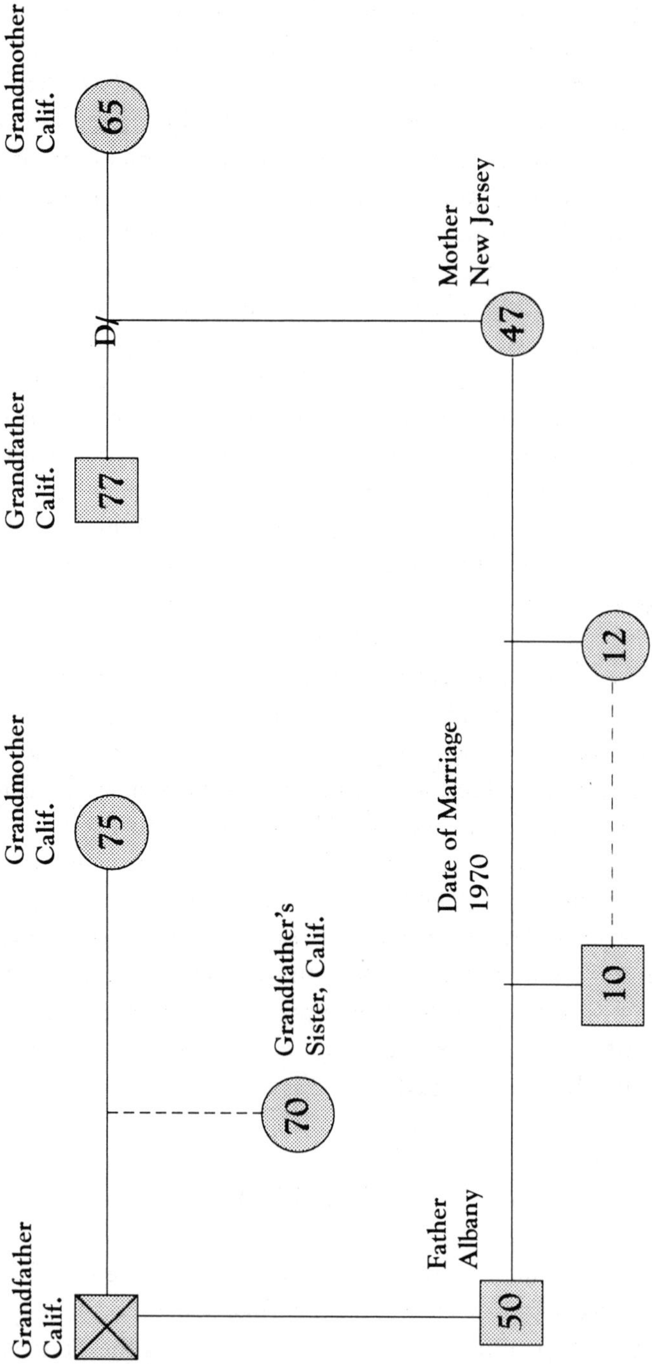

stressors in chronological order. The diagram is used to help understand the family dynamics over time. The symbols include:

□	Male
O	Female
– – –	Sibling
∅	Abortion/stillbirth
		Offspring
——	Marriage
D/	Divorce
X	Death

Construction of a genogram begins with the collection of facts about family members, their position in the family, and their relationships to other family members. Physical location is important for tracking distance and boundaries. Analysis of the genogram provides information about how conflicts are resolved as well as family secrets such as abortion. It is also helpful in identifying whether the family is cohesive or explosive. The genogram is used to spell out physical and emotional boundaries, characteristics of the membership, modal events, toxic issues, emotional cutoffs, a general openness/closedness index, and the available relationship options within the family.

The resulting diagram allows one to see at a glance the basic structural framework of the family including triangulation and repetitive family issues. Such information might otherwise require a lengthy document to record. General questions that should be explored include cultural, ethnic, and religious affiliations; socioeconomic level; and the way the family relates to the community socially and economically, and whether the family is cohesive or isolated.

Once the basic information is collected, including names, place of origin, ages, births, deaths, and divorces, the structure is expanded to include other significant data that indicate critical nodal points. As patterns of interaction emerge, other universal issues are exposed such as money, sex, power, control, parenting, children, and others. Does the family discuss problems or is there a conspiracy of silence? What events in the life cycle will shape the future? The genogram has proven to be an important tool for family therapists.

FAMILY SCULPTURING

Family sculpturing is a technique that emerged from attempts to translate family systems theory into physical form through spacial arrangements. It uses space as a metaphor for understanding human relationships quickly.

Sometimes called family choreography, sculpturing depicts emotional relationships that are always in motion. In a sense it choreographs important transactional patterns such as alliances, triangles, and shifting emotional currents. The technique can be used with any theoretical modality and modified to implement a variety of goals. The technique is also used to realign family relationships, create new patterns, and change the family system.

In practice, after defining or describing the family problem, each family member is asked to arrange family members as the individual experiences them or show a visual picture of the way he or she experiences the problem, to arrange the family members according to their emotional relationship with each member, and to identify their characteristic way of coping with this relationship. The technique can also be used to show how major stressors (death, illness) have altered the relationships over time. To help move the process along, the therapist might ask questions aimed at shedding light on the transactional patterns. Each members is asked to arrange the other family members as they would like to interact with them. In this way, family sculpturing or family choreography can be used to reveal human relationships within a social, psychological, and physical system and to realign those relationships when necessary. It is a silent motion picture of the family that removes the linguistic traps and cuts through the barrage of attack and counterattack that often characterizes family sessions.

23

Homework Assignments

Homework assignments grew out of managed care's strategy that patients take a more active role in their treatment to provide a quicker outcome. Homework is a technique that facilitates change outside of sessions and encourages clients to explore changes on their own.

The provider recertification form distributed by Merit Behavioral Care states, "Patients are expected to take an active part in their own therapy, often completing assignments between sessions."

To help providers deal more effectively with that request, this chapter offers some suggestions for homework as well as a list of available books that contain homework assignments.

ANGER MANAGEMENT*

Three Steps:

1. Time out. Remove yourself from situation temporarily. If cannot remove yourself, don't speak or act. You can feel the anger, but you can't act on it.

---

*Adapted from *Cognitive-Behavioral Treatment of Depression* by J. S. Klosko and W. C. Sanderson. Copyright © 1999 by Jason Aronson Inc., and used with permission.

2. Somatic and cognitive self-calming techniques: Somatic: self-calming exercises: meditation, breathing, imagery. Cognitive: think through the consequences of action. Insert thought between anger or impulse and action.
3. Apply principles of assertiveness:
   Equal respect for self and other person.
   Do what is best for the relationship.

Assertiveness is on the continuum between passivity and aggression: passivity—assertiveness—aggression. Both ends lead to depression. Passive fails to express preferences and needs, which fosters depression. Aggressive pushes others away and you end up disconnected and alone.

Maladaptive patterns: Seesaw from passive to aggressive, then in remorse go back to passive. Go passive-aggressive—say yes, but don't follow through.

Assertiveness principles:

1. Express your feelings.
2. Ask for what you need.
3. State your preferences.
4. Assert your rights.

Don'ts:

1. Don't yell.
2. Don't hit or physically dominate or intimidate the other.
3. Don't attack verbally or call names.
4. Don't say things to hurt.
5. Don't lose control of your anger.

Be assertive:

- Set a goal.
- Pick an appropriate setting—quiet, calm, private.
- Stay calm.
- Use assertive body language—eye to eye.

- Be brief and clear.
- Talk about your feelings, not about objective rightness. Don't preach.
- Don't get defensive.
- Request specific behavior changes.
- To say something negative, start and end with positives.
- If the other protests, just restate your position.

CHALLENGING COGNITIONS

This exercise involves identifying existing patterns of cognitive distortion and replacing them with rational thinking. Clients are given the Challenging Cognitions Worksheet (Table 23–1) and a list of Common Cognitive Distortions (Table 23–2). They are asked to identify their distortions and then to use the worksheet to get immediate feedback and discover their own ways to change their thinking based on evidence-based reality. They are then asked to bring the completed worksheet to the next session to discuss it with the therapist.

Table 23–1.
Challenging Cognitions Worksheet

Initial thought (belief rating 1–100):

Associated feelings:

Associated behavior (or behavioral urge):

Cognitive distortion:

Weigh the evidence:

Challenge (What are other possible ways of looking at this?):

From *Marital Distress* by J. H. Rathus and W. C. Sanderson. Copyright © 1999 by Jason Aronson Inc., and used with permission.

Table 23–2.
Common Cognitive Distortions

Can you identify those cognitive distortions that apply to you?

All-or-nothing thinking: Either your behavior is perfect or it is awful. Things are either black or white.

Emotional reasoning: You imagine that negative emotions are real: "John just doesn't like me."

Ignoring the positive: You disqualify positive experiences as if they don't count, yet hold on to negative beliefs: "I am just unlucky. The fact that my boss gave me a raise is a quirk."

Magical thinking: Thinking that if you do something or don't do something, it will cause some problem in someone else's life. "If I step on this crack in the sidewalk, so-and-so will get sick."

Maximization or catastrophizing: Making a mountain out of a molehill.

Minimization: Making a molehill out of a mountain.

Negative interpretation: You assume that someone is acting negatively toward you without checking it out.

Negative labeling: Attaching names to errors rather than describing the event: "I am stupid because I forgot to lock the door."

Overgeneralization: Taking one event and viewing it as a pattern that never ends.

Personalization: Giving yourself credit for being the cause of a negative or positive event for which you are not really responsible. "I didn't remind her, so she left the car unlocked."

Personification: A form of projection in which the desirable or undesirable properties of reality are attributed to some other person even if they are unrelated to what happened; for example, you send a letter to someone that is not delivered and accuse someone else of intercepting the letter.

Shoulds: Using the word *should* to motivate yourself and others. Using "should" directed at yourself creates guilt. When directed at others, it results in anger and frustration.

DEPRESSION

Clients are given a list of Suggested Pleasurable Activities (Table 23–3) and requested to engage in at least one activity for the week in order to expand the client's interests. Clients are also given a Pleasurable Activities Self-Monitoring Form (Table 23–4) to record their feelings before and after the event as well as their sense of self-mastery and pleasure.

The client may also be asked to keep a Thought Log (Table 23–5) of automatic thoughts during an upsetting event and a list of Common Cognitive Distortions of Depression (Table 23–6). The thought record is used to identify and rate the upsetting event, the associated emotions, and automatic thoughts, and then to replace them with rational responses (Table 23–7). Instructions are provided for identifying the distortions and building a rational response.

Homework may incorporate use of an integrated therapist–client package on *Overcoming Depression* by Gary Emery (2000), New Harbinger Press, Oakland, CA, which includes a therapist treatment protocol and client manual of exercises and worksheets.

Table 23–3.
Suggested Pleasurable Activities

Tend the garden.
Listen to music.
Read a book.
Go for a walk in a natural setting, such as the woods or a park.
Watch a movie.
Help someone.
Watch sports.
Exercise.
Play a board game.
Watch children play.
Play cards.
Ride a bicycle.
Go for a run.
Visit a friend.
Call someone on the phone.
Sing a song.
Play a musical instrument.
Play a computer game.
Surf the Internet.
Watch the sun rise or set.
Draw or paint outdoors.
Take photographs.
Write a letter to someone you love.
Get a massage.
Visit a new place.
Go to an amusement park.
Dance.
Go for a car ride.
Build a model.
Fix something that is broken.
Work on your car.
Attend a lecture.
Go to a museum.
Enroll in a class.
Learn a new craft.
Walk on the beach.
Solve a brainteaser.

Make a videotape.

Go to the library.

Go to a café.

Prepare a healthy meal.

Meditate.

Listen to a relaxation tape.

Go hiking.

Go fishing.

Go swimming.

Attend a political rally.

Pray.

Have a pleasant daydream.

Make love.

Take a bath.

Contemplate your career path.

Start a collection (of books, coins, dolls, etc.).

Go shopping for new clothes.

Go to a comedy club.

Go camping.

Arrange flowers.

Chop wood.

Go to a concert.

Redecorate a part of your home.

Follow the financial markets.

Educate yourself in some aspect of your profession.

Go to the racetrack.

Go to a casino.

Go to a nightclub.

Write a poem.

Play with an animal.

Go to a party.

Go scuba diving.

Do volunteer work.

Go bowling.

Go to the theater.

Get dressed up.

Play chess.

Go skating.

Table 23–3.
Suggested Pleasurable Activities (*continued*)

Go sailing.
Plan a trip.
Join a club.
Go sightseeing.
Go to the beauty parlor.
Join a discussion group.
Go out to a restaurant to eat.
Have a sexual fantasy.
Write in your journal.
Go on a picnic.
Do a crossword puzzle.
Read the Bible.
Go to a religious service.
Go horseback riding.
Put together a jigsaw puzzle.
Study your schoolwork.
Bird-watch.
Make a fire in the fireplace.
Repair something.
Participate in a discussion.
Read the newspaper.
Do an activity with children.
Play a game of pool.
Perform a community service.
Look at the night sky.
Go out for ice cream.
Have a glass of fine wine (if you do not have a drinking problem).
Figure out how something works.
Go skiing.
Go look at new cars.
Go to a country inn.
Go rock climbing.
Play golf.
Go boating.
Walk around the city.
Go to the zoo.
Go to the aquarium.

Go to a mall.
Invite a friend to visit.
Go to the mountains.
Tell a joke.
Do yardwork.
Play a word game.
Play frisbee.
Tell a story to a child.
Compliment someone.
Sew.
Attend an auction.
Give to charity.
Do woodworking.
Watch television.
Listen to talk radio.
Look at the stars through a telescope.
Have your fortune told.
Brush your hair.
Join a political group.
Go to a twelve-step meeting.
Go out on a date.
Practice yoga.
Go to a martial arts class.
Rake the leaves.
Go to a bookstore.
Go window shopping.
Finish some task you have been putting off.
Fly an airplane.
Observe animals in the wild.
Go to the ballet.
Fly a kite.
Have a conversation.
Learn a new song.
Build a bonfire at night.
Sit on the porch and watch the world.
Organize something (your closet, books, music, tools, etc.).
Send someone a fax or e-mail.
Go to sleep on clean sheets.

Table 23–3.
Suggested Pleasurable Activities (*continued*)

Manage your finances.
Invent a healthful drink.
Visit a planetarium.
Play tennis.
Play a lawn game (croquet, badminton).
Experience your five senses, one by one.
Dress up in a disguise.
Smile.
Light a candle and watch the flame.
Prepare a lovely table for a meal.
Look at beautiful pictures in a book.
Hug someone.
Make tea or hot chocolate.
Sit in the lobby of a beautiful, old hotel.
Listen to the rain.
Walk in the rain, stepping in puddles.
Skip.
Go on the swings.
Eat something sweet.
Take a sauna.
Buy or make someone a present.
Throw a party.
Prepare an elaborate holiday celebration.
Buy or make yourself a present.
Get a pet.
Go for a long walk with your dog.
Learn how to work an electronic device (cellular phone, VCR, computer, answering machine, etc.).
Install a new computer program.
Read interesting entries in the encyclopedia.
Refinish a piece of furniture.
Play baseball.
Have a barbecue.
Act.
Play football.
Put lotion on your body.
Take a shower.

Go to a video arcade.
Bake.
Play volleyball.
Get a good night's sleep.
Stay up all night watching movies.
Carry out an assertiveness exercise.
Go for a train ride along a scenic route.
Visit a relative.
Talk politics.
Conduct an experiment.
Play soccer.
Practice listening well to another person.
Make someone laugh.

From *Cognitive-Behavioral Treatment of Depression* by J. S. Klosko and W. C. Sanderson. Copyright © 1999 by Jason Aronson Inc., and used with permission.

Table 23–4.
Pleasurable Activities Self-Monitoring Form

Date:

Time:

Activity: _____

_____

_____

Intensity of emotion ratings

0------------25------------50------------75------------100
None   Mild   Moderate   Intense   Very Intense

	Before		After	
	Feeling	Rating	Feeling	Rating
Feelings	_____	_____	_____	_____
	_____	_____	_____	_____
	_____	_____	_____	_____
	_____	_____	_____	_____

Sense of mastery: _____

Sense of pleasure: _____

From *Cognitive-Behavioral Treatment of Depression* by J. S. Klosko and W. C. Sanderson. Copyright © 1999 by Jason Aronson Inc., and used with permission.

Table 23–5.
Automatic Thought Log

Fill out when you have a negative feeling or if a negative feeling becomes worse.

1. Feeling.
    How do you feel now? Check ✔ and rate how much on a scale of 0 (usual) to 100 (worst I can imagine).

    Anxious ( )
    Sad ( )
    Guilty ( )
    Angry ( )
    Other ( )   Specify which one _____

2. Situation
    What were you doing when you felt this way?

3. Automatic Thought
    What went through your mind that could have made you feel this way? List all thoughts here and rate each thought on how much you believe it — 0 (not at all) to 100 (completely).

4. Behavior
    What did you do? How did you cope with the situation?

Table 23–6.
Common Cognitive Distortions of Depression

1. Black or white thinking: Seeing things as either black or white, rather than in shades of gray.

Examples of black and white thinking when depressed: Feeling that if you are not perfect, then you are a complete failure; believing that if you do not have total control over a situation, then you are helpless; feeling that your relationships are either "all good" or "all bad."

2. Overgeneralizing: erroneously assuming that the specifics of one case are true of other cases.

Examples of overgeneralizing when depressed: Because you perform poorly in one situation, you erroneously view yourself as incompetent in other situations. Because a partner rejects you, you feel that no one will ever love you. Because your parent was critical of you, you feel that all authority figures are critical of you. Because something bad happened in one situation, you decide that all similar situations are hopeless.

3. Focusing on the negative: focusing on the negative aspects of a situation and ignoring the positive aspects, so that you see the situation as more negative than it is realistically.

Examples of focusing on the negative when depressed: You focus only on the bad aspects of yourself, the world, or the people around you, ignoring the good aspects. You focus only on the ways you lack control in a situation, rather than on the ways you could (and should) exert control. You focus on the ways you failed to cope with a challenge, rather than acknowledging the ways you succeeded in coping.

4. Jumping to conclusions: jumping to a conclusion without enough evidence to do so, when other conclusions are also possible.

Examples of jumping to conclusions when depressed: You notice a physical symptom and assume you have a serious illness. You hear a noise in the house, and assume that a criminal has broken in. A friend breaks a date, and you assume that the person no longer wants to be your friend. Your girlfriend is late coming home and you assume that she has gotten into a car accident.

5. Catastrophizing: thinking "what if" bad things happen, usually at great length and in imaginative detail.

Examples of catastrophizing: You vividly imagine something bad happening. You experience a manageable event as catastrophic. You imagine the worst possible outcome and then you play it out again and again in your mind.

Table 23–7.
Steps to Constructing a Rational Response

Automatic thoughts: _____

_____

_____

    Rate belief in automatic thoughts (0 to 100): _____

What evidence do you have to support your automatic thoughts?

What evidence do you have against your automatic thoughts?

What are some alternative explanations?

Have you made any cognitive distortions?

Can you design a test of your automatic thoughts?

Have you identified a realistic problem? If so, go through the steps of the problem-solving exercise, and write the results here. What solution have you chosen? What steps can you take to carry out this solution?

Has one of your schemas been triggered? Which one? What do you need to do to battle the schema in this case?

Summarized rational response: _____

_____

_____

    Rerate belief in automatic thoughts (0 to 100) _____

From *Cognitive-Behavioral Treatment of Depression* by J. S. Klosko and W. C. Sanderson. Copyright © 1999 by Jason Aronson Inc., and used with permission.

MARITAL ANGER

Couples can be given examples of Positive and Negative Aspects of Anger Expression (Table 23–8) to think about during the week and discuss at the next session. The Anger Worksheet (Table 23–9) can be given to clients to fill out at home and bring back to address further issues rather than blame each other.

Table 23–8.
Potential Positive and Negative Aspects of Anger Expression

Positive aspects of anger expression
  Signaling to oneself that a right or standard has been violated.
  Motivating oneself for action toward protecting rights or values.
  Maintaining self-respect.
  Getting one's way.
  Gaining a partner's attention.
  Punishing a partner.
  Quieting a partner or avoiding an uncomfortable topic.
  Communicating strong feelings.
  Providing a sense of empowerment.
  Releasing tension.

Negative aspects of anger expression (short-term)
  Hurting a partner's feelings.
  Frightening a partner.
  Saying something one later regrets.
  Provoking an escalation of conflict.
  Driving a partner to withdraw.
  Failing to resolve a problem.
  Causing an embarrassing situation (e.g., if in public).
  Sabotaging pleasant occasions or important events.
  Feeling *dis*empowered or out of control.
  Exasercbating one's own negative mood state.

Negative aspects of anger expression (long-term)
  Being a partner who is viewed as unapproachable, or who causes others
    to "walk on eggshells."
  Creating distance in the relationship.

Emotionally scarring one's partner.

Accumulating a roster of unresolved marital conflicts.

Creating a poor environment for children.

Frightening the children.

Causing difficulty at work.

Alienating outside relationships.

Increasing stress.

Creating health problems.

Table 23-9.
Anger Worksheet

Situation: Date:

Warning signs of increasing anger:

Physical:

Cognitive:

Behavioral:

Environmental:

Behavior (or behavioral urges):

From *Marital Distress* by J. H. Rathus and W. C. Sanderson. Copyright © 1999 by Jason Aronson Inc., and used with permission.

OBSESSIVE-COMPULSIVE DISORDER

This exercise also uses the Challenging Cognitions Worksheet (Table 23–1) combined with a list of Common Misconceptions Observed in Obsessive-Compulsive Disorder (Table 23–10). Clients can identify their irrational thoughts and behaviors and reframe them with more rational responses.

Homework may incorporate use of an integrated therapist–client package on *Overcoming Obsessive-Compulsive Disorder* by Gail Sketee (1998), New Harbinger Press, Oakland, CA, which includes a therapist treatment protocol and client manual of exercises and worksheets.

Table 23-10.
Common Misconceptions Observed in Obsessive-Compulsive Disorder

1. Catastrophizing:

   "I will have a nervous breakdown if the anxiety continues any longer."

   "My family will die in a fire unless I unplug all the electrical appliances in the house."

   "If Michael didn't call to say he will be late, it means that he is dead."

2. Overestimating the risk of harm or danger:

   "I will become ill if I use the public restroom."

   "I better wash my hands over and over again; otherwise, I am liable to fall sick."

   "Planes crash, so Michael shouldn't fly."

3. Underestimating ability to cope:

   "I am no good at handling my anxiety."

   "I am not sure I remembered to check, so let me check again."

   "I don't trust myself to decide one way or the other. What if I am wrong?"

4. Personalization/self-blame:

   "If Michael dies, it will be my fault."

   "I had better call and check to see if he is alive, or else I will be responsible for his death."

   "If I don't check the gas stove to see that it is off, it is as good as saying that I want him dead."

5. Negative labeling:

   "I am a sinner because I imagine my husband dying."

   "I am wicked, evil, wretched, a degenerate."

   "I am weak."

6. All-or-nothing thinking:

   "If I make even one mistake, it means I am no good."

   "Even the slightest anxiety is intolerable."

"Everything must be in perfect order; even the slightest disorder is not okay."

7. Magical reasoning:

"Michael will die if I touch the knife."

"If I say 'safe Mike,' I will prevent his death."

8. Should and must statements:

"I should be able to control my obsessions."

"I should never make a mistake."

"I should not feel anxious."

From *Treatment of Obsessive-Compulsive Disorder* by L. K. McGinn and W. C. Sanderson. Copyright © 1999 by Jason Aronson Inc., and used with permission.

PHOBIAS

There are multiple parts to this assignment. First, the client is asked to read "Things You Should Know About Social Phobia" (Table 23–11) and then to complete the Phobic Types Questionnaire (Table 23–12), the Phobic Objects, Situations, and Activities Questionnaire (Table 23–13), the Methods of Coping Questionnaire (Table 23–14), the Fearful Thoughts Questionnaire (Table 23–15), the Phobic Sensations Questionnaire (Table 23–16), and the Exposure Record Form (Table 23–17).

Homework may incorporate use of an integrated therapist–client package on *Overcoming Agoraphobia and Panic Disorder* by Elke Zuercher-White (1998), *Overcoming Generalized Anxiety Disorder* by John White (1998), or *Overcoming Specific Phobia* by Edmund J. Bourne (1998), New Harbinger Publications, Oakland, CA, which include a therapist treatment protocol and client manual of exercises and worksheets.

Table 23–11.
Things You Should Know About Social Phobia

1. It is a way of relating to the world.

2. At certain times, we all feel shy, and people who do not feel shy can often be inappropriate.

3. The reason people feel shy is not completely known.

4. People with social phobias are afraid of what other people will think about them.

5. Self-monitoring can provide information about your life to help overcome the problem.

Table 23–12.
Phobic Types Questionnaire

Check	Rank	Type of phobia
_____	_____	Animals: _____
_____	_____	Insects: _____
_____	_____	Heights: _____
_____	_____	Storms: _____
_____	_____	Water: _____
_____	_____	Blood: _____
_____	_____	Needles: _____
_____	_____	Dental work: _____
_____	_____	Seeing a doctor: _____
_____	_____	Bridges: _____
_____	_____	Driving: _____
_____	_____	Enclosed places: _____
_____	_____	Flying: _____
_____	_____	Elevators: _____
_____	_____	Choking: _____
_____	_____	Vomiting: _____
_____	_____	Getting a disease: _____
_____	_____	Other: _____

Table 23–13.
Phobic Objects, Situations, and Activities Questionnaire

Type of phobia: _____

Please use this scale to rate your *fear*.

0-----1-----2-----3-----4-----5-----6-----7-----8-----9-----
No fear　　　　Mild fear　　　Moderate　　　Strong　　　Severe

Please use the following scale to make your rating of *avoidance*:

0-----1-----2-----3-----4-----5-----6-----7-----8-----9-----

No　　　　　　Some　　　　　Often　　　　Mostly　　　　Always
avoidance　　avoidance　　avoid　　　　avoid　　　　avoid

Objects, situations, or activities	Fear (0–10)	Avoidance (0–10)

From *Social Phobia* by R. C. Rapee and W. C. Sanderson. Copyright © 1998 by Jason Aronson Inc., and used with permission.

Table 23–14.
Methods of Coping Questionnaire

Type of phobia: _____

Check   Method of coping:

_____   Avoid it _____

_____   Escape _____

_____   Keep my distance when in its presence _____

_____   Avert my attention _____

_____   Wear protective garments _____

_____   Have a safe person with me (who?) _____

_____   Have a safe object with me (what?) _____

_____   Talk to myself (what?) _____

_____   Pray _____

_____   Prepare for encounters (how?) _____

_____   Freeze or stand still _____

_____   Take medicine/alcohol/drugs (specify) _____

_____   Try to be informed/read/learn about object or situation _____

_____   Fight off feelings _____

_____   Try to relax _____

_____   Other _____

From *Social Phobia* by R. C. Rapee and W. C. Sanderson. Copyright © 1998 by Jason Aronson Inc., and used with permission.

Table 23–15.
Fearful Thoughts Questionnaire

Type of phobia _____

Please use this scale to rate *how often* the feared thought has occurred:

0-----1-----2-----3-----4-----5-----6-----7-----8-----9-----10

Never   Seldom   Half the time   Often   Always

Please use this scale to rate *how believable* the thought has been:

0-----1-----2-----3-----4-----5-----6-----7-----8-----9-----10

No belief   Mildly   Moderately   Strongly   Completely

Fearful thought	How often (0–10)	Belief (0-10)

Table 23–16.
Phobic Sensations Questionnaire

Type of phobia _____

Use this scale to rate the *intensity* (*strength*) and your *fear* of each sensation marked:

0-----1-----2-----3-----4-----5-----6-----7-----8-----9-----10
None   Mild   Moderate   Strong   Severe

Check	Feelings (Sensations)	Intensity (0–10)	Fear (0–10)
_____	Heart beats faster	_____	_____
_____	Heart pounds harder	_____	_____
_____	Breathing is faster	_____	_____
_____	Breathing is difficult	_____	_____
_____	Chest feels tight	_____	_____
_____	Feel faint, dizzy, unsteady	_____	_____
	Have you ever fainted? yes ____ no ____		
_____	Vision changes (How? _____)	_____	_____
_____	Weakness	_____	_____
	Have you ever collapsed? yes ____ no ____		
_____	Shaky or trembling	_____	_____
_____	Numbness/tingling	_____	_____
_____	Chills or hot flashes	_____	_____
_____	Feeling of choking	_____	_____
_____	Feeling detached from oneself	_____	_____
_____	Other things seem unreal	_____	_____
_____	Nauseous or other stomach distress	_____	_____
	Have you ever vomited? yes ____ no ____		
_____	Other (specify)	_____	_____

From *Social Phobia* by R. C. Rapee and W. C. Sanderson. Copyright © 1998 by Jason Aronson Inc., and used with permission.

Table 23–17.
Exposure Record Form

Immediately before the exposure phase, complete this page:

1. Date/time: _____

2. Briefly describe the exposure task and whether this is the first or second, etc. time you have done it _____

3. Please rate your anxiety level right now (0–10) _____

4. How confident are you that you can manage this exposure? (0–10) _____

5. Before doing the exposure, imagine doing it. As you do that, briefly list (one or two words) what you fear could happen during the encounter. List each and all fears that come to mind. Then rate how believable each fear *feels* on the following scale.

0-----1-----2-----3-----4-----5-----6-----7-----8-----9-----10
No belief   Mildly   Moderately   Strongly   Completely

Predicted fears and rated beliefs (0–10)

_____

_____

_____

_____

_____

_____

6. Now re-imagine the encounter. However, this time, instead of listing the feared events, list the most likely challenges you will face (be objective) and how you intend to cope with these. Remember to include that you might feel fear or doubt if that is most likely, indicate also how you plan to manage these feelings. Briefly describe the alternative prediction below. Finally, rate how believable it feels using the 0–10 scale. Immediately after the encounter, complete these questions:

1. Did any of the things you feared happen?
2. Did any other fears come up during the encounter?
3. What physical sensations did you experience during the encounter?
4. Did any of the sensations frighten you?
5. How did you try to cope with the encounter? (List all ways):
6. Why did you stop the exercise?

Other comments?

From *Social Phobia* by R. C. Rapee and W. C. Sanderson. Copyright © 1998 by Jason Aronson Inc., and used with permission.

Bibliotherapy for Clients

SELF-HELP BOOKS

Alcohol

Althauser, D. (1998). *You Can Free Yourself From Alcohol and Drugs*. Oakland, CA: New Harbinger. (A balanced twelve-step approach to recovery.)

Fanning, P., and O'Neill, J. (1996). *The Addiction Workbook*. Oakland, CA: New Harbinger. (A guide for quitting alcohol and drugs.)

Tanner, L. (1996). *The Mother's Survival Guide to Recovery*. Oakland, CA: New Harbinger. (Alcohol, drugs, and babies.)

O'Neill, J., and O'Neill, P. (1992). *Concerned Intervention*. Oakland, CA: New Harbinger. (What to do when your loved one won't quit alcohol or drugs.)

Anxiety

Barlow, D., and Crooke, M. G. (2000). *Mastery of Your Anxiety and Panic*. San Antonio: The Psychological Corp. (Client workbook including record and monitoring forms for panic attacks and agoraphobia.)

Bassete, L. (1995). *From Panic to Power*. New York: Harper Collins. (Techniques to calm your anxieties.)

Bodger, C. (1999). *Smart Guide to Relieving Stress*. New York: Wiley. (Customized plans for relieving stress.)

Bourne, E. J. (1997). *The Anxiety and Phobia Workbook*, 2nd ed. Oakland, CA: New Harbinger. (A comprehensive, practical guide.)

————— (1998). *Healing Fear*. Oakland, CA: New Harbinger. (Offers a range of healing strategies to overcome anxiety.)

Copeland, M. E. (1998). *The Worry Control Workshop*. Oakland, CA: New Harbinger. (Exercises and self-tests for worriers.)

Gallo, F. P., and Vincenzi, H. (2000). *Energy Tapping*. (Using "energy psychology" to eliminate anxiety, depression, and cravings.)

Gerzon, R. (1997). *Finding Serenity in the Age of Anxiety*. New York: Bantam. (New insights into anxiety.)

Jacobson, E. (1978). *You Must Relax*. New York: McGraw-Hill. (Practical methods for reducing tension and stress.)

Jeffers, S. (1988). *Feel the Fear and Do It Anyway*. New York: Fawcett Columbine. (A humorous ten-step plan to stop negative self-talk.)

Johnson, S. (1998). *Who Moved My Cheese?* New York: Putnam. (New ways to deal with changes in your work and life.)

Kopp, S. (1988). *Raise Your Right Hand Against Fear, Extend the Other One in Comparison*. Minneapolis: Compo Care. (Explains how to manage your fears.)

Wetherill, M. J. (2000). *The Eye of the Storm: Discovering Inner Calm Amidst Inner Pressure*. Holbrook, MA: Adams Media. (Using your inner strength to cope with pressure and anxiety.)

Wilson, R. R. (1996). *Don't Panic: Taking Control of Anxiety Attacks*. New York: HarperCollins. (A straightforward self-help program.)

Attention-Deficit Disorder

Hartman, T. (1995). *ADD Success Stories: A Guide to Fulfillment with Attention Deficit Disorder*. Grass Valley, CA: Underwood. (Practical knowledge to help deal with all areas of life.)

————— (1995). *Healing ADD: Simple Exercises that Will Change Your Daily Life*. Grass Valley, CA: Underwood. (Visualizations and positive thinking for change.)

Roberts, S., and Jansen, G. J. (1997). *Living with ADD*. Oakland, CA: New Harbinger. (A workbook of interactive exercises for adults with attention deficit disorder.)

Bereavement

Caplan, S., and Lang, G. (1995). *Grief's Courageous Journey*. Oakland, CA: New Harbinger. (A workbook to help cope with the loss of a loved one.)

Jozefowski, J. (1999). *The Phoenix Phenomenon: Rising from the Ashes of Grief*. Northvale, NJ: Jason Aronson. (Advice and inspiration for those suffering from loss.)

Viorst, J. (1986). *Necessary Losses*. New York: Simon & Schuster. (Coping with death and loss.)

Borderline Personality Disorder

Manson, P. T., and Kreger, R. (1998). *Stop Walking on Eggshells*. Oakland, CA: New Harbinger. (Taking your life back when someone you care about has borderline personality disorder. A guide for family and friends.)

Santoro, J., and Cohen, R. (1997). *The Angry Heart*. Oakland, CA: New Harbinger. (Exercises and techniques to overcome borderline and addictive disorders.)

Brief Therapy

Preston, J. D., Zarzos, N., and Liebert, D. S. (2000). *Make Every Session Count*. Oakland, CA: New Harbinger. (How to make the most of brief therapy.)

Depression/Suicide

Burns, D. (1999). *Feeling God*. New York: Avon. (How to eliminate depression, anxiety, and guilt without drugs.)

Copeland, M. E. (1992). *Living without Depression and Manic Depression*. Oakland, CA: New Harbinger. (A workbook for maintaining mood stability.)

Cousens, G., with Mayell, M. (2000). *Depression: Free for Life*. New York: Morrow. (An all-natural five-step plan to reclaim your zest for living.)

Ellis, T. E., and Newman, C. F. (1996). *Choosing to Live*. Oakland, CA: New Harbinger. (A self-help guide for individuals contemplating suicide.)

Gibson, M., and Freeman, A. (2000). *Overcoming Depression: A Cognitive Approach for Taming the Depression Beast*. San Antonio: Harcourt Brace. (Explores depression and its symptoms and provides exercises to deal with them.)

Medina, J. (1998). *Depression: How it Happens, How it's Healed*. Oakland, CA: New Harbinger. (How chemical changes in the brain contribute to feelings of depression.)

Owen, P. (1995). *I Can See Tomorrow*. Center City, MN: Hazelden. (A guide for living with depression.)

Ray, V. (1995). *Choosing Happiness*. Center City, MN: Hazelden. (The art of living unconditionally.)

Weisman, M. M. (1955). *Mastering Depression through Interpersonal Psychotherapy*. New York: Harcourt Brace. (A client workbook.)

Williams, K. (1995). *A Parents' Guide to Suicidal and Depressed Teens*. Center City, MN: Hazelden. (Help for recognizing if a child is in crisis and what to do about it.)

Young, J. E., and Kloso, J. S. (1964). *Reinventing Your Life*. New York: Penguin. (A set of tools for significant change.)

Dissociative Identity Disorder

Akderman, T., and Marshall, K. (1998). *Amongst Ourselves*. Oakland, CA: New Harbinger. (A self-help guide for living with dissociative identity disorder.)

Eating Disorders

Apple, R. F., and Agras, W. S. (1997). *Overcoming Eating Disorders: A Cognitive-Behavioral Treatment for Bulimia Nervosa and Binge Eating Disorders*. San Antonio: Harcourt Brace. (A guided plan to healthy eating patterns.)

Danowski, D., and Lazaro, P. (2000). *Why Can't I Stop Eating?* Center City, MN: Hazelden. (Recognizing, understanding, and overcoming food addiction.)

Ebbett, J. (1994). *The Eating Illness Workbook.* Center City, MN: Hazelden. (A blueprint of exercises for recovery.)

Edell, D. (1999). *Eat, Drink, and Be Merry.* New York: HarperCollins. (You can be fatter than you think.)

Nash, J. D. (1999). *Binge No More.* Oakland, CA: New Harbinger. (How to overcome disordered eating.)

Sandbek, T. (1993). *The Deadly Diet.* Oakland, CA: New Harbinger. (Proven cognitive techniques to overcome eating disorders.)

Schroder, C. R. (1992). *Fat Is Not a Four-Letter Word.* New York: Chronemed. (Help women to realize they don't have to be ashamed of their bodies if they don't look like fashion models.)

Sherman, R. T., and Thompson, R. A. (1996). *Bulimia: A Guide for Family and Friends.* San Francisco: Jossey-Bass. (A step-by-step guide to help family and friends deal with the disorder.)

Zerbe, K. J. (1993). *The Body Betrayed: Eating Disorders and Their Treatment.* Washington, DC: American Psychiatric Press. (Eating disorders that affect women and other factors associated with them.)

Emotional Abuse

Thompson, P. (1989). *Emotional Abuse.* Center City, MN: Hazelden. (Explains the differences between healthy and abusive relationships.)

Gambling

Heineman, M. (1988). *When Someone You Love Gambles.* Center City, MN: Hazelden. (Support for family members.)

Horvath, A. T. (2000). *Sex, Drugs, Gambling, and Chocolate.* Atascardero, CA: Impact. (An easy-to-follow workbook to deal with cravings.)

Lesieur, H. R. (1986). *Understanding Compulsive Gambling.* Center City, MN: Hazelden. (A resource for clients and their families.)

Lorenz, V. (1988). *Releasing Guilt about Gambling.* Center City, MN: Hazelden. (Explains how guilt is often accompanied by other destructive emotions.)

Guilt/Shame

Black, C., and Drozd, L. (1995). *The Missing Piece: Solving the Puzzle of Self.* New York: Ballantine. (Offers a road map and exercises for discovering hidden aspects of yourself.)

Breitman, P., and Hatch, C. (2000). *How to Say No without Feeling Guilty.* New York: Broadway. (A practical guide to setting boundaries without guilt.)

Efron, R. P., and Efron, F. P. (1989). *Letting Go of Shame: Understanding How Shame Affects Your Life.* Center City, MN: Hazelden. (Practical information for coping with shame.)

Hypnosis/Visualization

Austin, V. (1998). *Free Yourself from Fear: Self-Hypnosis for Anxiety, Panic, Attacks, and Phobias.* London: HarperCollins. (A step-by-step self-hypnosis guide.)

Davis, M., Eshelman, E. R., and McKay, M. (1995). *The Relaxation and Stress Reduction Workbook.* Oakland, CA: New Harbinger. (Client workbook including step-by-step instruction in relaxation training.)

Epstein, G. (1987). *Healing Visualizations: Creating Health through Imagery.* New York: Bantam. (A guide to visualizations to heal medical problems and other disorders.)

Fanning, P. (1999). *Visualization for Change.* Oakland, CA: New Harbinger. (Instruction in the classic applications of hypnosis.)

Fisher, S. (1991). *Discovering the Power of Self-Hypnosis: A New Approach for Enabling Health and Promoting Healing.* San Antonio: HarperCollins. (Exercises for learning self-hypnosis.)

Gawain, S. (1982). *Creative Visualization.* New York: Bantam. (How the power of your imagination can create the life you want.)

——— (1995). *The Creative Visualization Workbook.* Novato, CA: New World Library. (Discover and use the power of your imagination.)

Hadley, J., and Staudacher, C. (1996). *Hypnosis for Change.* Oakland, CA: New Harbinger. (Hypnosis for weight loss, smoking, pain, anxiety, performance, and childbirth.)

Napier, N. (1990). *Recreating Yourself: Building Self-Esteem through Imaging and Self-Hypnosis.* New York: Norton. (How to use self-hypnosis to reclaim your life.)

Medical

Caufield, J., Hansen, M. V., Aubry, P., and Mitchell, N. M. (1996). *Chicken Soup for the Surviving Soul*. Deerfield Beach, FL: Health Communications. (101 inspiring stories.)

Doka, K. J. (1998). *Living with Life-Threatening Illness: A Guide for Patients, Their Families, and Caregivers*. San Francisco: Jossey-Boss. (Practical suggestions grounded in personal experience.)

Kabat-Zinn, J. (1990). *Full Catastrophic Living: Using the Wisdom of Your Body and Mind to Face Stress, Pain, and Illness*. New York: Dell. (Teaches clients how to live their lives more fully.)

Pitzele, S. K. (2000). *Finding the Joy in Today*. Center City, MN: Hazelden. (Living with chronic illness.)

Register, C. (2000). *Living with Chronic Illness*. Center City, MN: Hazelden. (Embracing the imperfect life.)

Obsessive-Compulsive Disorder

C., Roy. (2000). *Obsessive-Compulsive Disorder*. Center City, MN: Hazelden. (A survival guide for the client's family and friends.)

Hyman, B. M., and White, K. (1990). *The OCD Workbook*. Oakland, CA: New Harbinger. (A self-directed program for breaking free from obsessive-compulsive disorder.)

Personality Disorders

Basco, M. R. (1999). *Never Good Enough: How to Use Perfectionism to Your Advantage without Letting It Ruin Your Life*. New York: Simon & Schuster. (How to use perfectionism in a positive way.)

Kreisman, J. J., and Straus, H. (1999). *I Hate You, Don't Leave Me*. New York: HarperCollins. (Advice on how to address the troubling issues associated with borderline personality disorder.)

Linehan, M. M. (1993). *Skills Training Manual for Treating Borderline Personality Disorders*. New York: Guilford. (Guide for teaching clients mindfulness, interpersonal effectiveness, emotional regulation, and frustration tolerance.)

Masterson, J. F. (1988). *The Search for the Real Self: Unmasking the Personality Disorder of Our Age*. New York: Free Press. (Practical suggestions on gaining the power to alter your life.)

Phobias

Antony, M. M., Craske, M. G., and Barlow, D. H. (1995). *Mastering Your Special Phobia.* San Antonio: Harcourt Brace. (Exploring phobias and strategies to overcome them.)

Colas, E. (1998). *Scenes from the Life of an Obsessive-Compulsive.* New York: Pocket Books. (A world where kitchen utensils become instruments of contamination.)

Foa, E. B., and Kozak, M. J. (1997). *Mastery of Obsessive-Compulsive Disorder: A Cognitive-Behavioral Approach.* San Antonio: Harcourt Brace. (Control of ritualistic behavior.)

Gravitz, H. L. (1998). *New Help for the Family.* Santa Barbara, CA: Healing Visions Press. (Family help for obsessive-compulsive disorder.)

Robinson, B. E. (2000). *Don't Let Your Mind Stunt Your Growth.* Oakland, CA: New Harbinger. (Stories, fables, and techniques to change the way you think.)

Schwartz, J. M., and Bigette, B. (1996). *Brain Lock.* New York: HarperCollins. (A four-step approach to gaining control of your life.)

Zuercher-White, E. (1997). *Treating Panic Disorder and Agoraphobia.* Oakland, CA: New Harbinger. (A step-by-step cognitive-behavioral guide.)

Posttraumatic Stress Disorder

Matsakis, A. (1998). *Trust After Trauma.* Oakland, CA: New Harbinger. (A guide to relationships for survivors and those who love them.)

——— (1999). *I Can't Get Over It.* Oakland, CA: New Harbinger. (A handbook for trauma survivors.)

——— (1999). *Survivor Guilt.* Oakland, CA: New Harbinger. (A self-help guide for coming to terms with guilt.)

Rothluum, B. O., and Foa, E. B. (2000). *Reclaiming Your Life After Rape.* San Antonio: Harcourt Brace. (Cognitive-behavioral therapy for posttraumatic stress disorder.)

Procrastination

Knaus, W. J. (1998, 1979). *Do It Now: Break the Procrastination Habit.* New York: Wiley. (Identifies causes of procrastination and develops a workable action plan to overcome it.)

Roberts, M. S. (1995). *Living without Procrastination*. Oakland, CA: New Harbinger. (Techniques for unlearning counterproductive habits.)

Relational Problems—Partner/Parent-Child

Asherson, S. (1992). *Wrestling with Love: How Men Struggle with Intimacy with Women, Children, Parents, and Each Other*. New York: Fawcett. (Deals honestly with the problems men have with intimacy.)

Basoff, E. S. (1992). *Mothering Ourselves: Help and Healing for Adult Daughters*. (How to transform past disappointments into a meaningful relationship.)

Beck, A. (1988). *Love Is Never Enough: How Couples Can Overcome Misunderstandings and Resolve Relationship Problems through Cognitive Therapy*. New York: Harper Perennial. (Insights, advice, and exercises to help a failing marriage.)

Brown, E. M. (1999). *Affairs: A Guide to Working Through the Repercussions of Infidelity*. San Francisco: Jossey-Bass. (A pull-no-punches guide to the problems of infidelity.)

Davies, M. W. (1998). *A Woman's Guide to Changing Her Man (without His Even Knowing)*. New York: Golden Books. (Helpful in improving relationships.)

Fraiberg, S. H. (1996). *The Magic Years: Understanding and Handling the Problems of Early Childhood*. New York: IDG. (Development theory from birth through age six.)

Gookin, S. H. (1995). *Parenting for Dummies*. New York: IDG. (A parenting guide for the '90s and beyond.)

Heitler, S. (1997). *The Power of Two*. Oakland, CA: New Harbinger. (The secrets of a strong and loving marriage.)

Hendrix, H. (1990). *Getting the Love You Want: A Guide for Couples*. New York: Harper Perennial. (Transforming couples into passionate friends.)

Larsen, J. H. (2000). *Should We Stay Together?* San Francisco: Jossey-Bass. (Provides couples with the tools to make better decisions about their relationships.)

Lassen, M. K. (2000). *Why Are We Still Fighting?* Oakland, CA: New Harbinger. (How to end the fighting and connect with the people you love.)

Markman, H., Stanley, S., and Blumberg, S. (1995). *Fighting for Your Marriage*. San Francisco: Jossey-Bass. (Strategies for enhancing your marriage.)

McGraw, P. C. (2000). *Relationship Recovery.* New York: Hyperion. (An insightful program to get you back on track with your partner.)

McKay, M., Fanning, P., and Paleg, K. (1995). *Couple Skills—The Book.* Oakland, CA: New Harbinger. (How to make your relationship work. Focuses on action rather than theory. See video and audiotape versions of this program.)

Metcalf, J. (1996). *Parenting Toward Solutions.* New York: Prentice Hall. (A solution-oriented approach to parenting problems.)

Newman, M. G. (1998). *Helping Your Kid Cope with Divorce the Sandcastle's Way.* New York: Random House. (Covers all problems faced by children of divorcing parents and suggests special activities to improve communications.)

Schaes, A. W. (1990). *Escape from Intimacy: Untangling the Love Addictions—Sex, Romance, Relationships.* New York: Harper and Row. (Codependency and the road to recovery.)

Spring, J. A., with Spring, M. (1996). *After the Affair: Healing the Pain and Rebuilding Trust When a Partner Has Been Unfaithful.* New York: HarperCollins. (Reconstructing your marriage.)

Weiner-Davis, M. (1993). *Divorce Busting.* New York: Fireside. (Solution-oriented methods to stop divorce.)

Schizophrenia

Muesler, K., and Gingerich, S. (1994). *Coping with Schizophrenia.* Oakland, CA: New Harbinger. (A strategy guide for families.)

Self-Esteem

Blank, C., and Drozd, L. (1995). *The Missing Piece: Solving the Puzzle of Self.* New York: Ballantine. (A road map to self-awareness.)

Brander, N. (1997). *The Art of Living Consciously: The Power of Awareness to Transform Everyday Life.* New York: Fireside. (Mindfulness for survival.)

Carlson, R. (1997). *Don't Sweat the Small Stuff . . . and It's All Small Stuff.* New York: Hyperion. (Don't go nuts over the little things.)

Caufield, J., and Hansen, M. V. (1993). *Chicken Soup for the Soul.* Deerfield Beach, FL: Health Communications. (An inspirational approach to awareness.)

Emerick, J. J., Jr. (1997). *Be the Person You Want to Be*. Rocklin, CA: Prima. (Help with running your own life.)

McGraw, P. S. (2000). *The Life Strategies Workbook*. New York: Hyperion. (Help to identify your problems, confront them and work toward permanent solutions.)

McKay, M., and Fanning, P. (2000). *Self-Esteem*. Oakland, CA: New Harbinger. (Cognitive-behavioral techniques for assessing, improving, and maintaining your self-esteem. A classic.)

Napier, N. (1990). *Recreating Your Self*. New York: Norton. (Teaches adult children of dysfunctional families how to use self-hypnosis to reclaim their lives.)

O'Hanlon, W. (1999). *Do One Thing Different and Other Uncommonly Simple Solutions to Life's Persistent Problems*. New York: Morrow. (A bold, humorous approach to changing your life.)

Sexual Abuse

Kunzman, K. (1989). *Healing from Childhood Sexual Abuse*. Center City, MN: Hazelden. (A guide for recovering women.)

Sexual Dysfunction

Carnes, P. (1992). *Out of the Shadows: Understanding Sexual Addictions*. Center City, MN: Hazelden. (A twelve-step program with worksheets and checklists for sexual addicts.)

———— (1997). *Sexual Anorexia*. Center City, MN: Hazelden. (An in-depth study of the problem and its causes.)

Goodwin, A. J., and Agronin, M. E. (1997) *A Woman's Guide to Overcoming Sexual Fear and Pain*. Oakland, CA: New Harbinger. (Self-guided exercises to help work through individual sexual problems.)

Week, E., and Gombescia, N. (2000). *Erectile Dysfunction*. New York: Norton. (Regards erectile dysfunction as a systemic problem and integrates couples therapy, sex therapy, and medical treatment.)

Wineze, J. P., and Barlow, D. H. (1999). *Enhancing Sexuality: A Problem-Solving Approach*. San Antonio: Harcourt Brace. (A cognitive-behavioral workbook to help target the sources of problems and how to solve them. The differences between male and female sexuality are explained.)

Sleep

Ancoli-Israet, S. (1996). *All I Want Is a Good Night's Sleep*. St. Louis: Mosby Year Book. (Suggested ways to help you sleep better.)

Smoking

Stevic-Rust, L., and Maximin, A. (1996). *The Stop Smoking Workbook*. Oakland, CA: New Harbinger. (The tools to quit smoking.)

Substance Abuse

Alcoholics Anonymous (1976). *The Big Book*. New York: AA. (The AA bible that outlines the twelve-step program.)

———— (2000). *Alcoholics Anonymous World Service*. New York: AA. (65th printing of the AA introductory handbook.)

Anonymous (2000). *How to Get Sober and Stay Sober*. Center City, MN: Hazelden. (A five-step workbook.)

Byrofsky, S. (1990). *Me Five Years from Now*. New York: Warner. (An interactive book with strategy charts to help change your life.)

Daley, D. C. (1988). *Surviving Addiction: A Guide for Alcoholics, Drug Addicts, and their Families*. New York: Gardner. (A realistic and hopeful perspective for clients and their families.)

Daley, D. C., and Marlatt, G. A. (1997). *Managing Your Drug and Alcohol Problem*. San Antonio: Harcourt Brace. (A workbook that helps uncover underlying causes and develop ways to cope with the problems.)

Dupont, R. L. (2000). *The Selfish Brain*. Center City, MN: Hazelden. (An updated view of alcoholism.)

Ellis, A., and Velten, E. (1992). *When AA Doesn't Work for You: Rational Steps to Quitting Alcohol*. New York: Barricade. (An alternative to AA.)

Johnson, V. E. (1980). *I'll Quit Tomorrow*. New York: HarperCollins. (A practical guide to alcoholism treatment for clients and family members.)

Potter-Efron, R., and Potter-Efron, P. (1989). *Letting Go of Shame*. Center City, MN: Hazelden. (Understanding how shame affects your life.)

Rosellini, G., and Worden, M. (1997). *Of Course You're Angry*. Center City, MN: Hazelden. (Dealing with the emotions associated with chemical dependency.)

Rustin, T. A. (1996). *Keep Quit!* Center City, MN: Hazelden. (A motivational guide to life without smoking.)

—— (1996). *Quit and Stay Quit.* Center City, MN: Hazelden. (A personal program to stop smoking.)

Simon, S. (1988). *Getting Unstuck: Breaking through Your Barriers to Change.* New York: Warner. (A workable blueprint for self-directed change.)

Swanson, J., and Cooper, A. (1995). *Finding Your Strengths.* Center City, MN: Hazelden. (Relapse prevention strategy.)

W., Anne. (1985). *What Do I Do for Fun?* Center City, MN: Hazelden. (Suggested ways to fill free time.)

Washton, A. (1990). *Cocaine Recovery Workbook: Quitting Cocaine, Staying off Cocaine, and Maintaining Recovery.* Center City, MN: Hazelden. (Three-book collection on recovery.)

Vocational and Financial Problems

Chope, R. C. (2000). *Dancing Naked.* Oakland, CA: New Harbinger. (How to break through the emotional limitations that keep you from the job you want.)

Bolles, R. (2000). *What Color Is Your Parachute?* California: Ten-Speed Press. (A workbook for job-seekers.)

Casanova, K. (2000). *Letting Go of Debt.* Center City, MN: Hazelden. (Mediations on growing richer one day at a time.)

Hazelden (1993). *Managing Money; Living Skills.* Center City, MN: Hazelden. (Pamphlet with exercises to teach money management.)

Mudaner, T. (2000). *Coach Yourself to Success.* Chicago, IL: Contemporary Books. (101 tips for recycling your work and life goals.)

O'Hara, V. (1995). *Wellness at Work.* Oakland, CA: New Harbinger. (Building resistance to job stress.)

Robbins, A. (1991). *Awaken the Great Wisdom.* New York: Fireside Books. (Tools for focusing your thoughts and emotions to attain your goals.)

Tieger, P. D., and Barron-Tieger, B. (1992). *Do What You Are.* Boston: Little, Brown. (Discover the perfect career through analysis of personality type.)

SELF-HELP AUDIOTAPES

The following audiotapes are available from New Harbinger Publications, Oakland, CA.

Anxiety and Stress

Time Out from Stress: Vol. One: *Lakeside* and *The Path to Lookout
     Mountain.* Vol. Two: *Five Finger Exercise* and *Country Inn.*
Body Relaxed, Mind at Ease. 1993. (Harriett Sanders)
Peaceful Body, Relaxed Mind. 1995. (Harriett Sanders)

Cognition

Combating Distorted Thinking
Thought Stopping
Systematic Desensitization & Visualizing Goals
Covert Modeling and Covert Reinforcement
Pain Control and Healing

Communication Skills

Assertiveness Training
Effective Self-Expression
Becoming a Good Listener
Making Contact
Sexual Communication
Fair Fighting

Couples

Conflict Resolution for Couples (Susan Heitler)

The following series is based on McKay and colleagues (1994).

Exchanging Favors
Constructive Conflict Resolution
Listening
Expressing Feelings

Clean Communication
Negotiation
Time Out from Anger
Coping with an Angry Partner

Depression

Depression and Anxiety Management (John Preston)
Living with Depression and Manic Depression (M. E. Copeland)

General

Visualizations for Change (Patrick Fanning)
Stress Reduction
Allergies and Asthma
Healing Injuries
Curing Infectious Disease
Shyness
Transforming Your Chronic Pain

Hypnosis

Self-Hypnosis
Hypnosis for Weight Control
Hypnosis for Non-Smoking
Hypnosis for Sleep
Hypnosis for Self-Esteem
Hypnosis for Improved Learning
Hypnosis for Motivating Change and Problem Solving
Hypnosis to End Anxiety and Panic Attacks
Hypnosis for Overcoming Depression
Hypnosis for Coping Before and After Surgery

Phobias (E. J. Bourne)

Flying
Shopping in a Supermarket
Driving Freeways
Giving a Talk
Speaking in Public
Fear of Illness
Driving Far from Home
Heights

25

Self-Help Groups and 800 Numbers

Alcohol

Al-Anon and Alateen: 888-425-2666
American Council on Alcohol Addiction: 800-527-5344
National Council on Alcohol Addiction: 800-622-2255
National Clearinghouse for Alcohol and Drug Information: 800-729-6686
Alcohol and Drug Abuse Testing Center: 900-942-3784
National Council on Alcoholism and Drug Dependence: 800-475-HOPE

Child Abuse

If a child is in immediate danger or risk, call: 800-THE-LOST
National Child Abuse Hotline: 800-25-ABUSE

Depression

National Depressive and Manic Depressive Association: 800-826-2632

DAD (Depression After Delivery): 800-944-4773

National Foundation for Depressive Illness: 800-926-3632

Drug Abuse

Narcotics Anonymous: 888-994-9484

National Council on Alcoholism and Drug Dependence Inc.: 800-622-2255

Schick Shadel Hospital: 800-CRAVING (800-272-9464)

National Parents Resource Institute for Drug Education (PRIDE): 800-241-794

National COCAINE Hotline: 800-COCAINE

Office of Substance Abuse Prevention: 900-638-2045; Marijuana Anonymous: 800-766-6779

Teen Help Adolescent Resources: 800-637-0701

National Substance Abuse Hotline: 800-DRUG-HELP or 900-HELP-III

Mental Health

National Alliance for the Mentally Ill: 800-950-NANG (6264)

PART IV

APPENDIX

26

On-Line Resources[*]

General

Internet Index Home Page
http://www.openmarket.com/intindex/

Pharmaceutical Information Network home page
http://pharminfo.com/

Psychology organizations on the web
http://www.wesleyan.edu/spn/psych.htm

Search page for articles in psychology and social science journals
http://www.shef.ac.uk/~psych/journals/jsearch.html

Social work and social services web sites
http://www.gwbweb.wustl.edu/websites.html

The Social Statistics Briefing Room
http://www.whitehouse.gov/fsbr/ssbr.html

Child welfare home page
http://www.childwelfare.com/

Internet Mental Health
http://www.mentalhealth.com/

Mental Health Net
http://www.cmhc.com/

NIMH home page
http://www.nimh.nih.gov/

Psyjourn, Inc.
http://www.psyjourn.com

Psychscapes Worldwide
http://www.mental-health.com

The Shrink Tank BBS web site
http://www.shrinktank.com/testing.htm

Professional Organizations

American Academy of Child and Adolescent Psychiatry home page
http://www.aacap.org/web/aacap/

American Psychiatric Association Online
http://www.psych.org/

American Psychoanalytic Association Online
http://apsa.org/

American Psychological Association PsychNet
http://www.apa.org

California Coalition for Ethical Mental Health Care
http://www.pw1.netcom.com/~donmar/home.html

National Coalition of Mental Health Professionals and Consumers
http://www.execpe.com/~mastery/coalitionMain.html

Clinical Social Work Federation
http://www.cswf.org

NASW Online
http://www.socialworkers.org/main.htm

Self-Help and Support Group Resources

Emotional Support on the Internet
http://www.cix.co.uk/~net-services/care

Mental Health Net—Self-Help Questionnaires
http://www.cmhc.com/guide/quizes.htm

Mental Health Net—Self-Help Resources Index
http://www.cmhc.com/selfhelp.htm

Support-Group.com
http://support-group.com

Specific Disorders

Alcoholics Anonymous
http://www.alcoholics-anonymous.org/

ANXIETY-PANIC Internet resource-articles
http://www.algy.com/anxiety/

Bipolar and other mood disorders: Pendulum Resources
http://www.pendulum.org

Children and Adults with Attention Deficit Disorders
(C.H.A.D.D.)
http://chadd.org/

COLA—Center for Online Addiction
http://netaddiction.com/

Cyber-Psych: Eating Disorders
http://www.cyber-psych.com/eat.html

Death, Dying, and Grief Resources: The WEBster
http://www.cyberspy.com/%7Ewebster/death.html

Depression Central
http://www.psycom.net/depression.central.html

Futur.com (schizophrenia and other psychoses)
http://www.futur.com/

International Society for the Study of Dissociation
http://www.issd.org/

Mental Health Resources
http://gopher.bu.edu/COHIS/hsource/mh.htm

Obsessive-Compulsive Disorders
http://www.cmhc.com/guide/ocd.htm

The Samaritans (Suicide)
http://www.samaritans.org.uk/

Completing the Forms

OUTPATIENT TREATMENT REPORT (OTR/TAR)

The Outpatient Treatment Report, sometimes called a Treatment Authorization Request (TAR), is required for continuing patient certification and authorization of additional treatment sessions. Most insurance companies supply their own OTR forms for provider use. Some OTRs require that you estimate how much your intervention has helped the client reach targeted goals, stated in percentage terms. At this time, there are no published criteria to guide you. The percentage is a subjective estimate made by the provider. What you write in these reports, and how you write it, will often determine how many sessions the insurance company will allocate for treatment. The following completed form is provided to give you a better idea of the information usually required.

SAMPLE OUTPATIENT TREATMENT REPORT

Check One: Initial OTR _✔_   Continuing OTR ____

DEMOGRAPHICS

Patient: _Jane Doe_   ID: _xxx-xx-xxxx_   Group #: _0000_
Date of Birth: _xx/xx/xxxx_ First Date of Service _xx/xx/xxxx_ Gender: M F

DSM-IV DIAGNOSIS

Axis I: 300.4
          309.28
Axis II: V71.09
Axis III: None
Axis IV: Problems with primary support group, occupation, and economics.
Axis V: (GAF) - Current: 55   Highest Last Year: _?_
          Expected GAF at Discharge: 71

Global Assessment of Functioning (GAF)

91–100	Superior functioning	81–90	Good functioning, minimal symptoms
71–80	Transient symptoms, slight impairment	61–70	Minor symptoms, functions fairly well
51–60	Moderate symptoms, functioning	41–50	Serious symptoms, impairments
31–40	Impairments in reality testing or communication	21–30	Major impairment or delusions/ hallucinations
11–20	Risk of harm to self/others, poor personal hygiene	1–10	Serious danger to self or others, or actively suicidal
0	Not enough information		

Practitioner's Name: _Dr. James Morton, DSW, CSW_
Practitioner's Address: _xxx East xth Street_
City: _New York_   State: _NY_   Zip: _xxxxx_
Telephone number: _212-xxx-xxxx_
Discipline, State License and Number: _MD, PR0xxxx-xx_
Federal Tax ID Number: _SS# 000-00-0000_

Name: <u>Jane Doe</u>　　　**OTR**　　　SS#: <u>xxx-xx-xxxx</u>

ASSESSMENT
Previous Treatment (*Please check all that apply*):

<u>Psychiatric</u>	<u>Substance Abuse</u>	<u>Treatment Outcomes</u>
None ✔	None ✔	_____
Outpatient ____	Outpatient ____	_____
Inpatient ____	Inpatient ____	_____
within last 12 months ____	within last 12 months ____	_____
one prior admission ____	one prior admission ____	_____
2 or more prior admissions ____	2 or more prior admissions ____	_____

Symptoms (*Please check symptoms that apply*):

✔	Anxiousness	✔	Hyperactivity	✔	Substance Use (check if applicable)	
	Concomitant Medical Condition	✔	Irritability		Active Substance Abuse	
✔	Lack of Energy		Impulsiveness		Early Full Remission	
	Delusions	✔	Obsessions/ Compulsions		Early Partial Remission	
✔	Depressed Mood		Oppositionalism		Sustained Full Remission	
	Dissociative State		Panic Attacks		Sustained Partial Remission	
	Elevated Mood		Paranoia		Other—specify:	
✔	Grief		Somatic Complaints		Other—specify:	
	Guilt	✔	Thought Disruption			
	Hallucinations		Trauma Victim			
✔	Hopelessness	✔	Worthlessness			

Duration of symptoms:
　　Less than one month ____1–6 months ____7–11 months ____more than a year ____

page 2

Name: <u>Jane Doe</u> **OTR** SS#: <u>xxx-xx-xxxx</u>

Functioning (please assess the current level of impairment and anticipated level at discharge):

Impairment Level
(Please circle appropriate level)

Categories	None	Mild	Moderate	Marked	Extreme	Discharge
Activities of daily living (hygiene)	①	2	3	4	5	<u>2</u>
Ability to concentrate	1	2	③	4	5	<u>2</u>
Ability to control temper	1	2	③	4	5	<u>1</u>
Eating habits	①	2	3	4	5	<u>2</u>

Weight loss/gain _____ lbs. Current weight _____ lbs. Height _____

Categories	None	Mild	Moderate	Marked	Extreme	Discharge
Financial Situation	1	2	3	④	5	<u>2</u>
Friendship/peer relationship	1	2	3	④	5	<u>2</u>
Hobbies/Interests/play activities	1	2	3	④	5	<u>2</u>
Job/school/performance	1	2	3	④	5	<u>2</u>
Marriage/relationship/ family	1	2	3	④	5	<u>2</u>
Physical health	①	2	3	④	5	<u>1</u>
Sexual functioning	1	2	③	4	5	<u>2</u>
Sleeping habits	①	2	3	4	5	<u>2</u>

Difficulty falling asleep ___ Difficulty staying asleep ___ Early awakening ___

RISK ASSESSMENT (*Check all that apply*)

Suicide: None ___ Ideation ✔ Plan ___ Means ___
Prior attempt date: _____
Homicide: None ___ Ideation ___ Plan ___ Means ___
Prior attempt date: _____
Other risk behaviors:
(If Yes to any risk issues, provide plan: Patient has suicidal ideation, and has agreed to inform me or her psychiatrist of her intentions before taking any action.)

TREATMENT PLAN

Primary Treatment Approach (Check one)
Problem focused _____ Symptom focused _____ Complex case _____
Therapeutic stabilization _____ Medication management only _____

Progress in treatment (Check one)
Continues with/or recurrence of acute presenting problems _✔_
Somewhat improved _____
Much improved _____
Needs support/maintenance only _____
Near completion of treatment _____
Other: _____

Expected treatment outcomes (Check all that apply)
Reduction in symptoms and discharge from active treatment _____
Return to highest GAF and discharge from active treatment _✔_
Transfer to self-help/other supports and discharge from active treatment _____
Provide ongoing supportive counseling and maintain stabilization of
    symptoms _____
Provide ongoing medication management _____

Did patient concur with goals and strategies of treatment plan? Yes___ No___

Medication (List all psychotropic and other medications)

Has patient been evaluated for medication?   Yes _✔_ No _____
Current Medication: None _____ Psychotropic _✔_ Medical _____
                    Other: _____
Does patient follow medication regime?   Yes _✔_ No _____
Prescribing physician (indicate if PCP
    or Psychiatrist):   Dr. Mary Simon, MD (Psychiatrist)

Name of Medication	Current Dosage /Frequency	Start Date	Side Effects
Celexa	40 mg/day	7/30/2000	Yes _____ No _____
			Dizziness

Name: <u>Jane Doe</u>   **OTR**   SS#: <u>xxx-xx-xxxx</u>

Care Planning

Problem: Suicidal Ideation
Goal: Eliminate or reduce suicidal thoughts.   **Est. Time:** 1 mo.
Intervention: Implement a 'suicide pact' in which client informs therapist of active plan and promises to contact therapist before taking any action.
Progress since start of tx: <u>25%</u> **of goal as evidenced by:** Client has entered into 'suicide pact' with Dr. Mary Smith and me.

Problem: Adjustment Disorder with Anxiety and Depression due to loss.
Goal: Decrease anxiety/depression, feelings of humiliation.   **Est. Time:** 2 mos.
Intervention: Investigate with client available resources to deal with occupational and financial problems.
Progress since start of tx: <u>10%</u> **of goal as evidenced by:** Client is actively researching resources and self-help groups for future use when issues of embarrassment are reduced.

Problem: Dysthymia
Goal: Reduce symptoms of depression.   **Est. Time:** 4 mos.
Intervention: Investigate with client the symptoms of depression and their origins and triggers prior to her losing her job.
Progress since start of tx: <u>10%</u> **of goal as evidenced by:** Client is able to recognize symptoms of depression and their origins.

Name: <u>Jane Doe</u>　　　　　**OTR**　　　　　SS#: <u>xxx-xx-xxxx</u>

Clinical Summary:

Client has worked as an accountant, and entered treatment because she lost her job as a result of mistakes in client billing. She has never been married and has very little familial or social support in place. Her depression is both acute and chronic. Therefore, she is suffering from dysthymia and an adjustment disorder related to her loss. She also feels humiliated and tends to blame herself for the billing error. However, her self-blame is more global. She has suicidal ideations, but has not developed a plan of action. Although Miss Doe has some savings, her biggest fear is of becoming homeless. The client is highly intelligent and well-educated, and once she works through her depression and anxiety and overcomes her fear of failure, she should be employable.

Clinical Coordination: What arrangements have been made to refer client to psychiatrist or PCP?

Patient was referred to Dr. Mary Smith, MD, for psychiatric evaluation and medication. She has also promised to see her primary care physician within the next month.

Treatment Frequency and Duration

Date first seen:　<u>xx/xx/xxxxx</u>　　Date last seen:　<u>xx/xx/xxxxx</u>
Total number of visits used to date for this course of treatment: <u>Nine (9)</u>
Estimated total visits for entire course of treatment: <u>Twenty (20), 1x/week</u>

Procedure Code

[Note: Some OTRs require CPT codes. For a complete list, see CPT Codes, this chapter.]

What other treatment or community service is the patient receiving?

None ____	Individual ____	Group ____	EAP ____
Medication Management ____	Family ____	AA/NA ____	Structures Program ____
Other ____			

Medical Treatment (Date of last physical examination?)   xx/xx/xxxx

Last date of contact to coordinate treatment: Behavioral: xx/xx/xxxx
                                                  Medical: xx/xx/xxxx
Are other family members in treatment?   Yes ____   No ____
                              With you?   Yes ____   No ____

Treating Provider's Signature: *Dr. James Morton, DSW, CSW*
Date: xx/xx/xxxx

MEDICAL MANAGEMENT-PSYCHIATRIST'S REPORT

[To be completed by psychiatrist and submitted to the insurance company. The referring therapist, if any, should receive a copy.]

Client Information:	Provider Information:
Name: Jane Doe **DOB:** xx-xx-xxxx	**Name:** Dr. Mary Smith, MD
Case #: xxxxxx	**Title:** Psychiatrist
Treatment Start Date: xx/xx/xxxx	**Address:** xxx East xxth
Treatment End Date: xx/xx/xxxx	**State:** New York **Zip:** xxxxx
SS#: xxx-xx-xxxx	**Telephone:** xxx/xxx-xxxx
Employer: ABC Corporation	**Tax ID: SS#** xxx-xx-xxxx

***DSM-IV* Multi-Axial Diagnosis: Based on current symptoms.**

Axis I: 300.4
             309.28
Axis II: V71.09
Axis III: None
Axis IV: Problems with primary support, occupation, economics
Axis V: GAF: Current: <u>55</u>   At treatment start: <u>50</u>   Highest Last Year: <u>?</u>

Current Medication:

Medication	Dosage/Freq.	Start date	Reaction
Celexa	40 mg./once a day	xx/xx/xxxx	Dizziness

Substance Abuse:
Current problem: Yes ____ No ✔ Past Problem: Yes ____ No ____

Clinical Synopsis:
Client entered treatment because she lost her job. She is an accountant and had worked at the same firm since she graduated from college. Client lives alone and has never been married. She feels depressed, anxious, and humiliated. Claims she has probably been depressed most of her life. She has suicidal ideation, but no plan of action. Client has been self-sufficient with practically no familial supports. She is now terrified of becoming homeless.

Name: <u>Jane Doe</u>   **MM-PR**   SS#: <u>xxx-xx-xxxx</u>

However, she is bright and well-educated, and should find other employment when she comes out of this crisis and works through her fear of failure.

Risk:
   Suicidal   ____   Violent ____
   Homicidal ____   Other ____

Safety plan in place? If so, please describe:
Patient has suicidal ideation, and has entered into a "suicide pact" with both her therapist and me. She has agreed to inform either of us, or both, of her intentions before taking action.

Procedure Code
<u>Pharmacological Management CPT 90862</u>   Frequency: <u>1x/month</u>
Start Date: <u>xx/xx/xxxx</u>   End date: <u>xx/xx/xxxx</u>

I certify that personally direct treatment to this client and that the above information is accurate to the best of my knowledge.
Signature: <u>**Dr. Mary Smith**</u>, MD   Date: <u>xx-xx-xxxx</u>

page 2

BILLING

Despite some inroads in electronic billing, notably by Medicare, GHI, and others, the HCFA 1500 (12-90) is now the universal form for billing, and all insurance companies require that it be filled out accurately (see Chapter 27). If not, the form may be discarded. It is rare that an insurance company will return a form to you indicating why it has been rejected. Providers must keep accurate records and be prepared to follow up by telephone or rebilling when not paid within sixty days. Insurance companies frequently misplace claims, pay incorrect feets, and ignore some billed sessions. Benefit statements should be reviewed as they are received and all discrepancies followed up promptly.

CPT CODES

Current procedural terminology (CPT) codes represent the procedures and services performed by providers. The codes for psychiatric treatment procedures include the following:

Description of Services	CPT Code
Initial diagnostic interview	90801
Individual psychotherapy—20–30 minutes	90804
Individual psychotherapy—45–50 minutes	90806
Individual psychotherapy—75–80 minutes	90808
Family psychotherapy—without patient present	90846
Family/conjoint psychotherapy—with patient present	90847
Group psychotherapy (other than multiple family group)	90853
Interactive group psychotherapy	90857
Pharmacological management	90862

HCFA-1500

NONAME INSURANCE CO.   (201) 477-6868
1 MAPLE STREET
HAWTHORNE, NY 07075

HEALTH INSURANCE CLAIM FORM

PICA

PATIENT AND INSURED INFORMATION

1. MEDICARE (Medicare #) MEDICAID (Medicaid #) CHAMPUS (Sponsor's SSN) CHAMPVA (VA File #) GROUP HEALTH PLAN (SSN or ID) FECA BLK LUNG (SSN) OTHER (ID) X

1a. INSURED'S I.D. NUMBER
100010111-002

2. PATIENT'S NAME (Last Name, First Name, Middle Initial)
JONES JESSICA J

3. PATIENT'S BIRTH DATE MM DD YY 01 01 1948 SEX M F

4. INSURED'S NAME (Last Name, First Name, Middle Initial)
JONES JESSICA J

5. PATIENT'S ADDRESS (No., Street)
120 EAST 70TH STREET
CITY NEW YORK STATE NY
ZIP CODE 10022 TELEPHONE (Include Area Code) (212) 8828888

6. PATIENT RELATIONSHIP TO INSURED
Self X Spouse Child Other

7. INSURED'S ADDRESS (No., Street)
SAME
CITY STATE
ZIP CODE TELEPHONE (INCLUDE AREA CODE) (   )

8. PATIENT STATUS
Single Married X Other
Employed X Full-Time Student Part-Time Student

9. OTHER INSURED'S NAME (Last Name, First Name, Middle Initial)

a. OTHER INSURED'S POLICY OR GROUP NUMBER

b. OTHER INSURED'S DATE OF BIRTH MM DD YY SEX M F

c. EMPLOYER'S NAME OR SCHOOL NAME

d. INSURANCE PLAN NAME OR PROGRAM NAME

10. IS PATIENT'S CONDITION RELATED TO:

a. EMPLOYMENT? (CURRENT OR PREVIOUS) YES NO X

b. AUTO ACCIDENT? YES NO X PLACE (State)

c. OTHER ACCIDENT? YES NO X

10d. RESERVED FOR LOCAL USE

11. INSURED'S POLICY GROUP OR FECA NUMBER
17999021C

a. INSURED'S DATE OF BIRTH MM DD YY 02 04 1946 SEX M X F

b. EMPLOYER'S NAME OR SCHOOL NAME
ABC CONSTRUCTION

c. INSURANCE PLAN NAME OR PROGRAM NAME
LIBERTY PLAN

d. IS THERE ANOTHER HEALTH BENEFIT PLAN?
YES NO X   If yes, return to and complete item 9 a-d.

12. PATIENT'S OR AUTHORIZED PERSON'S SIGNATURE I authorize the release of any medical or other information necessary to process this claim. I also request payment of government benefits either to myself or to the party who accepts assignment below.

SIGNED SIGNATURE ON FILE   DATE 07 01 2000

13. INSURED'S OR AUTHORIZED PERSON'S SIGNATURE I authorize payment of medical benefits to the undersigned physician or supplier for services described below.

SIGNED SIGNATURE ON FILE

READ BACK OF FORM BEFORE COMPLETING & SIGNING THIS FORM.

(FOR PROGRAM IN ITEM 1)

SECOND FOLD

SS-AN   NY-SS

PHYSICIAN OR SUPPLIER INFORMATION

14. DATE OF CURRENT: MM | DD | YY — ILLNESS (First symptom) OR INJURY (Accident) OR PREGNANCY (LMP)

15. IF PATIENT HAS HAD SAME OR SIMILAR ILLNESS GIVE FIRST DATE MM | DD | YY

16. DATES PATIENT UNABLE TO WORK IN CURRENT OCCUPATION
FROM MM | DD | YY   TO MM | DD | YY

17. NAME OF REFERRING PHYSICIAN OR OTHER SOURCE

17a. I.D. NUMBER OF REFERRING PHYSICIAN

18. HOSPITALIZATION DATES RELATED TO CURRENT SERVICES
FROM MM | DD | YY   TO MM | DD | YY

19. RESERVED FOR LOCAL USE

20. OUTSIDE LAB? YES NO ☒ $ CHARGES 0 00

21. DIAGNOSIS OR NATURE OF ILLNESS OR INJURY (RELATE ITEMS 1,2,3 OR 4 TO ITEM 24E BY LINE)

1. 300.02   3.
2.   4.

22. MEDICAID RESUBMISSION CODE   ORIGINAL REF. NO.

23. PRIOR AUTHORIZATION NUMBER

24.

A. DATE(S) OF SERVICE From MM DD YY	To MM DD YY	B. Place of Service	C. Type of Service	D. PROCEDURES, SERVICES, OR SUPPLIES (Explain Unusual Circumstances) CPT/HCPCS	MODIFIER	E. DIAGNOSIS CODE	F. $ CHARGES	G. DAY'S OR UNITS	H. EPSDT Family Plan	I. EMG	J. COB	K. RESERVED FOR LOCAL USE
07 01 2000	07 01 2000	11	1	90806	AJ	300 02	100 00	0				
07 08 2000	07 08 2000	11	1	90806	AJ	300 02	100 00	0				
07 15 2000	07 15 2000	11	1	90806	AJ	300 02	100 00	0				
07 22 2000	07 22 2000	11	1	90806	AJ	300 02	100 00	0				
07 29 2000	07 29 2000	11	1	90806	AJ	300 02	100 00	0				

25. FEDERAL TAX I.D. NUMBER 000-00-0000 SSN EIN ☒

26. PATIENT'S ACCOUNT NO. 1234

27. ACCEPT ASSIGNMENT? (For govt. claims see back) YES ☒ NO

28. TOTAL CHARGE $ 500 00

29. AMOUNT PAID $

30. BALANCE DUE $ 500 00

31. SIGNATURE OF PHYSICIAN OR SUPPLIER INCLUDING DEGREES OR CREDENTIALS (I certify that the statements on the reverse apply to this bill and are made a part thereof)

SIGNED Robert Sample, M.D.   DATE 08 27 2000

32. NAME AND ADDRESS OF FACILITY WHERE SERVICES WERE RENDERED (If other than home or office)

33. PHYSICIAN'S, SUPPLIER'S BILLING NAME, ADDRESS, ZIP CODE
PHONE NO.

DR. ROBERT SAMPLE, MD
XXX EAST X STREET
NEW YORK, NY 10021
PIN# 22102   GRP#

PLEASE PRINT OR TYPE

(APPROVED BY AMA COUNCIL ON MEDICAL SERVICE 8/88)

WHCFA-1500-CS-90 (10/93)

FORM HCFA-1500   (12-90)
FORM OWCP-1500
FORM RRB-1500

FIRST FOLD : WHCF 10-F/NV : WHCF 10-E

PSYCHOSOCIAL INTAKE REPORT

[To be completed at intake and retained for the therapist's records]

Date: _____

First name:		Last name:	
Address			
SS#		Birth date:	
Presenting problem:			

Assessment of mental status:			
Affect: (Check)	☐ – Poor	☐ – Okay	☐ – Good
Explain:			
Mood:	☐ – Poor	☐ – Okay	☐ – Good
Explain:			
If suicidal	☐ – With plan		☐ – Ideation
Speech	☐ – Poor	☐ – Okay	☐ – Good
Explain:			
Thought content:	☐ – Poor	☐ – Okay	☐ – Good
Explain:			
Judgment:	☐ – Poor	☐ – Okay	☐ – Good
Explain:			
Insight	☐ – Poor	☐ – Okay	☐ – Good
Explain:			
Concentration:	☐ – Poor	☐ – Okay	☐ – Good
Explain:			
Memory:	☐ – Poor	☐ – Okay	☐ – Good
Explain:			
Relevant medical conditions:			

Provider: Name: _____

Signed: _____ Date:_____

PAYMENT AND SESSION MONITOR*

It is well worth your time and effort to use the Basic Session Monitor for all managed care patients. It is designed to organize all critical information in one place, and advises you when future outpatient treatment reports (OTRs) are due. In addition to client data, it provides space to track client sessions and payments. The form should be started right from the initial telephone referral from an insurance company. It can be entered into your computer or kept in a notebook for manual notation.

The form also provides space to enter the telephone numbers and contacts for the client's insurance company. This eliminates the need to pore through a lengthy provider manual every time you must contact the insurer to confirm coverage, co-pay amounts, and treatment authorizations. It is recommended that the completed form be checked weekly.

Record keeping can be a nightmare, and the requirements are a lot more extensive than many providers realize. However, the more complete your documentation and the more behavioral it is, the better your chances of getting the authorized sessions your client needs.

---

*This section, including the form that follows, is from *The Psychotherapists' Guide to Managed Care in the 21st Century* by S. Tuckfelt, J. Fink, and M. P. Warren. Copyright © 1997 by Jason Aronson Inc., and used with permission.

PAYMENT AND SESSION MONITOR

CLIENT NAME:	PRIMARY INSURANCE CO.:
Address:	Billling Address:
City, State, Zip	City, State, Zip
Tel. Home: Work:	Telephone: Fax:
SS# DOB:	Contact:
Ins. Member #:	Your Provider #:
Date of First Visit:	SECONDARY INSURANCE CO.:
CPT 1st Visit—90801	Billing Address:
90806 Individual; 90847 Couples/Family	City, State, Zip
MANAGED CARE PROTOCOL:	Telephone: Fax:
	Contact:
	Your Provider #:
	PCP:
	Address:
	City, State, Zip
AUTHORIZATIONS:	Telephone: Fax:
No. # of Visits Date:	PSYCHIATRIST:
	Address:
	City, State, Zip
	Telephone: Fax:

PAYMENT AND SESSION MONITOR—*continued*

OTR Alert	Auth. Start #	Auth. End	Visit #	Date Of Visit	Date OTR Filed	Ins. Amt.	Date Paid	Co-Pay Amt.	Date Paid:	Ins. Bal.	Pt. Bal.
			1								
			2								
			3								
			4								
			5								
			6								
			7								
			8								
			9								
			10								
			11								
			12								
			13								
			14								
			15								

PROGRESS NOTES

These guidelines for progress notes have been recommended by the National Committee on Quality Assurance (NCQA), and are required by many insurance companies, including Magellan.

Progress notes must be kept for each session. The notes must include the name of the client, the date, a summary of what transpired in the session, including your intervention, and an evaluation of progress toward a treatment goal. The progress notes for each session must be signed by the provider. Dictated notes are considered preliminary until the transcription is reviewed and signed.

PROGRESS NOTES

Client:	Date:
Address:	Insurance co.
City, State, Zip	
SS#	ID#

Session summary:

Intervention

Evaluation of Progress

Provider: _____   Date: _____

Signed: _____

DISCHARGE SUMMARY

Some, but not all, insurance companies require a discharge summary. Since many companies are tracking your success rate and duration of treatment, it is a good idea to submit a discharge summary even if you suspect the client may return to treatment and you have authorized sessions left. You can always open the case again.

DISCHARGE SUMMARY

CLIENT:	DATE:
SS#:	INSURER:
DATE OF FINAL VISIT:	
REASONS FOR DISCHARGE: (Check)	
☐ Treatment Objective Achieved	☐ Client Relocated
☐ Treatment Regarded as Ineffectual by Therapist	☐ Referred to New Therapist
☐ Treatment Regarded as Ineffectual by Client	☐ Quit Treatment
☐ Substantial Progress Made and Client Satisfied	Other:
☐ Client No Longer Eligible for Service	
Describe Situation at Discharge:	
Diagnosis at Discharge:	
Axis 1:	
Axis 2:	
Axis 3:	
Axis 4:	
Axis 5:	
GAF (at Discharge):	
GAF (at Start of Treatment):	
Client Attitude Toward Treatment:	
☐ Well Motivated ☐ Somewhat Motivated ☐ Unmotivated ☐ Uncooperative	
Prognosis:	

Provider: _____ Date: _____

Signature: _____

28

State Insurance Departments

Alabama	201 Monroe Street (Suite 1700) Montgomery, AL 36104 334/269-3550; Fax: 241-4192
Alaska	3601 C Street (Suite 1324) Anchorage, AK 99503-5948 907/269-7912; Fax: 269-7900
American Samoa	American Samoa Government Pago Pago, American Samoa 96799 011-684/633-4116; Fax: 633-2269
Arizona	2910 North 44th Street (Suite 210) Phoenix, AZ 85018-7256 602/912-8400; Fax: 912-8452
Arkansas	1200 West Third Street Little Rock, AR 72201-1904 501/371-2600; Fax: 371-2629

California

300 Capitol Mall (Suite 1500)
Sacramento, CA 95814
916/492-3500; Fax: 445-5280

445 Fremont Street (23rd Floor)
San Francisco, CA 94102
415/538-4040; Fax: 904-5889

300 South Spring Street
Los Angeles, CA 90013
213/346-6400; Fax: 897-6771

Colorado

1560 Broadway (Suite 850)
Denver, CO 80202
303/894-7499; Fax 894-7455

Connecticut

PO Box 816
Hartford, CT 06142-0816
860/297-3800; Fax: 566-7410

Delaware

841 Silver Lake Boulevard
Dover, DE 19904
300/739-4251; Fax: 739-5280

District of Columbia

810 First Street, NE (Suite 701)
Washington, DC 20002
202/727-8000; Fax: 535-1196

Florida

State Capital—Plaza Level Eleven
Tallahassee, FL 32399-0300
850/922-3101; Fax: 488-3334

Georgia

2 Martin Luther King Jr. Drive
Floyd Memorial Building
Atlanta, GA 30334
404/656-2056; Fax: 657-7493

Guam	Building 113-3, First Floor Mariner Avenue Tiyan Barrigada, Guam 96913 671/475-1843; Fax: 472-2643
Hawaii	250 South King Street, Fifth Floor Honolulu, Hawaii 96813 808/586-2790; Fax: 586-2806
Idaho	700 West State Street, Third Floor Boise, ID 83720-0043 208/334-4250; Fax: 334-4398
Illinois	320 West Washington Street, Fourth Floor Springfield, IL 62767-0001 217/785-0116; Fax: 524-6500 100 West Randolph Street (Suite 15-100) Chicago, IL 60601-3251 312/814-2420; Fax: 814-5435
Indiana	311 West Washington Street (Suite 300) Indianapolis, IN 46204-2787 317/232-2385; Fax: 232-5251
Iowa	330 East Maple Street Des Moines, IA 50319 515/281-5705; Fax: 281-3059
Kansas	420 S.W. Ninth Street Topeka, KS 66612-1678 785/296-7801; Fax: 296-2283
Kentucky	PO Box 517 215 West Main Street Frankfort, KY 40602-0517 502/564-6027; Fax: 564-1453

Louisiana   950 North Fifth Street
                          Baton Rouge, LA 70802
                          225/342-5423; Fax: 342-8622

Maine   State Office Building, Station 34
                          Augusta, ME 04333-0034
                          207/624-8745; Fax: 924-8599

Maryland   525 St. Paul Place
                          Baltimore, MD 21202-2272
                          410/468-2090; Fax: 468-2020

Massachusetts   One South Station, 4th Floor
                          Boston, MA 02110
                          617/621-7301; Fax: 521-7758

Michigan   611 West Ottawa Street, 2nd Floor North
                          Lansing, MI 48933-1020
                          517/373-9273; Fax: 335-4978

Minnesota   121 Seventh Place East (Suite 200)
                          St. Paul, MN 55101-2145
                          651/296-6025; Fax: 282-2568

Mississippi   1804 Walter Sillers
                          550 High Street
                          Jackson, MS 39201
                          601/359-3569; Fax: 359-2474

Missouri   301 West High Street (6 North)
                          Jefferson City, MO 65102-0690
                          573/751-4126; Fax: 751-1165

Montana   840 Helena Avenue
                          Helena, MT 59601
                          406/444-2040; Fax: 444-3497

Nebraska	Terminal Building (Suite 40) 941 'O' Street Lincoln, NE 68508 702/471-2201; Fax: 471-4610
Nevada	788 Fairview Drive Carson City, NV 89701-5753 775/687-4270; Fax: 687-3937
New Hampshire	56 Old Suncook Road Concord, NH 03301 603/271-2261; Fax: 271-1406
New Jersey	20 West State Street (CN325) Trenton, NJ 08625 609/292-5360; Fax: 984-5273
New Mexico	PO Drawer 1269 Santa Fe, NM 87504-1269 505/827-4601; Fax: 476-0326
New York	25 Beaver Street New York, NY 10004-2319 212/480-2289; Fax: 480-2310 Agency Building One Empire State Plaza Albany, NY 12257 518/474-6600; Fax: 473-6814
North Carolina	PO Box 26387 Raleigh, NC 27611 919/733-3058; Fax: 733-6495
North Dakota	600 East Boulevard Bismarck, ND 58505-0320 701/328-2240; Fax: 328-4880

Ohio	2100 Stella Court Columbus, OH 43215-1067 614/644-2658; Fax: 644-3743
Oklahoma	2401 N.W. 23rd Street (Suite 28) Oklahoma City, OK 73107 405/521-2828; Fax: 521-6635
Oregon	350 Winter Street N.E. (Room 200) Salem, OR 97310-0700 503/947-7980;Fax: 378-4351
Pennsylvania	1326 Strawberry Square (13th Floor) Harrisburg, PA 17120 717/783-0442; Fax: 772-1969
Puerto Rico	Cohan's Plaza Building 1607 Ponce de Leon Avenue Santurce, Puerto Rico 00909 787/722-8686; Fax: 722-4400
Rhode Island	233 Richmond Street (Suite 233) Providence, RI 02903-4233 401/222-2223; Fax: 222-5475
South Carolina	1612 Marion Street Columbia, SC 29201 803/737-6100; Fax: 727-6229
South Dakota	118 West Capitol Avenue Pierre, SD 57501-2000 605/773-3536; Fax: 773-5369
Tennessee	500 James Robertson Parkway Nashville, TN 37243-0565 615/741-2241; Fax: 532-6934

Texas	333 Guadalupe Street Austin, TX 78701 512/463-6464; Fax: 475-2005
Utah	3110 State Office Building Salt Lake City, UT 84114-1201 801/538-3800; Fax: 538-3829
Vermont	89 Main Street, Drawer 20 Montpelier, VT 05620-3101 802/828-3301; Fax: 828-3306
Virgin Islands	18 Konders Gade, Charlotte Amalie St. Thomas, Virgin Islands 00/802 340/773-6449; Fax: 773-4052
Virginia	PO Box 1157 Richmond, VA 23218 804/371-9694; Fax: 371-9873
Washington	PO Box 40255 Olympia, WA 98504-0255 360/753-7301; Fax: 586-3535
West Virginia	PO Box 50540 Charleston, WV 25305-2540 304/558-3354; Fax: 558-0412
Wisconsin	121 East Wilson Madison, WI 53702 208/267-1233; Fax: 267-8570
Wyoming	122 West 25th Street (Third Floor East) Cheyenne, WY 82002-0440 307/777-7401

29

Glossary of Managed-Care Terms

Allowable: A fee decided by the third-party payer that the provider is paid or allowed to charge. It's usually lower than the therapist's normal fee.

Appeal: A request to an insurance company for reconsideration of sessions that have been denied as unauthorized. It may be written or oral, depending on the requirements of a particular insurance company. Many companies have multiple levels of appeal from telephone review to consideration by an external committee of experts.

Assignment: The client designates or assigns the third-party payer or insurance company to pay the therapist or provider directly.

Authorization: The process by which insurance companies approve a number of therapeutic sessions within a specific amount of time based on medical necessity. Precertification is usually required before the first session.

Biofeedback: A technique similar to hypnosis in which monitoring equipment is used to teach clients relaxation control. The monitor can display whether the client is in a trance state and how deep.

Capitation: A system developed by insurance companies to pay a group or organization of providers a set fee over time to provide services to a designated population. The population is usually confined to a state, city, or community. In practice, the capitation company is responsible for treatment decisions. The system has been criticized as creating a conflict of interest for capitation providers since the more treatment is denied or withheld, the higher the profits.

Case manager: A clinician who monitors client sessions for medical necessity at the least intensive level that is appropriate.

Certification: The number of treatment sessions approved by an insurance company as medically necessary.

Coding: Communications short-hand used by insurance companies and providers to describe the diagnosis (*DSM-IV*) and services performed in Current Procedural Terminology (CPT).

Cognitive behavioral therapy: Systematic use of behavioral strategies to help clients gain mastery over unwanted behaviors. Procedures include (1) identification of dysfunctional or distorted cognitions and the realization that they result in negative feelings and behaviors; (2) self-monitoring of negative thoughts (self-talk); (3) identification of the relationship of thoughts to underlying beliefs and feelings; (4) identification of alternative thinking patterns based on reality; and (5) hypothesis testing of the validity of the client's basic assumptions about self, the world, and the future.

Concurrent review: The process of assessing justification of treatment authorizations from initial session to discharge. The review focuses on appropriateness of treatment, measurable goals, and progress toward termination.

Consent form: A standard form signed by a client authorizing the provider to release confidential information about the client to his/her insurance company.

Coordination of benefits: A procedure of coordinating payments by more than one insurance company to assure that no more than 100 percent of costs are reimbursed to the client or paid to the provider. When two insurance companies are involved, the primary plan pays a portion of the allowable amount, and an explanation of benefits from the primary plan is then sent to the secondary insurance company which may pay some of the remaining portion of the allowable amount.

Copayment: The portion of the total fee for which an insured client is responsible. The amount is usually fixed by the insurance company.

Current Procedural Terminology (CPT): A systematic listing of coded procedures and services performed. The codes are changed periodically. The CPT codes in year 2000 for psychotherapy include:

Individual psychotherapy, 90806
With medical management, 90807
Families couples, 90846, 90847
Group psychotherapy, 90849
Pharmacological management, 90802
Biofeedback training, 96100
Electroconvulsive therapy, 90870

Deductible: The amount payable by the client before insurance benefits become payable.

Diagnosis: The *Diagnostic and Statistical Manual of Mental Disorders,* fourth edition (*DSM-IV*), and the *International Classification of Diseases,* ninth revision (*ICD-9*), provide classification codes of clients' conditions.

Drug utilization review: The goal of this insurance company review is to reduce the cost of drug therapy by substituting generic drugs for name brands or using a formulary to limit drugs physicians are permitted to prescribe. Since some drug companies own or are owned by insurance companies, use of a formulary has been criticized as a possible conflict of interest.

Dual diagnosis: Comorbid Axis I mental disorders.

Emergency: A medical or behavioral condition that is sudden and severe, and places the client's life or health in jeopardy.

Employment Retirement Income Security Act (ERISA): Regulates employee benefit plans, including health insurance. ERISA regulations supersede state regulations.

Explanation of Benefits (EOB): A statement that accompanies insurance company payment and describes the session dates and amounts per session covered by the enclosed check.

Fee for service: Payment on a session-by-session basis.

Focal therapy: A treatment modality focused on restoring a client to his/her level of functioning prior to onset of an acute or chronic disorder. Focal therapy uses a brief intervention designed to bring about a specific outcome. It structures the treatment by asking "Why now?" which reveals the client's expectations and develops an alliance toward change. Much of the work is performed outside the therapy sessions as homework assignments. Focal therapy and "Why now?" are service marks of Merit Behavioral Care.

Formulary: A list of select medications and approved dosages. In some managed care plans, providers can prescribe only from the formulary.

Gatekeeper: A clinician or case manager who controls access to health care services to keep costs in check.

Global assessment of functioning (GAF): A scale that indicates the overall functioning of a client on Axis V of the *DSM-IV* multiaxial assessment system.

Grievance: A formal complaint to an insurance company by either a client or provider regarding dissatisfaction with access to, administration of, or reimbursement for services.

Group practice: A number of providers who come together as a single practice and bill insurance companies under a single tax identification number.

Health Care Financing Administration (HCFA): Overseer of Medicare and Medicaid, which thus has a major impact on health insurance policies and procedures. The HCFA-1500 is the standard form for submission of claims to insurance companies.

Health Maintenance Organization (HMO): Provider of health care services to enrolled members, usually using primary care physicians as gatekeepers to keep costs down.

Hypnosis: An induced altered state of consciousness or trance state in which the individual is more susceptible to suggestion. People are imprinted with mind sets that originate in their families of origin and are incorporated into the unconscious. People organize their personalities and act around these imprints. We don't operate directly on the world, but through a map or model of the world, a created representation of what we believe. In hypnosis, the therapist aims at changing or otherwise influencing the maps we hold in our minds.

Hypnosis can be a highly effective therapeutic tool. When the clients have slipped into trance after induced relaxation, they may be instructed to imagine themselves the way they would like to be. For example, in hypnosis, smokers may be asked to imagine themselves as nonsmokers and through visualization begin to change their belief systems.

Hypnosis appears to work well with the cognitive-behavioral modality. However, insurance company reaction to the technique is mixed. Although many companies find it an acceptable psychotherapeutic technique, some prefer to call it a relaxation technique rather than hypnosis. It is best to find out where the insurance company stands on the issue.

Impairments: Objective, observable reasons why a client seeks treatment. Impairments are not the disorder, but rather behavioral expressions of *DSM-IV* codes.

Individual practice association (IPA): An HMO that provides services through an association of self-employed providers in their own offices under a contract negotiated with the group.

Individual practitioner: An individual clinician who provides behavioral case services to managed care companies. These clinicians must meet specific insurance company credentialing criteria.

Inpatient treatment: A program that provides 24-hour care, usually in a hospital or similar health care facility, with multiple treatment disciplines licensed by the Joint Commission on Accreditation of Healthcare Organizations (JCAHO).

Intensive outpatient care: A structured treatment program outside of a health care facility consisting of multiple sessions accessing various treatment modalities.

Joint Commission on Accreditation of Healthcare Organizations (JCAHO): An accrediting organization for health care companies.

Level of care: Specific structural and staffing components that support the designated level of treatment required. Level of care may evolve during an episode of treatment.

Managed behavioral health organization (MBHO): Manager of benefits under a special arrangement with a managed behavioral health program. This may include everything from provision of services to organizing a provider network.

Managed health care: A system created to control health care costs. It uses management techniques and financial incentives to direct clients to providers who will provide appropriate care in the most cost-effective manner.

Medical necessity: The criterion used by insurance carriers to approve treatment services. Medical necessity may vary from company to company.

Member: A subscriber, or eligible dependent, who participates in an insurance plan.

National Committee for Quality Assurance (NCQA): An accrediting agency for managed behavioral health care or HMOs that sets standards and reviews and reports on performance.

Peer review: Evaluation by a therapist of the quality of care given. Also used to determine the number of treatment sessions required before termination.

Place of Service Code: Standardized codes used by providers to report the location where the billed services were performed.

Point of service (POS): A benefit plan in which the subscriber can elect to use a nonparticipating provider usually at a level of reduced coverage and higher out-of-pocket costs.

Practice guidelines: Standardized clinical specifications for specific *DSM-IV* diagnoses to assist provider and client make appropriate health care decisions.

Precertification: Treatment approval by insurance company following review to determine medical necessity.

Preferred provider organization (PPO): A group of practitioners who contract with a health care payer to provide services at competitive rates.

Primary care physician (PCP): A doctor who assumes responsibility for the fundamental care of a patient. A PCP provides patient referrals to medical specialists as required.

Primary insurance: An insurance company that provides reimbursement of medical costs regardless of any other insurance coverage.

Problem-focused: A treatment modality, usually limited to one to ten sessions, that has a high probability of solving a concrete problem in daily living. This approach is typically educative and identifies and directs the client to use available resources.

Psychoanalysis: Treatment modality that analyzes past and present emotional experiences to determine sources of pathology and reduce unconscious conflicts by making clients aware of their existence and origins. This modality is not usually acceptable to insurance companies, who regard it as unfocused, lengthy, and costly compared to behavioral modalities.

Psychodynamic: Aspect of psychoanalytic theory that explains thoughts, feelings, and behaviors as the result of opposing goal-directed or motivational forces.

Quality management: A program designed by the insurance company to provide systematic quality control and risk management.

Rehabilitation Accreditation Commission (CARF): An accreditation authority for the disabled that accredits programs and services, not organizations.

Relaxation technique: A treatment technique used in hypnosis in which clients are taught how to progressively relax their muscles and thus calm themselves. Breathing and pulse slow down and blood pressure is lowered. Relaxation itself is thought to be healing. When completely relaxed, it is impossible to feel negative emotions (*see* Hypnosis).

Site visits: As part of the insurance companies' agreement with NCQA, they conduct site visits to provider offices to review treatment records and have developed criteria as part of the credentialing and recredentialing processes.

Symptom-focused: Treatment modality, usually brief, that targets maladaptive thoughts and feelings and interpersonal problems. Interventions are focused on the symptom or problem that has caused a decline in the client's level of functioning.

Utilization Management (UM): Process of determining and evaluating treatment. UM oversees preauthorization reviews and discharge planning.

Visualization: Use of creative imagery for the purpose of change. Through visualization, clients are taught how to cancel out negative thinking and acting. Used in hypnosis.

30

Resources for Providers

BOOKS

Antisocial Behavior

Black, D. W., and Larson, C. H. (1999). *Bad Boys, Bad Men: Confronting Antisocial Personality Disorder*. New York: Oxford University Press.

Anxiety

American Psychiatric Association. (1998). *Practice Guidelines for the Treatment of Patients with Panic Disorders*. Washington, DC: APA.

Barlow, D. H. (2000). *Anxiety and Its Disorders: The Nature and Treatment of Anxiety and Panic*. San Antonio: Harcourt Brace. (Therapist version.)

Barlow, D. H., and Cerny, J. (2000). *Psychiatric Treatment of Panic*. New York: Guilford.

Craske, M. G., and Barlow, D. H. (2000). *Mastery of Your Anxiety and Panic*, 3rd ed. San Antonio: Harcourt Brace. (Therapist version.)

Davis, M. (1995). *The Leader's Guide to the Relaxation and Stress Reduction Workbook.* Oakland, CA: New Harbinger. (Therapist's guide that accompanies the client workbook.)

Attention Deficit Disorder

Wren, C. (2000). *Hanging by a Twig: Understanding and Counseling Adults with Learning Disorders and ADD.* New York: Norton.

Bereavement

C., Roy. (2000). *Obsessive-Compulsive Disorder.* Center City, MN: Hazelden. (A survival guide for the client's family and friends.)

Jozefowski, J. T. (1999). *The Phoenix Phenomenon: Rising from the Ashes of Grief.* Northvale, NJ: Jason Aronson.

Sanders, C. M. (1998). *Grief: The Mourning After: Dealing with Adult Bereavement.* New York: Wiley.

Walsh, F., and McGoldrick, M. eds. (1995). *Living Beyond the Losses: Death in the Family.* New York: Norton.

Bipolar

American Psychiatric Association. (1990). *American Psychiatric Association Practice Guidelines for the Treatment of Patients with Bipolar Disorder.* Washington, DC: APA.

Goldberg, G. F., and Harrow, M., eds. (1999). *Bipolar Disorders: Clinical Course and Outcomes.* Washington, DC: American Psychiatric Press.

Depression

American Psychiatric Association. (1993). *American Psychiatric Association Practice Guidelines for Depressive Disorders in Adults.* Washington, DC: American Psychiatric Press.

Beck, A. T., Rush, A. J., and Emery, G. (1979). *Cognitive Therapy of Depression.* New York: Guilford.

Blackburn, M., and Davidson, K. M. (1995). *Cognitive Therapy for Depression and Anxiety.* Washington, DC: American Psychiatric Press.

Klerman, G. L, Weissman, M. M., Rounsaville, B. J., and Chevron, E. (1984). *Interpersonal Psychotherapy of Depression.* San Antonio: Harcourt Brace. (Therapist version.)

Klosko, J. S., and Sanderson, W. C. (1999). *Cognitive-Behavioral Treatment of Depression.* Northvale, NJ: Jason Aronson.

Dissociative Disorders

Braun, B. G., ed. (1985). *Treatment of Multiple Personality Disorders.* Washington, DC: American Psychiatric Press.

Brenner, J. D., and Marmar, C. R. (1985). *Trauma, Memory and Dissociation.* Washington, DC: American Psychiatric Press.

DSM-IV–Related

American Psychiatric Association. (1994). *Diagnostic and Statistical Manual of Mental Disorders,* 4th ed. Washington, DC: APA.

Cole, C. J. (1998). *Practical Guide to DSM-IV Diagnosis and Treatment,* 2nd ed. Huntington Beach, CA: Cole.

La Bruzza, A. L., with Mendez-Villarrubia, J. M. (1999). *Using DSM-IV.* Northvale, NJ: Jason Aronson.

Munson, C. E. (2000). *The Mental Health Diagnostic Desk Reference: Visual Guides and More for Learning to Use the Diagnostic and Statistical Manual.* Binghamton, NY: Hawthorn.

Eating Disorders

Agras, W. S., and Apple, R. F. (1997). *Overcoming Eating Disorders: A Cognitive-Behavioral Treatment for Bulimia Nervosa and Binge-Eating Disorder.* San Antonio: Psychological Corp. (Therapist version.)

American Psychiatric Association. (1993). *American Association Practice Guidelines for Eating Disorders.* Washington, DC: American Psychiatric Press.

Levenkron, S. (2000). *Anatomy of Anorexia.* New York: Norton.

Wilson, C. P., ed. (1987). *Fear of Being Fat: The Treatment of Anorexia Nervosa and Bulimia.* Northvale, NJ: Jason Aronson.

Factitious Disorders

Feldman, M. D., and Eisendrath, S. J. (1996). *The Spectrum of Factitious Disorders*. Washington, DC: Psychiatric Press.

Gambling

Horvath, A. T. (1998). *Sex, Drugs, Gambling and Chocolate*. Atascadero, CA: Impact.

McCown, W. G., and Chomberlain, L. L. (2000). *Best Possible Odds: Contemporary Treatment Strategies for Gambling Disorders*. New York: Wiley.

Genograms

McGoldrick, M., Gerson, R., and Shellenberger, S. (1999). *Genograms: Assessments and Interventions*. New York: Norton.

Homework

Hecker, L. L., Deacon, S. A., et al. (1998). *The Therapist's Notebook*. New York: Haworth.

Korb-Khalsa, K. L., Azok, S. D., and Leutenberg, E. A. *Life Management Skills Series* (reproducible handouts). Beachwood, OH: Wellness.

LM-1 (1993): Assertion, discharge planning, emotion identification, exercise, goal-setting, leisure, motivation, nutrition, problem-solving, risk-taking, role-satisfaction, self-awareness, self-esteem, sleep, stress management support systems, time management, values classification.

LM-2 (1993): Activities of daily living, anger management, assertion, communication—verbal, communication—nonverbal, coping skills, grief/loss, humor, life balance, money management, parenting, reminiscence safety issues, self-esteem image, steps to recovery, stress management, support systems, time management.

LM-3 (1994): Aging, body image, communication, conflict resolution, coping skills, creative expression, feedback, healthy living, job readiness, nurturance, relapse prevention, relationships, roles, self-awareness, self-empowerment, self-esteem, social skills, stress management.

LM-4 (1996): Activities of daily living, combating stigma, communication, coping with serious mental illness, home management, humor, job readiness, journalizing, leisure, parenting, relationships, responsibility, self-esteem, sexual health, social skills, stress management, suicide issues, values.

LKM-5 (1999): Abuse, aging, coping skills, grief, interpersonal skills, leisure, making changes, medication management, parenting, positive, recovery, relationships, self-esteem, self expression, supports supplement: confiding in someone, groups, keep on growing, lightening up, mood swing, pick and choose our battle, recovery, stressed to deserts backwards, wellness in bloom.

Schultheis, G. M., O'Hanlon, B., and O'Hanlon, S. (1999). *Brief Couples Therapy Homework Planner*. New York: Wiley.

Hypnosis, Relaxation, Visualizations, and Biofeedback Techniques

Davis, M. (1995). *Relaxation/Stress Leaders Guide*. Oakland CA: New Harbinger.

Dowd, E. T. (2000). *Cognitive Hypnotherapy*. Northvale, NJ: Jason Aronson.

Epstein, G. (1989). *Healing Visualizations: Creating Health through Imagery*. New York: Bantam.

Fanning, P. (1988). *Visualization for Change*. Oakland, CA: New Harbinger.

Fisher, S. (1991). *Discovering the Power of Self Hypnosis. A New Approach for Enabling Change and Promoting Healing*. New York: HarperCollins.

Fuller, G. D. (1984). *Clinical Biofeedback Methods*. San Francisco: Institute of San Francisco.

Gafner, G., and Benson, S. (2000). *Handbook of Hypnotic Inductions*. New York: Norton.

Garvain, S. (1982). *Creative Visualization*. New York: Bantam.

Haley, J., and Stoudacher, C. (1989). *Hypnosis for Change. A Practical Manual of Proven Hypnotic Techniques*. Oakland, CA: New Harbinger.

Hammond, D. C., ed. (1990). *Handbook of Hypnotic Suggestion and Metaphors*. New York: Norton.

Udolf, R. (1992). *Handbook of Hypnosis for Professionals*. Northvale, NJ: Jason Aronson.

Internet-Related

Fink, J. (1999). *How to Use Computers and Cyberspace in the Clinical Practice of Psychotherapy*. Northvale, NJ: Jason Aronson.

Managed Care

Berghuis, D. J., and Jongsma, A. E., Jr. (2000). *The Severe and Persistent Mental Illness Treatment Planner*. New York: Wiley.

Bjorck, J. P., Brown, J. A., and Goodman, M. (2000). *Casebook for Managing Managed Care: A Self-Study Guide for Treatment Planning, Documentation and Communication*. Washington, DC: American Psychiatric Press.

Blount, L., Mendoza, E. M., Udell, C. J., and Walters, J. M. (1998). *Mastering the Reimbursement Process*, 2nd ed. Chicago, IL: American Medical Association.

Dattilio, F. M., and Jongsma, A. E., Jr. (2000). *The Family Therapy Treatment Planner*. New York: Wiley.

Frager, S. (2000). *Managing Managed Care; Secrets from a Former Case Manager*. New York: Wiley.

Frazer, D. W., and Jongsma, A. E., Jr. (1998). *The Older Adult Psychotherapy Treatment Planner*. New York: Wiley.

Goodman, M., Brown, J. A., and Dietz, P. M. (1996). *Managing Managed Care II: A Handbook for Mental Health*, 2nd ed. Washington, DC: American Psychiatric Press.

Jongsma, A. E., Jr. (2000). *The Child and Adolescent Psychotherapy Treatment Planner*. New York: Wiley.

———. (2000). *The Adult Psychotherapy Progress Notes Planner*. New York: Wiley.

———. (1998). *The Couples Therapy Treatment Planner*. New York: Wiley.

———. (1998). *The Older Adult Psychotherapy Treatment Planner*. New York: Wiley.

Jongsma, A. E., Jr., and Perkinson, L. M. (1999). *The Complete Adult Psychotherapy Treatment Planner*, 2nd ed. New York: Wiley.

O'Leary, K. D., Heymon, R. E., and Jongsma, A. E., Jr. (1998). *The Couples Therapy Treatment Planner*. New York: Wiley.

Perkinson, R. R., and Jongsma, A. E., Jr. (1997). *The Chemical Dependence Treatment Planner*. New York: Wiley.

Wiger, D. (1999). *The Clinical Documentation Sourcebook*, 2nd ed. New York: Wiley.

————. (1999). *The Psychotherapy Documentation Primer*. New York: Wiley.

Medical Issues

Derogatis, L. R., and Wise, T. N. (1989). *Anxiety and Depression in the Medical Patient*. Washington, DC: American Psychiatric Press.

France, R. D., and Krishnan, R. R. (1988). *Chronic Pain*. Washington, DC: American Psychiatric Press.

Hodges, M., and Moorey, S. (1993). *Psychological Treatment in Disease*. Washington, DC: American Psychiatric Press.

Keller, P. (1991). *Psychosomatic Syndromes and Somatic Symptoms*. Washington, DC: American Psychiatric Press.

Maximin, A., and Stevic-Rust, L. (2000). *Treating Depression in the Medically Ill*. Oakland, CA: New Harbinger.

Obsessions and Phobias

Benson, A. L., ed. (2000). *I Shop, Therefore I Am: Compulsive Buying and the Search for Self*. Northvale, NJ: Jason Aronson.

Browning, C. H., and Browning, B. J. (1994). *How to Partner with Managed Care*. Los Alamitos, CA: Duncliff International.

Bruce, J., and Sanderson, W. C. (1998). *Specific Phobias: Clinical Applications of Evidence-Based Psychotherapy*. Northvale, NJ: Jason Aronson.

Craske, M. G., and Antony, M. M. (1997). *Mastering Your Specific Phobia*. San Antonio, TX: Harcourt Brace. (Therapist version.)

Hope, D. A., Heimberg, R. G., Jusher, H. R., and Turk, C. L. (2000). *Managing Social Anxiety: A Cognitive-Behavioral Therapy Approach*. San Antonio, TX: Harcourt Brace. (Therapist version.)

McGinn, L. K., and Sanderson, W. C. (1999). *Treatment of Obsessive Compulsive Disorder*. Northvale, NJ: Jason Aronson.

Rapee, R. M. (1999). *Overcoming Shyness: A Step by Step Guide*. Northvale, NJ: Jason Aronson.

Rapee, R. M., and Sanderson, W. C. (1998). *Social Phobia: Clinical Application of Evidence-Based Psychotherapy*. Northvale, NJ: Jason Aronson.

Personality Disorders

Beck, A. T., and Freeman, A. (1990). *Cognitive Therapy of Personality Disorders*. New York, NY: Guilford.

Cloninger, C. R., ed. (1999). *Personality and Psychopathology*. Washington, DC: American Psychiatric Press.

Linehan, M. M. (1996). *Cognitive Behavior Treatment of Borderline Personality Disorders*. New York: Guilford.

Masterson, J. F. (1988). *The Search for the Real Self: Unmasking the Personality Disorder of Our Age*. New York: Free Press.

Preston, J. (1999). *Shorter Term Treatments for Borderline Personality Disorders*. Oakland, CA: New Harbinger.

Ronington, E., ed. (1997). *Disorders of Narcissism: Diagnostic, Clinical, and Empirical Implications*. Washington, DC: American Psychiatric Press.

Pharmacology

Good, D. E., Crawford, A. L., and Jongsma, A. E., Jr. (1999). *Behavioral Meds*. New York: Wiley.

Konopasek, D. E. (2000). *Medication "Fact Sheet" in a Medication Reference Guide for the Non-Medical Professional*. Anchorage, AK: Arctic Tern Publishing.

Preston, J. D., O'Neal, J. H., and Talga, M. C. (1999). *Handbook of Clinical Psychopharmacology for Therapists*. Northvale, NJ: Jason Aronson.

Posttraumatic Stress Disorder

Allen, G. G. (1999). *Coping With Trauma*. Washington, DC: American Psychiatric Press.

Brenner, J. D., and Marmar, C. R. (1998). *Post Traumatic Stress Disorder: DSM-IV and Beyond*. Washington, DC: American Psychiatric Press.

Davidson, J. R. T., and Foa, E. B. (1992). *Trauma, Memory and Dissociation*. Washington, DC: American Psychiatric Press.

Psychosis

American Psychiatric Association. (1997). *American Psychiatric Association Practice Guidelines for the Treatment of Patients with Schizophrenia*. Washington, DC: American Psychiatric Press.

American Psychiatric Press. (1998). *American Association Practice Guidelines for the Treatment of Patients with Delirium*. Washington, DC: American Psychiatric Press.

Bellach, A. S., Mueser, K., Gingrich, S., and Agreata, K. (1997). *Social Skills Training for Schizophrenia: A Step-by-Step Guide*. New York: Guilford.

Benveniste, D. (1996). *Diagnosis and Treatment of Sociopaths and Clients with Sociopathic Traits*. Oakland, CA: New Harbinger.

Bishee, C. C. (1999). *Educating Patients and Families about Mental Illness*. Birmingham, AL: Partnership for Recovery.

Jonston, B. (1999). *Enhancing Recovery from Psychosis: A Practical Guide*. Woodsville, South Australia: North Western Adelaide Mental Health Service.

Mueser, K., and Glynn, S. M. (1999). *Behavioral Family Therapy for Psychiatric Disorders*. Oakland, CA: New Harbinger.

Preston, J. D. (1997). *Shorter Term Treatments for Borderline Personality Disorders*. Oakland, CA: New Harbinger.

Wurmser, L. (2000). *The Power of the Inner Judge: Psychodynamic Treatment of the Severe Neuroses*. Northvale, NJ: Jason Aronson.

Relational Problems/Parent–Child, Partner

Donovan, J. M. (2000). *Short-Term Couple Therapy*. New York: Guilford.

Everett, C. A., and Everett, S. V. (1999). *Family Therapy for ADHD: Treating Children, Adolescents and Adults*. New York: Guilford.

Gottman, J. M. (1999). *The Marriage Clinic*. New York: Norton.

Guerin, P. J. (1976). *Family Therapy: Theory and Practice*. New York: Gardner.

McCormack, C. C. (2000). *Treating Borderline States in Marriage: Dealing with Oppositionalism, Ruthless Aggression and Severe Resistance*. Northvale, NJ: Jason Aronson.

Papp, P., ed. (2000). *Couples and the Fault Line*. New York: Guilford.

Rathus, J. H., and Sanderson, W. C. (1998). *Marital Discord: Clinical Applications of Evidence-Based Psychotherapy*. Northvale, NJ: Jason Aronson.

———. (1999). *Marital Distress: Cognitive Behavioral Interventions for Couples*. Northvale, NJ: Jason Aronson.

Satir, V. (1997). *Conjoint Family Therapy*. Palo Alto, CA: Science & Behavior.

———. (1998). *The New Peoplemaking*. Mountainview, CA: Science & Behavior.

Sharpe, S. A. (2000). *The Ways We Love: A Developmental Approach to Treating Couples.* New York: Guilford.

Siskind, D. (1997). *Working with Parents: Establishing the Essential Alliance in Child Psychotherapy and Consultation.* Northvale, NJ: Jason Aronson.

Wexiler, D. B. (2000). *Domestic Violence 2000.* New York: Norton.

Self-Help

Donovan, K. (1994). *The Self-Help Directory: A Sourcebook for Self-Help in the US and Canada.* Denville, NJ: American Self-Help Clearinghouse.

White, B. J., and Mandara, E. J., eds. (1998). *The Self-Help Sourcebook: Your Guide to Community and Online Support Groups,* 6th ed. Denville, NJ: Self-Help Clearinghouse.

Sexuality

Carnes, P. (1992). *Out of the Shadows: Understanding Sexual Addictions.* Center City, MN: Hazelden.

Castillo, R., Jr. (1999). *What Predators Do to Sexually Abuse and Silence Children.* Carson City, NV: United Youth Security.

Lieblum, S. R., and Rosen, R. C. (2000). *Principles and Practice of Sex Therapy,* 3rd ed. New York: Guilford.

Milstein, R., and Slowinski, J. (1999). *The Sexual Male: Problems and Solutions.* New York: Norton.

O'Hanlon, B., and Bertolino, B. (1998). *Even from a Broken Web: Brief, Respectful, Solution-Oriented Therapy for Sexual Abuse.* New York: Wiley.

Shaw, J. A., ed. (1999). *Sexual Aggression.* Washington, DC: American Psychiatric Press.

Wincze, J., and Borlow, D. H. (1997). *Enhancing Sexuality: A Problem-Solving Approach.* San Antonio: Harcourt Brace. (Therapist version.)

Wincze, J., and Carey, M. P. (1991). *Sexual Dysfunction: A Guide for Assessment and Treatment.* San Antonio: Harcourt Brace.

Sleep Disorders

Poceta, J. S., and Mitler, M. M. (1998). *Sleep Disorders: Diagnosis and Treatment.* (Current Clinical Practice Series.) Washington, DC: American Psychiatric Press.

Reite, M., Ruddy, J., and Nagel, K. (1997). *Concise Guide to Evaluation and Management of Sleep Disorders*, 2nd ed. Washington, DC: American Psychiatric Press.

Substance Abuse

Alcoholics Anonymous. (1975). *The Big Book*. New York: AA World Services.

———. (1975). *Living Sober*. New York: AA World Services.

American Psychiatric Association. (1995). *American Psychiatric Association Practice Guidelines for the Treatment of Patients with Substance Use Disorders: Alcohol, Cocaine, Opioids*. Washington, DC: American Psychiatric Press.

———. (1996). *American Psychiatric Association Practice Guidelines for the Treatment of Patients with Nicotine Dependence*. Washington, DC: American Psychiatric Press.

Beattie, M. (1989). *Crack*. Center City, MN: Hazelden.

Brown, S., and Lewis, V. (2000). *The Alcoholic Family in Recovery*. New York: Guilford.

Brown, S., ed., and Yalom, I., gen. ed. (1997). *Treating Alcoholism*. San Francisco: Jossey-Bass.

Cook, D. (1998). *Substance Abuse: The Meaning of Addiction*. San Francisco: Jossey-Bass.

Cummings, N. A., and Cummings, J. L. (2000). *The First Session with Substance Abuse: A Step-by-Step Guide*. San Francisco: Jossey-Bass.

Daley, D. C., and Marlatt, G. A. (1997). *Managing Your Drug or Alcohol Problem*. (Therapist guide.) San Antonio: Harcourt Brace.

Diamond, J. (2000). *Narrative Means to Sober Ends: Treating Addictions and Its Aftermath*. New York: Guilford.

Ellis, A., McInerney, J. F., DiGiuseppe, R., and Yeager, R. J. (1988). *Rational Emotive Therapy with Alcoholics and Substance Abusers*. Boston: Allyn & Bacon.

Evans, K., and Sullivan, J. M. (1990). *Dual Diagnosis: Counseling the Mentally Ill Substance Abuser*. New York: Guilford.

Fernandez, H. (1998). *Heroin*. Center City, MN: Hazelden.

Hafen, B., and Soulier, D. (1989). *Cocaine and Crack*. Center City, MN: Hazelden.

———. (1989). *Marijuana*. Center City, MN: Hazelden.

Miller, N. S., ed. (1999). *Treating Coexisting Psychiatric and Addictive Disorders.* Center City, MN: Hazelden.

O'Connell, D. F. (1999). *Dual Disorders: Essentials for Assessment.* New York: Haworth.

Peele, S. (1998). *The Meaning of Addiction.* San Francisco: Jossey-Bass.

Roberts, L. J., Shouer, A., and Eckman, T. A. (1999). *Overcoming Addictions: Skills Training for People with Schizophrenia.* New York: Norton.

Suicide

Blumenthal, S. J., and Kuper, D. J., ed. (1990). *Suicide Over the Life Cycle: Risk Factors, Assessment, and Treatment of Suicidal Patients.* Washington, DC: American Psychiatric Press.

Chiles, J., and Strosahl, K. (1996). *The Suicidal Patient: Principles of Assessment, Treatment, and Case Management.* Washington, DC: American Psychiatric Press.

Ramsey, R. F., Tanney, B. L., Kinzel, T., and Turley, B. (1999). *Suicide Intervention Handbook.* Calgary, Alberta, Canada: Living Work Education.

Theory

American Psychiatric Association. (1995). *Practice Guidelines for Psychiatric Evaluation of Adults.* Washington, DC: American Psychiatric Publishing Group.

———. (1996). *Psychiatric Evaluation of Adults: Eating Disorders, Major Depressive Disorders, Bipolar Disorders, Substance Abuse Disorders.* Washington, DC: American Psychiatric Press.

Barlow, D. H. (1993). *Clinical Handbook of Psychological Disorders.* New York: Guilford.

Beck, A. T., Freeman, A., et al. (1976). *Cognitive Therapy and the Emotional Disorders.* Madison, CT: International Universities Press.

———. (1990). *Cognitive Therapy of Personality Disorders.* New York: Guilford.

Beck, J. (1995). *Cognitive Therapy: Basics and Beyond.* New York: Guilford.

Blau, S., and Ellis, A., eds. (1998). *The Albert Ellis Reader: A Guide to Well Being Using Rational Emotive Behavior Techniques.* New York: Carol.

Craighead, L. W., Craighead, W. E., Kazdin, A. E., and Mahoney, M. J.

(1994). *Cognitive and Behavioral Interventions: An Empirical Approach to Mental Health Problems*. Boston: Allyn & Bacon Inc.

Dobson, K. S. (1988). *Handbook of Cognitive Behavioral Therapies*. New York: Guilford.

Dryden, W., and DiGuiseppe, R. (1990). *A Primer on Rational Emotive Therapy*. Champaigne, IL: Research Press.

Fish, R., and Schlanger, K. (1998). *Brief Therapy with Intimidating Cases: Changing the Unchangeable*. San Francisco: Jossey-Bass.

Flagelheimer, W. V. (1993). *Techniques of Brief Psychotherapy*. Northvale, NJ: Jason Aronson.

Greenberg, L. S., and Sarafon, J. D. (1987). *Emotion in Psychotherapy*. New York: Guilford.

Guidano, V. F., and Lotto, G. (1983). *Cognitive Processes and Emotional Disorders*. New York: Guilford.

Haley, J. (1991). *Problem-Solving Therapy*. San Francisco: Jossey-Bass.

Leahy, R., ed. (1997). *Practicing Cognitive Therapy: A Guide to Interventions*. Northvale, NJ: Jason Aronson.

Madanes, C., and Keim, J. P. (1995). *Violence of Men*. San Francisco: Jossey-Bass.

Mazel, B. (1996). *Better, Deeper and More Enduring Brief Therapy: The Rational Emotive Behavior Therapy Approach*. Florence, KY: Taylor & Francis.

McClintock, E. (1999). *Room for Change: Empowering Possibilities for Therapists and Clients*. Northvale, NJ: Jason Aronson.

McMullen, R. E. (1999). *The New Handbook of Cognitive Therapy Techniques*. New York: Norton.

———. (2000). *The New Handbook of Cognitive Therapy Techniques*. Northvale, NJ: Jason Aronson.

Miller, S. D., Hubble, M., and Duncan, B. L., ed. (1996). *Handbook of Solution-Focused Brief Therapy*. San Francisco: Jossey-Bass.

Northcut, T. B. (1999). *The Union of Cognitive and Psychodynamic Approaches*. Northvale, NJ: Jason Aronson.

Northcut, T. B., and Heller, N. R. (1999). *Enhancing Psychodynamic Therapy with Cognitive Behavioral Techniques*. Northvale, NJ: Jason Aronson.

O'Hanlon, B., and Beadle, S. (1999). *A Guide to Possibility Land: Fifty-One Methods for Doing Brief Respectful Therapy*. New York: Norton.

O'Hanlon, W. H., and Weiner-Davies, M. (1988). *In Search of Solutions: A New Direction in Psychotherapy*. New York: Norton.

Persons, J. B. (1989). *Cognitive Therapy in Practice: A Case Formulation*. New York: Norton.

Pollack, W. S., and Levant, R. F. (1998). *New Psychotherapy for Men.* Northvale, NJ: Jason Aronson.

Sarafon, J., and Segal, Z. (1990). *Interpersonal Process in Cognitive Therapy.* New York: Basic Books.

Turner, S. M., Calhoun, K. S., and Adams, H. E. (1992). *Handbook of Clinical Behavior Therapy,* 2nd ed. New York: Wiley.

Vocational and Financial

Browne, D., Brooks, L., et al. (1996). *Career Choice and Development,* 3rd ed. San Francisco: Jossey-Bass.

Hansen, L. S. (1996). *Integrative Life Planning: Critical Tasks for Career Planning and Changing Life Patterns.* San Francisco: Jossey-Bass.

St. John, M. (2000). *Release from Debtor's Prison.* Center City, MN: Hazelden.

Weisenger, H. (1996). *Emotional Intelligence at Work: The Untapped Edge for Success.* San Francisco: Jossey-Bass.

VIDEOTAPES

The following audio- and videotapes are available from New Harbinger Publications, Oakland, CA:

Anxiety

Clinical Hypnosis for Stress and Anxiety Reduction (B. Shalhehn)

Cognitive Techniques

Cognitive-Behavioral Assessments (Matthew McKay)
Guided Discovery Using Socratic Dialogue (Christine Padesky)
Testing Automatic Thoughts with Thought Records (Christine Padesky)
Stress Inoculation (Matthew McKay)
Educating Clients about the Cognitive Model (Valerie Hearn)

Depression

Coping with Depression (M. E. Copeland)

AUDIOTAPES

Anxiety/Stress

The following series of audiotapes is based on Davis and colleagues (1994).

Applied Relaxation Training
Autogenics and Meditation
Body Awareness and Imagination
Progressive Relaxation and Breathing
Stress Inoculation

References

American Psychiatric Association. (1994). *Diagnostic and Statistical Manual of Mental Disorders, 4th Ed. (DSM-IV)*. Washington, DC: Author.

Bourne, E. J. (1998). *Overcoming Specific Phobia*. Oakland, CA: New Harbinger.

Bruce, T. J., and Sanderson, W. C. (1998). *Specific Phobias: Clinical Applications of Evidence-Based Psychotherapy*. Northvale, NJ: Jason Aronson.

Emery, G. (2000). *Overcoming Depression*. Oakland, CA: New Harbinger.

Fink, J. (1999). *How to Use Computers and Cyberspace in the Clinical Practice*. Northvale, NJ: Jason Aronson.

Klosko, J. S., and Sanderson, W. C. (1999). *Cognitive-Behavioral Treatment of Depression*. Northvale, NJ: Jason Aronson.

McGinn, L. K., and Sanderson, W. C. (1999). *Treatment of Obsessive-Compulsive Disorder*. Northvale, NJ: Jason Aronson.

Rapee, R. C., and Sanderson, W. C. (1998). *Social Phobia*. Northvale, NJ: Jason Aronson.

Rathus, J. H., and Sanderson, W. C. (1999). *Marital Distress: Cognitive Behavioral Interventions for Couples*. Northvale, NJ: Jason Aronson.

Sketee, G. (1998). *Overcoming Obsessive-Compulsive Disorder*. Oakland, CA: New Harbinger.

Value Options: More Choices for More People. (1999). Provider Handbook, New York State Department of Civil Services.

White, J. (1998). *Overcoming Generalized Anxiety Disorder.* Oakland, CA: New Harbinger.

Zuercher-White, E. (1998). *Overcoming Agoraphobia and Panic Disorder.* Oakland, CA: New Harbinger.

Index

ABOUT THE AUTHOR

Muriel Prince Warren, DSW, ACSW, is a psychotherapist, author, and educator. She is engaged in private practice in New York City and Rockland County, New York. Dr. Warren is the Executive Director of the Psychoanalytic Center for Communicative Education as well as a senior training and supervising analyst there. She is past president of the International Society for Communicative Psychoanalysis and Psychotherapy where she has received many awards for excellence. She holds degrees in psychology and social work from Fordham, Columbia, and Adelphi Universities, and a certificate in psychoanalysis from Lenox Hill Hospital in New York. Dr. Warren is the author of two books: *A Psychotherapist's Guide to Managed Care in the 21st Century* (with Sondra Tuckfelt and Jeri Fink) and *SONS: A Mother's Manual* (with Elise Karlin). Among her published articles in various professional journals are "Coding and Decoding: Comparing Milton Erickson's Hypnotherapy with Robert Langs' Communicative Approach," "Phases of Treatment: Termination and Death Anxiety," and "The Role of Culture in the Development of Narcissistic Personality Disorder in America, Japan, and Denmark."